IMAGES
of America

The Schuylkill Canal

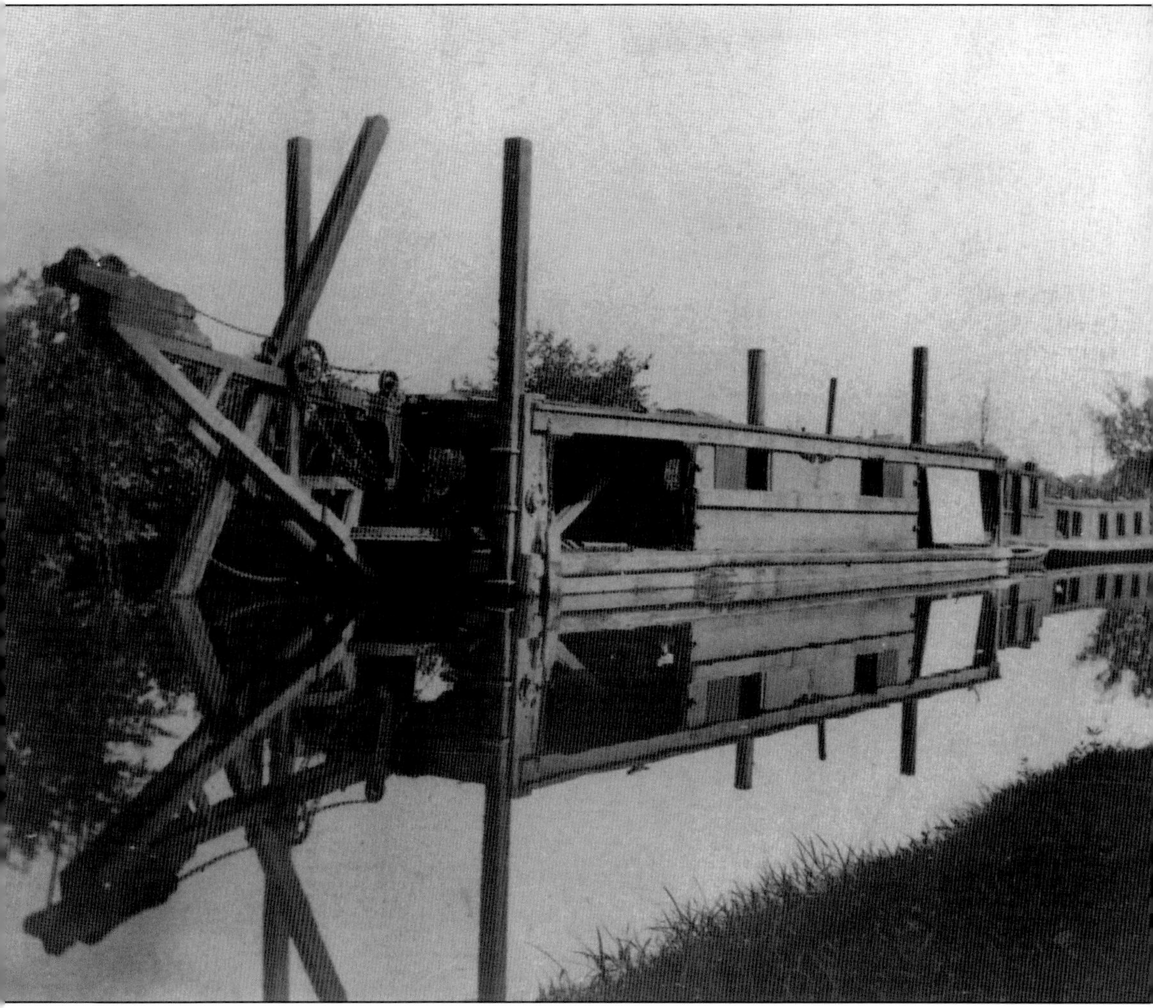

Dredging equipment is banked at an unknown location on the Schuylkill Canal. A dredge was a boat-mounted shovel, manipulated by the boat operator, used to clear sediment and other obstructions from the canal bed to keep the waterway passable. Dredging was a necessary operation year-round, except in cold winter months, when ice frequently shut down the canal. (Courtesy of the Schuylkill Canal Association.)

On the Cover: This 1958 photograph looks up the Oakes Canal at lock 60. This stretch of the Schuylkill Navigation System originally flowed for nearly three and a half miles from lock 60, just below Black Rock Dam (which still stands), past the settlements of Quincyville (now Mont Clare) and Jacobs (later called Lumberville and now Port Providence), to lock 61 at Oaks. From there, it entered the upriver end of the dam pool created by Pawlings Dam and the junction of the Perkiomen Creek and the river. (Courtesy of the Schuylkill Canal Association.)

IMAGES
of America

THE SCHUYLKILL CANAL

Karen Rodemich Roman

ARCADIA
PUBLISHING

ISBN 978-1-4671-2344-0

Published by Arcadia Publishing
Charleston, South Carolina

Printed in the United States of America

Library of Congress Control Number: 2014954869

For all general information, please contact Arcadia Publishing:
Telephone 843-853-2070
Fax 843-853-0044
E-mail sales@arcadiapublishing.com
For customer service and orders:
Toll-Free 1-888-313-2665

Visit us on the Internet at www.arcadiapublishing.com

Dedicated to the Schuylkill Canal Association, its tireless board members (both past and present), and its faithful volunteers

Contents

ACKNOWLEDGMENTS

First, I would like to thank an organization that I hold near and dear, the Schuylkill Canal Association (SCA), for welcoming me as a member and teaching me so much about an amazing spot in my own backyard. My deepest appreciation goes out to my fellow board members: Dan Daley, Gary Drennen, Roger Harris, Dave Hendricks, Strickland Kneass, Wayne Martin, Rich Matosky, Kevin McDonnell, Tim Parlapiano, Dave Williams, Carrie Wilson, and Chris Zeliznak. They supported me in the undertaking of this book, showing patience in answering my many questions and taking the time to review these materials. Special thanks go to former board member Tony Geyelin for putting me in touch with the SCA's earliest founding member, Ms. Neal Thorpe, who has many fond memories and entertaining stories from her years of service to the association, and to the SCA's past executive director, Betsy Daley, who did an amazing job of stewarding the organization through the formidable years and guiding the restoration of lock 60, as well as keeping the archives, records, and other information organized and easily accessible. Unless otherwise noted, all images appear courtesy of the SCA, many of which were acquired over the years from numerous sources, including the Smithsonian Institute, the City of Philadelphia Archives; the Pennsylvania Canal Society, the Pennsylvania Department of Forests and Waters, the Reading Company, the Philadelphia Free Library, the Pennsylvania Historical and Museum Commission, and Charles Heister.

I would also like to express my sincerest gratitude to my husband, Matt Roman, and my family and friends for putting up with the craziness that goes along with my taking on yet another project. Finally, I owe a great debt to Matt Egger for his consultation with image preparation and to my editor at Arcadia Publishing, Abby Walker. Without her, this book would not have been possible.

INTRODUCTION

For many, when they hear the word "canal," their first thoughts are of the Panama Canal—and why not? To say it is well known internationally would be an understatement. The 48-mile canal connects the Atlantic Ocean to the Pacific Ocean by way of the Caribbean Sea and is still in use today. For others, they may immediately start humming "Fifteen Years on the Erie Canal." Written by Thomas S. Allen in 1905, the song has been recorded by numerous artists and taught in schools around the country. But, while the Panama and Erie Canals may be famous in their own rights, they were not the first of their kind. To those from or living in Southeastern Pennsylvania, there is a canal that holds a great deal of historical significance.

In 1815, the Schuylkill Navigation Company was hired to build a navigable waterway between the Schuylkill and Susquehanna Rivers, which both flowed north to south. Generally speaking, canals can refer to artificial, man-made interconnected channels or river navigations that combine a series of locks and dams to create slackwater pools, navigable water behind a dam. By 1827, the Schuylkill Navigation Company had created a 108-mile navigable stretch from Port Carbon, Pennsylvania (above Pottsville), to Philadelphia. The Schuylkill Navigation System, commonly referred to as the Schuylkill Canal, was one of three canal systems that linked the eastern half of Pennsylvania. It was the first major canal in the state. For years, the navigation company maintained the locks and dredged the channels of the canal to collect sediment and keep the waterways deep enough to be passable. Dredging was an almost continuous operation between March and November.

Work began on the Schuylkill Canal with the first dam at the falls on the Schuylkill River, followed by the construction of Flat Rock Dam in Manayunk. When finished, it consisted of 62 miles of separate canals, often referred to as "reaches," with 46 miles of slackwater pools, 1 tunnel, and 120 locks, 92 of which were lift locks, used to overcome a difference of 588 feet in elevation between the navigation's terminal points. The Schuylkill Canal became a main transportation artery, allowing inexpensive shipment of anthracite coal—in barges pulled by mules—from Port Carbon to Philadelphia. The coal then made its way to New York markets.

The Schuylkill Navigation Company earned its income mainly by collecting tolls (according to tonnage) along the canal. Fares were collected at tollhouses located by each lock, though it is said that the Schuylkill Navigation Company did not have a fixed schedule of tolls. A lock tender's shanty would also be found at almost every lock site and was used as a business office for record keeping and a place of shelter during bad weather. Most canal boats were privately owned and measured roughly 60 feet in length by 7 feet in width, though beds, locks, and boat sizes experienced several enlargements through the years. The Schuylkill Canal was between 32 and 40 feet wide and accommodated barges eight feet wide. Because the canal was six feet deep, boats traveling on it could carry up to 200 tons of cargo. Providing waterpower was another source of income for the company. In 1819, John Towers opened the first mill to use waterpower from the canal.

The year 1859 was the most active and profitable one for the Schuylkill Canal. Then, in the 1860s, the Civil War, drought, and damage caused by flooding resulted in a downturn in usage and profitability. In 1870, the Schuylkill Navigation Company leased the canal to the Philadelphia & Reading Railroad Company—the very entity blamed for the demise of the Schuylkill Canal—but the waterway continued to decline. Eventually, coal silt filled the river, and navigation ceased, with the last barge navigating the canal in 1928. Use of excursion vessels and pleasure boats continued. In 1945, the Schuylkill River Desilting Project was approved by legislators to dredge the river and remove silt, but the project undid a good deal of the engineering that facilitated the navigation of the Schuylkill River. The canal was almost completely filled in the 1950s, with some locks buried and several dams removed.

The now-abandoned transportation canal is mostly filled in. Many of the dams remain today, but only two watered stretches (Oakes Reach and Manayunk Reach) are still in use recreationally. The photographs in each chapter of this book span from the end of the canal, near Fairmount, to the Girard Canal section of the Schuylkill Canal, with a specific concentration on the Oakes and Manayunk sections.

Black Rock Dam is the head of Oakes Reach, which is named after Thomas Oakes, the chief engineer for the Schuylkill Navigation Company. The canal passes through the dam structure at lock 60 and runs under Pennsylvania Route 29 in Mont Clare, then through Port Providence. In 1828, the company built the Phoenixville Branch Canal, which connected the slackwater pool of the Schuylkill Canal above the Black Rock Dam to Phoenixville. This canal ran parallel to the top end of Oakes Reach on the opposite side of the Schuylkill River. This branch canal provided waterpower to a new nail works in Phoenixville and conducted scheduled passenger service between Phoenixville and Norristown.

The final mile of the reach has been filled in; now, roughly 2.5 miles of the original 3.5-mile-long Oakes Reach is used recreationally by thousands each year. The Schuylkill Canal Association has restored the exterior of the 1836 lock tender's house, the vital water control gate flume opening at lock 60—as well as the lock itself—and the twin lock control gate. Today, lock 60 is the only operating lock on the Schuylkill River; lock 61 was filled in.

The Manayunk Reach opened for use in 1819. The head of this canal is at the Flat Rock Dam near Shawmont. The canal passed through the dam structure at lock 68 and ran through Manayunk at the downstream end of this reach, returning to the Schuylkill River by way of locks 69 and 70. A one-mile stretch of the Manayunk Reach in Manayunk is still used recreationally, and the area is maintained and protected by the Friends of the Manayunk Canal.

One

The Early Years of Canal Transportation

Construction of the Schuylkill Navigation System, or Schuylkill Canal, took nearly 10 years, persevering through floods, epidemics, and short capital. The canal was Pennsylvania's first major canal and marked the beginning of a canal-building boom. Operating between 1825 and 1917, the Schuylkill Navigation Company was quite successful for many years, primarily because of the demand for coal generated by the industrial revolution. Indeed, the downstream trade from the rich anthracite coal deposits at its northern terminals was essentially the canal's sole reason for being. The canal sections, or levels, generally paralleled the river, and each were named. Each canal was entered through a guard lock at the dam, and these locks were numbered sequentially from the head of the canal but were generally known to boatmen by the lock tender's or adjacent landowner's name. Towpaths were constructed along the canals and slackwater pools to provide level footing for the mules that labored for more than 100 years. Many mills and factories along the canal's banks leased waterpower from the Schuylkill Navigation Company, which they used to operate. They also shipped their wares on the canal.

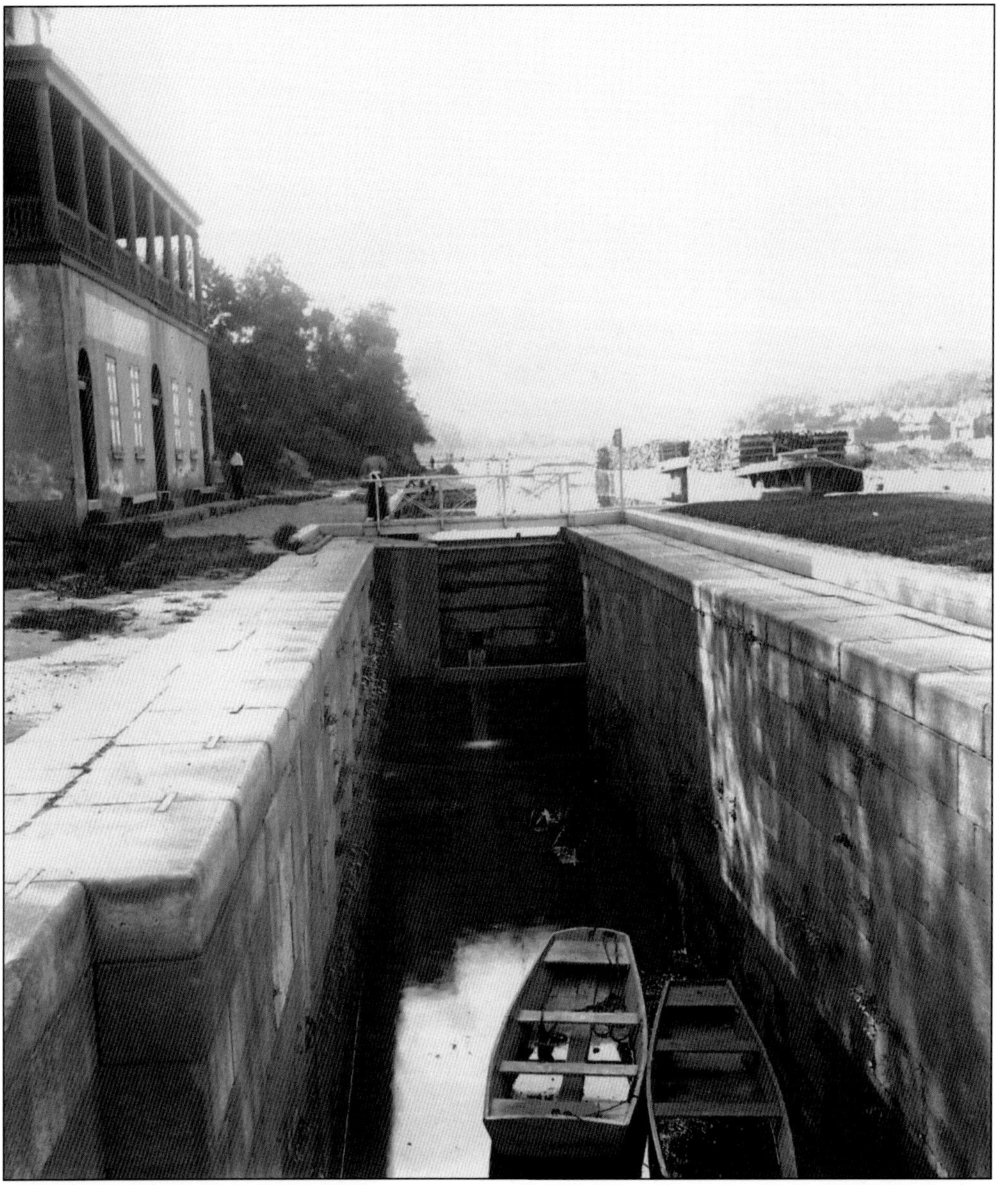

This photograph, taken on September 4, 1896, looks up at the former small lift lock at Fairmount Dam during low water. Note that the upper end of the lock is timbered up, as it was no longer in use. Lift locks are a conventional type of canal lock that enable a boat to be raised or lowered from one level to another by allowing water to flow in or out. Ariel Cooley, of Chicopee, Massachusetts, was contracted to build the Fairmount Dam, canal, and locks, which he began working on in 1819. In the 1950s, construction of West River Drive and the Schuylkill Expressway resulted in the destruction of locks 71 and 72 in this location. The old lock tender's house (left) was removed at a later date, and a new building was erected in its place.

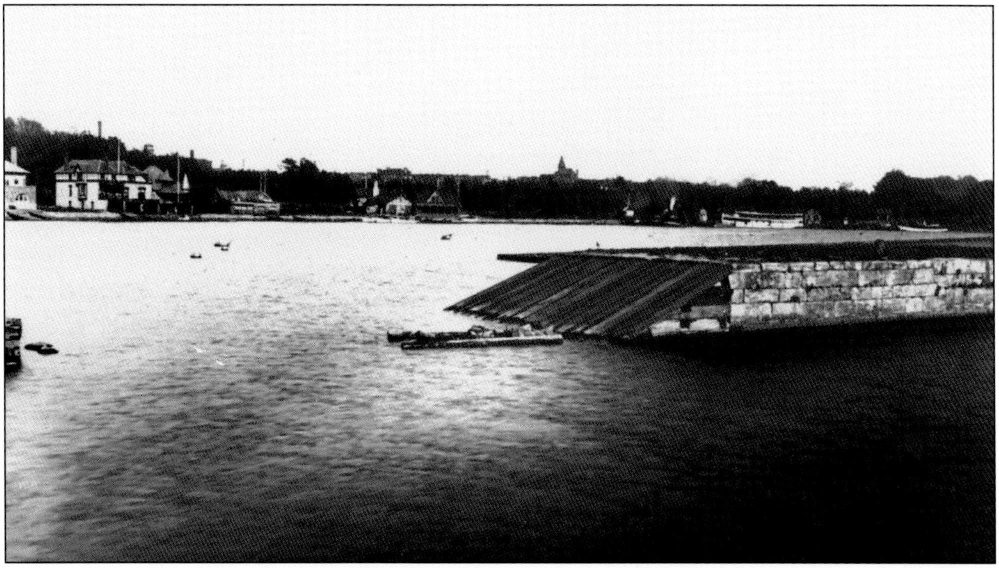

The entrance to guard lock 71 at Fairmount Dam is seen here on August 29, 1895. A guard lock is the lock at the head of a canal or dam that provides access to an impoundment of water. Most canal boats were towed to Port Richmond once they cleared lock 71.

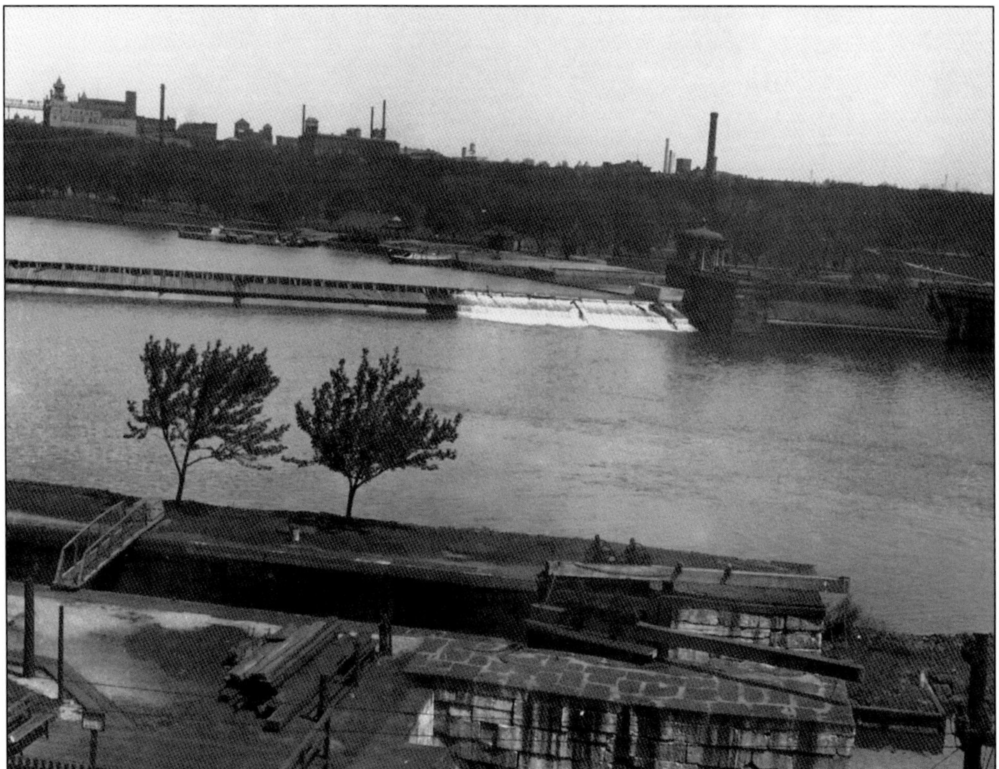

This photograph, taken in July 1919, shows the outlet gate of the outlet lock at Fairmount Dam (in the background). An outlet lock's main purpose is to move boats to and from a canal to the farther shore of a river—in this case, the Schuylkill River.

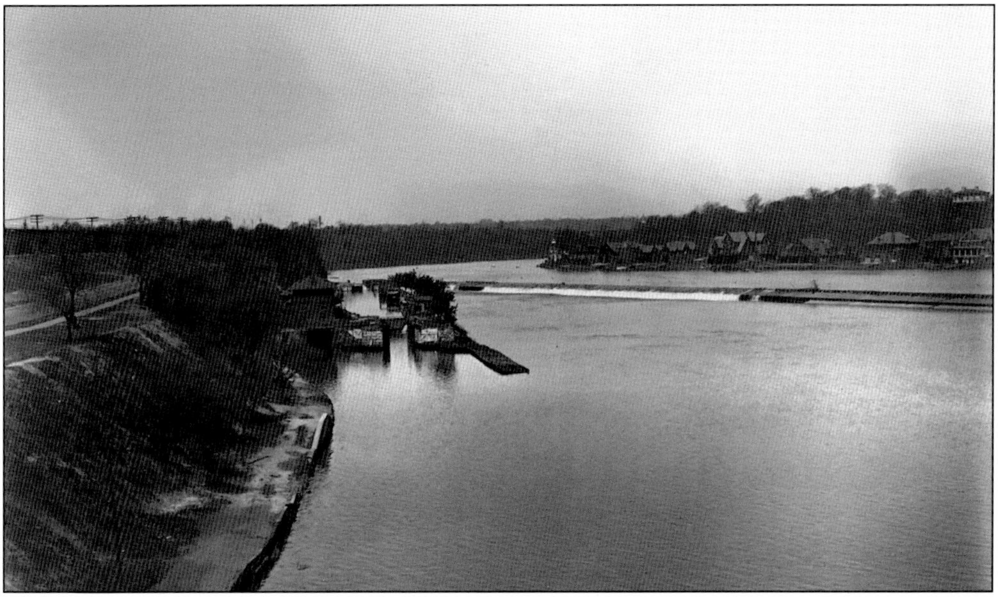

This photograph of the outlet lock at Fairmount Dam was taken in April 1919. This is the west bank of the Schuylkill River, with the dam in the background. Also seen here is the collector's house (dark building to the left of the lock). On the east (right) bank are the houses that make up what is referred to as Boathouse Row.

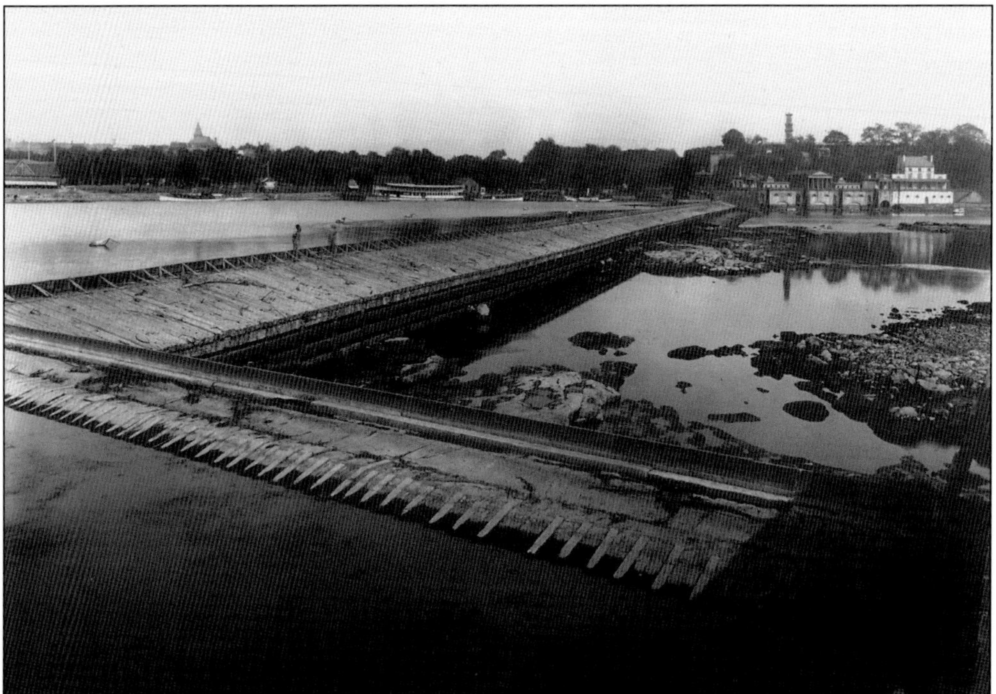

In this 1896 photograph of the Fairmount Dam, the Fairmount Water Works can be seen at far right. The city of Philadelphia was given access to water from the Fairmount Dam for its public works. Note the temporary fenders built on the dam comb; these were used to increase the water height.

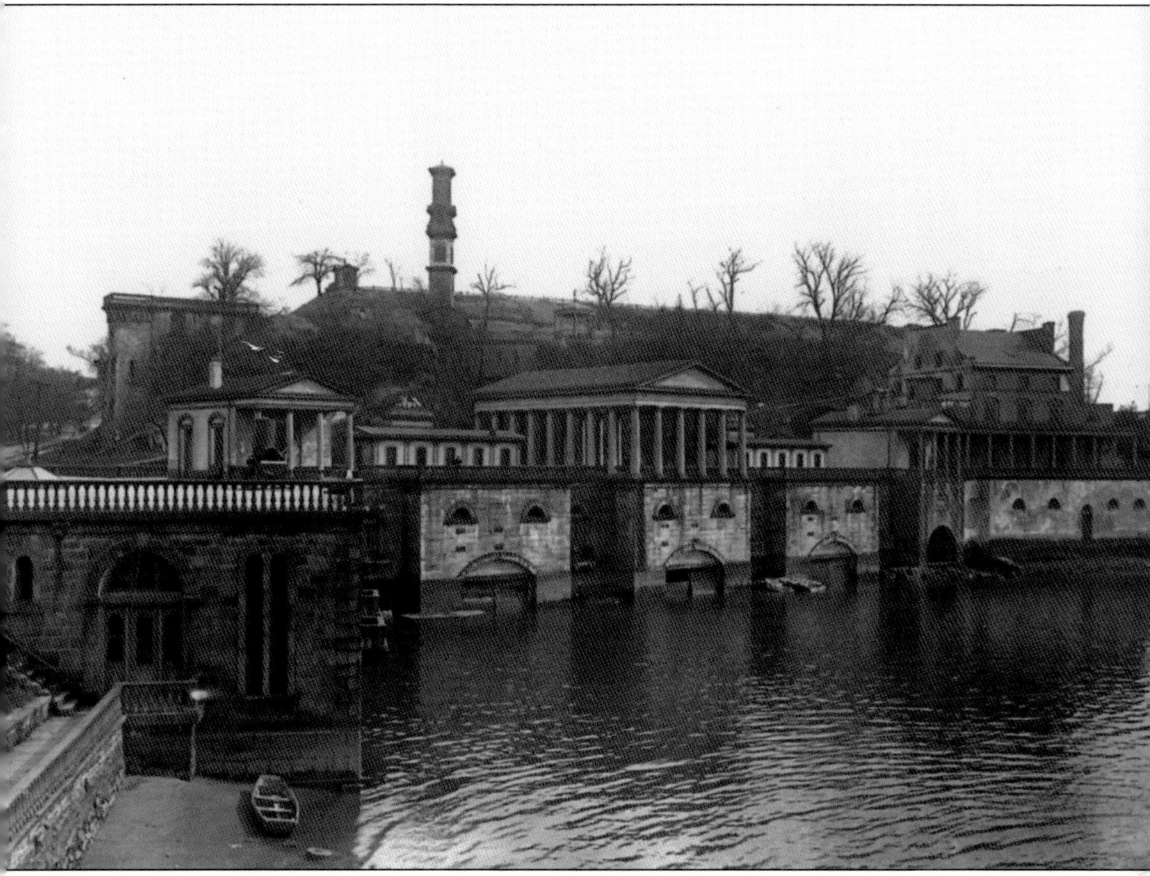

The Fairmount Water Works in Philadelphia is seen here at the turn of the century. Situated on the east bank of the Schuylkill River between historic Boathouse Row and the Philadelphia Museum of Art, the Fairmount Water Works opened its doors in 1815 as the nation's first major urban water-supply system. It was in a prime location, being the highest point in the area; this worked well with the gravity-fed water systems that the city used in those days. Water was pumped from the river into a reservoir (which existed where the art museum now stands) and was then distributed through the city by way of wooden water mains. In 1909, the Fairmount Water Works was decommissioned as a pumping station. It is now a National Historic Landmark, a Civil Engineering Landmark, and a National Mechanical Engineering Landmark. It also serves as the Fairmount Water Works Interpretive Center.

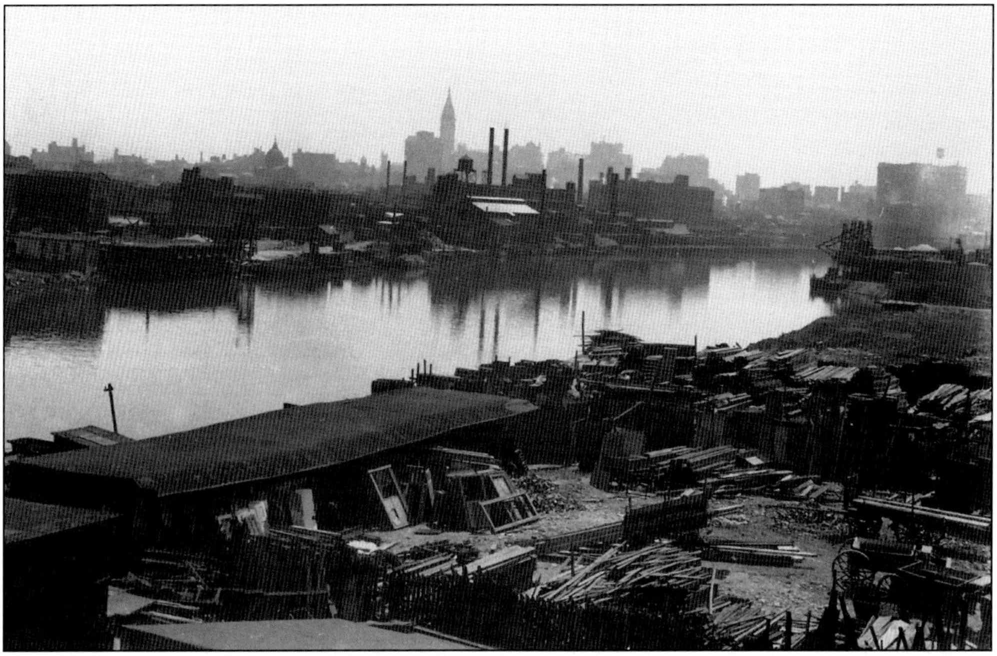

This 1919 photograph looks down the Schuylkill River from the Spring Garden Street Bridge, with the storage lot of a wrecking company in the foreground. This bridge carried West Spring Garden Street in West Philadelphia over the Schuylkill River to the site of the Fairmount Water Works.

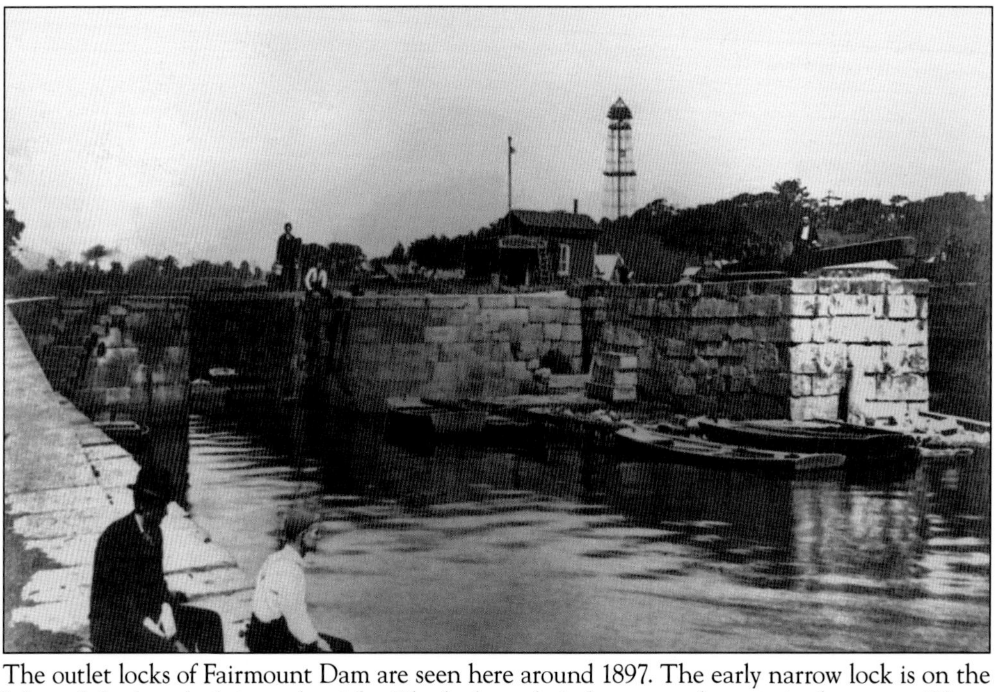

The outlet locks of Fairmount Dam are seen here around 1897. The early narrow lock is on the left, and the later lock is on the right. The lock tender's shanty can be seen in the center. These locks were located near the downriver end of a strip of land that ran along the west side of the Schuylkill River and met the dam at its upriver end.

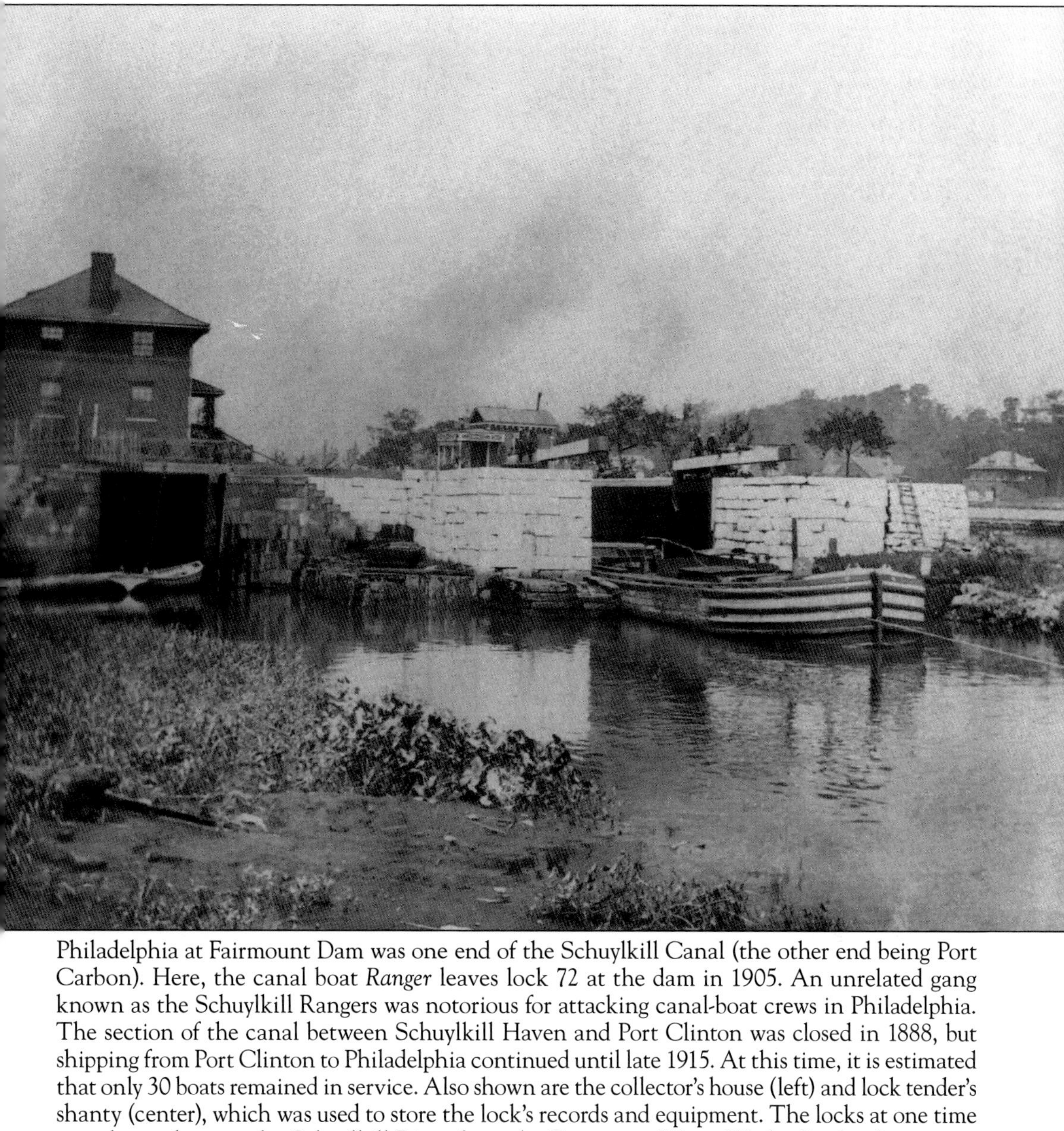

Philadelphia at Fairmount Dam was one end of the Schuylkill Canal (the other end being Port Carbon). Here, the canal boat *Ranger* leaves lock 72 at the dam in 1905. An unrelated gang known as the Schuylkill Rangers was notorious for attacking canal-boat crews in Philadelphia. The section of the canal between Schuylkill Haven and Port Clinton was closed in 1888, but shipping from Port Clinton to Philadelphia continued until late 1915. At this time, it is estimated that only 30 boats remained in service. Also shown are the collector's house (left) and lock tender's shanty (center), which was used to store the lock's records and equipment. The locks at one time were located across the Schuylkill River from the Fairmount Water Works. In the distance to the right lies Boathouse Row.

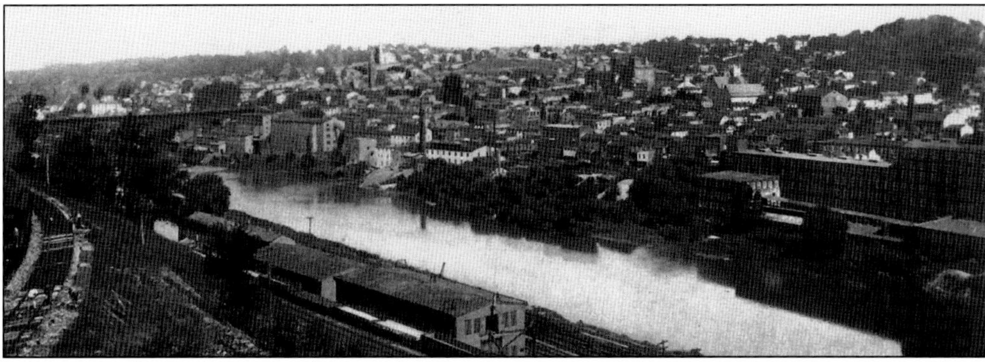

This 1902 photograph of the Schuylkill River provides a nice view of Manayunk, a section of Philadelphia originally named Flat Rock, after a natural rock formation in the river above Manayunk. The tracks of the Pennsylvania Railroad are at left. Across the river are several textile mills, beyond which lies the Schuylkill Canal (not visible).

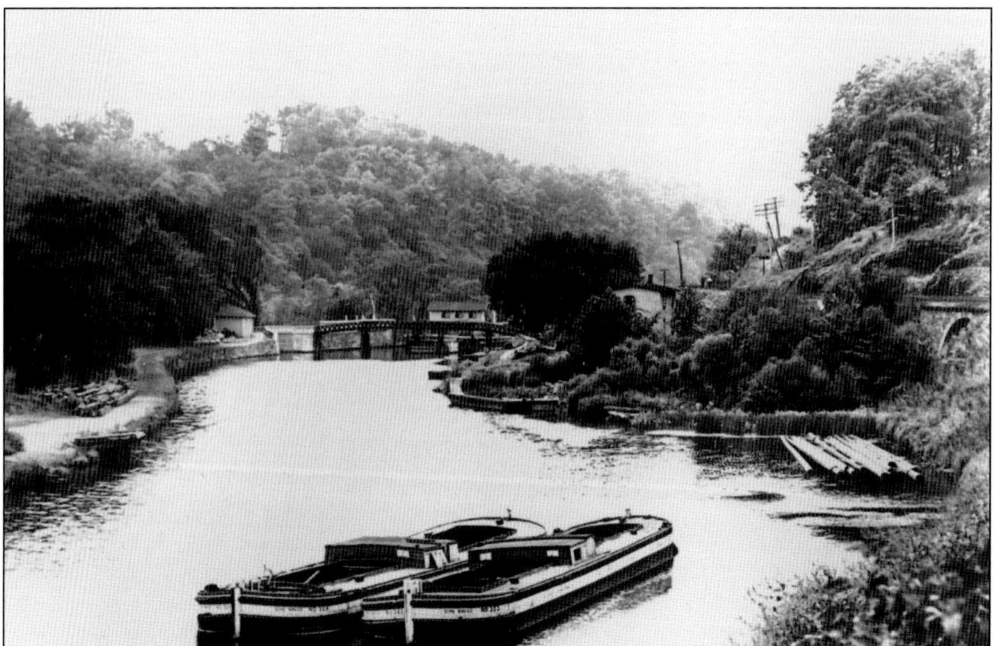

Shown here in 1909 is the Manayunk Canal at the canal feeders and lock 68 at Flat Rock Dam. In the foreground are Pennsylvania canal boats used in the last days of the canal.

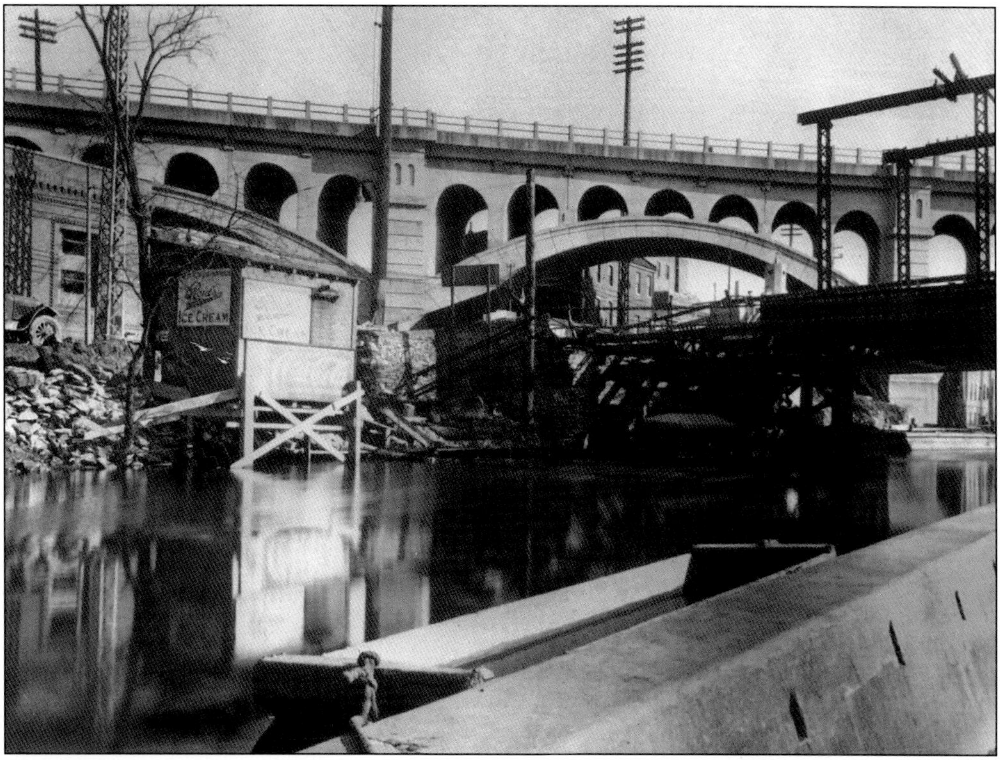

The Green Lane Bridge (background) was built in 1832. This photograph, taken on January 11, 1928, provides a view of the Manayunk Canal just above the bridge. The canal flows into the Schuylkill River at locks 69 and 70. Construction of the canal was completed in 1819.

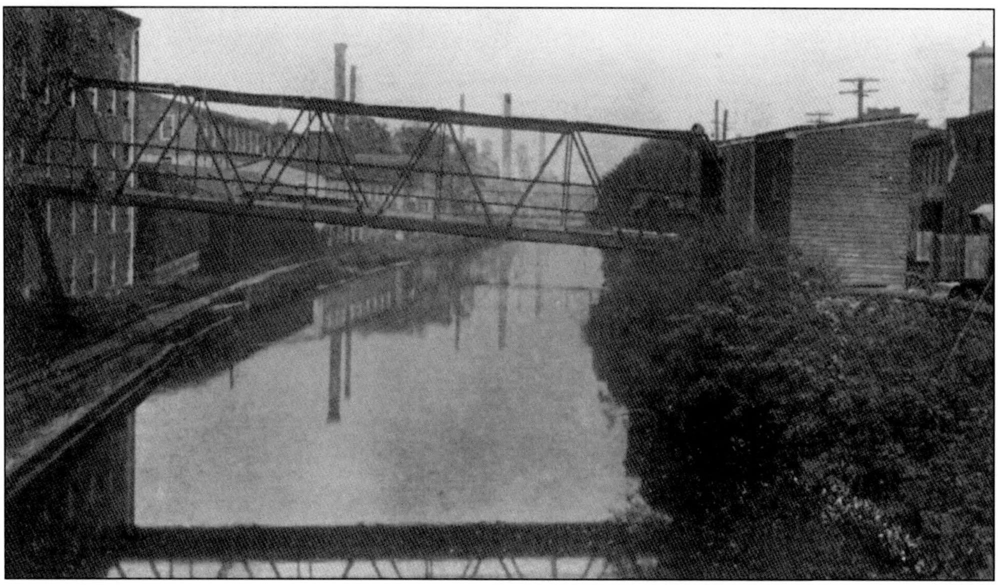

Joseph Ripka had one of the largest textile manufacturing businesses in the United States. This is believed to be the entrance bridge to one of the mill buildings, situated between the east bank of the Schuylkill River and the Manayunk Canal. Ripka filed for bankruptcy before the end of the Civil War, which proved to be a tough time for many.

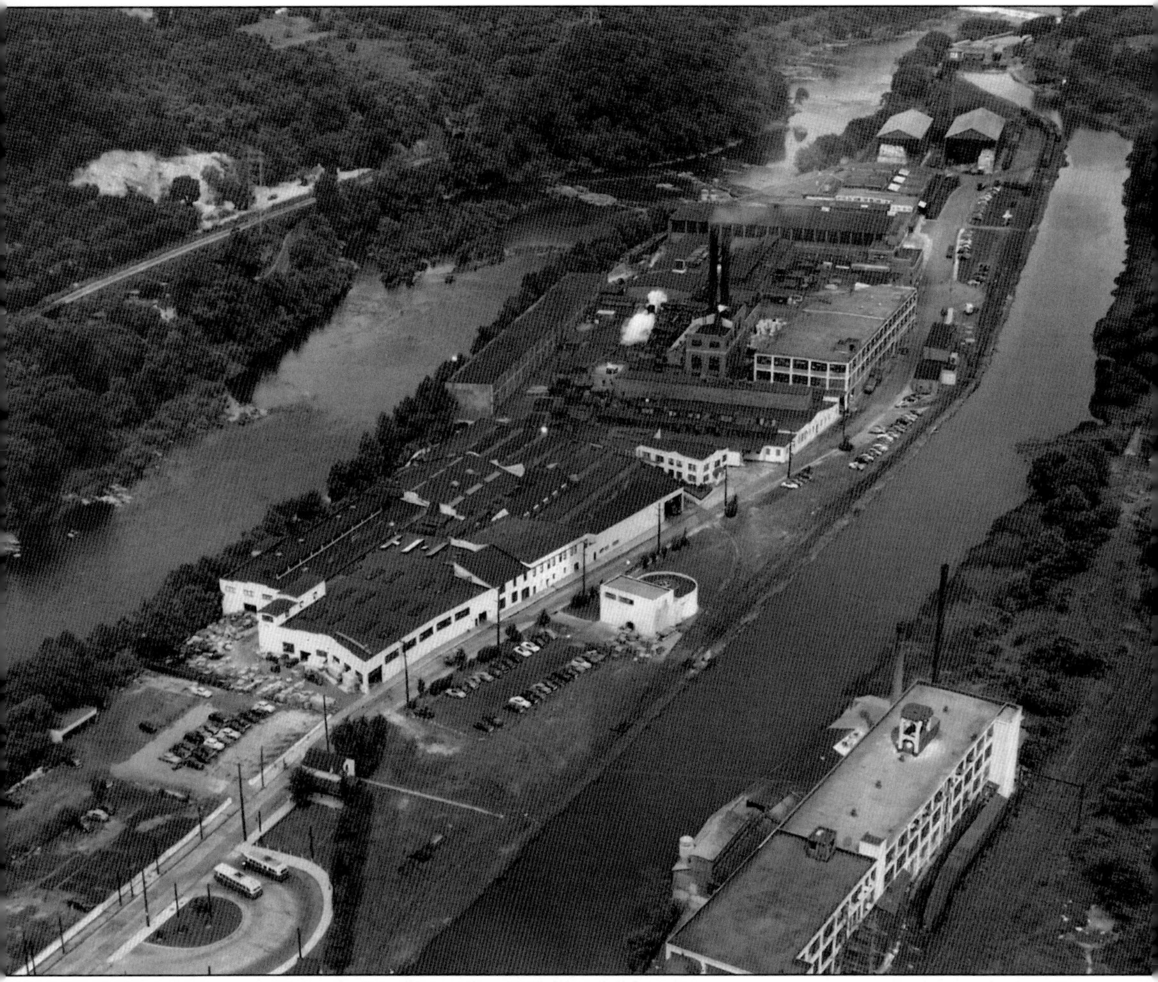

The natural resources offered by the Schuylkill River and its surrounding area drew immigrant workers to settle the hills rising up from the river. The Flat Rock Dam backed up the river for four miles and created a fall of 26 feet, which provided enough power to turn waterwheels. At this time, the Schuylkill Navigation Company began to sell waterpower to the mills built along these waterways. These factories produced everything from lumber to textiles and many commodities in between. This aerial photograph shows the river (left) and the Manayunk Canal (right). Flat Rock Dam, lock 68, and feeders are visible at upper right. Manayunk to Flat Rock Dam makes up the second reach (section of flat water between two locks) of the Schuylkill Navigation. The building complex in the center is the Container Corporation of America, which was founded in 1926 and manufactures corrugated boxes.

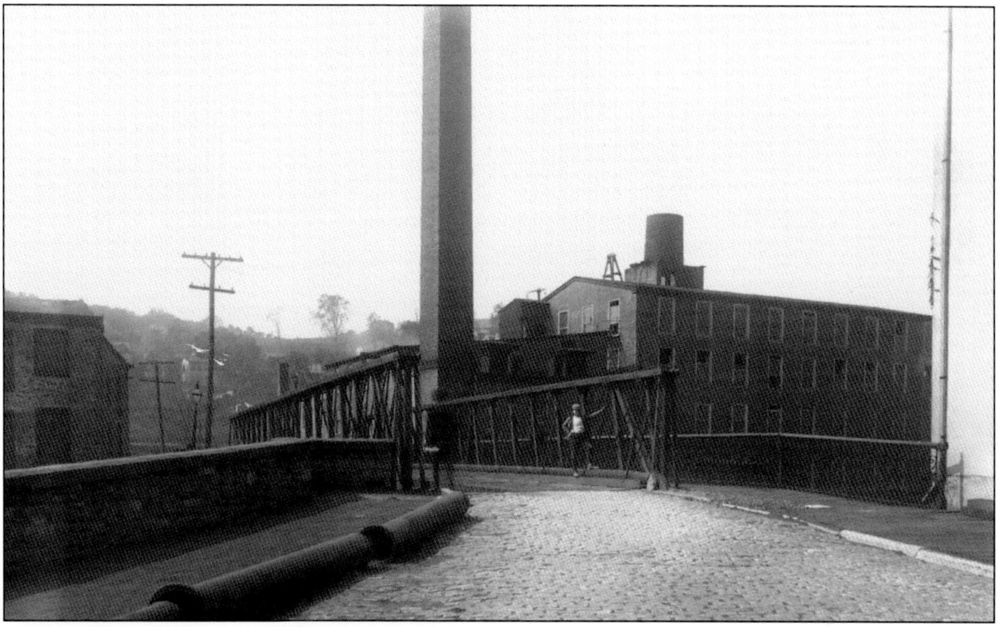

This bridge runs over the canal in Manayunk at the intersection of Leverington Avenue and Main Street. The building on the left once belonged to the Blankin Yarn Company. The building on the right was constructed in 1876 by Samuel Streeper Keely for his planing mill. This photograph was taken in 1901.

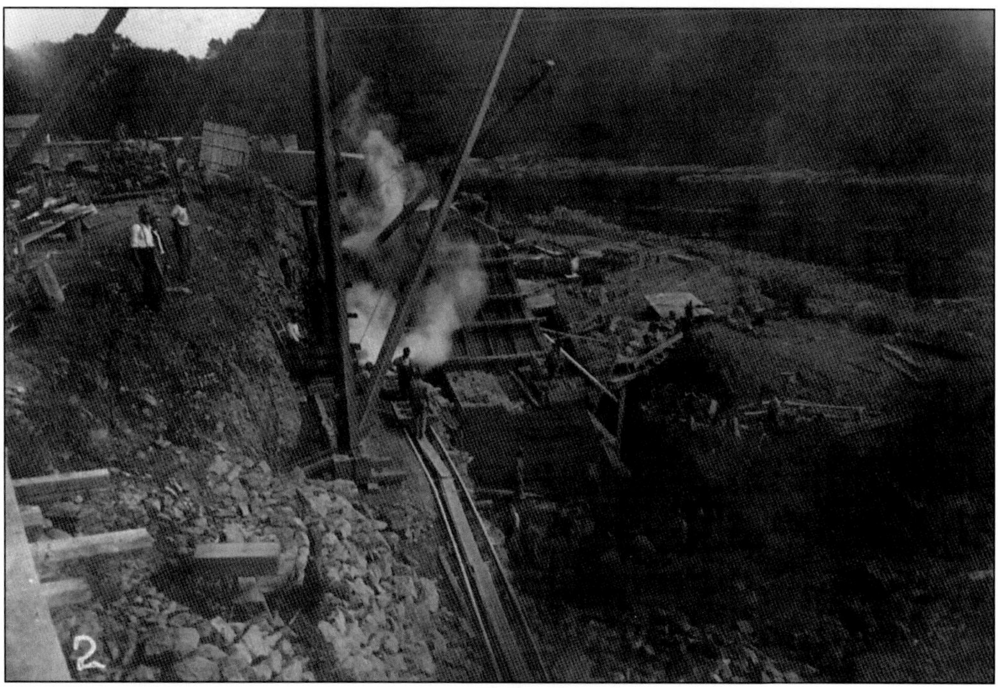

In 1815, construction began on the Flat Rock Dam. The intention was to make seven dangerous miles of the Schuylkill River into navigable water. This undated photograph shows men hard at work building the canal retaining wall at Flat Rock Dam. The canal itself was constructed through a low-lying swamp area, referred to at the time as "dead waters."

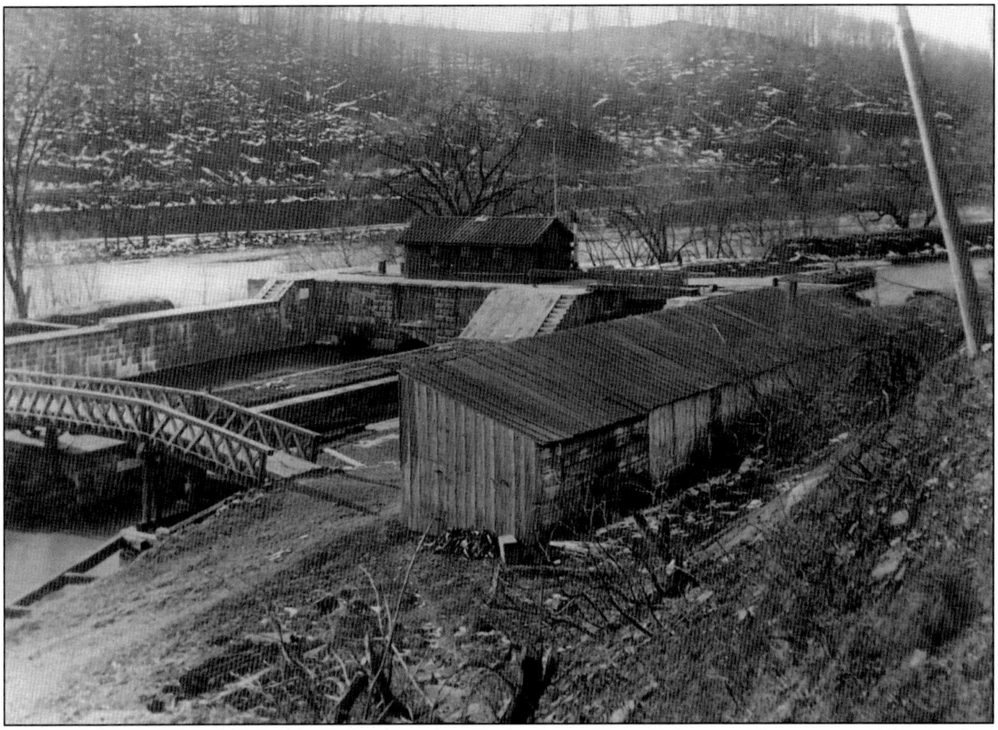

The head of the Manayunk Reach is at Flat Rock Dam (Dam 31) near Shawmont. The feeders and feeder house in this area at lock 68 are shown in the winter of 1904–1905. In winter, it was not uncommon for the canal to shut down due to the formation of ice.

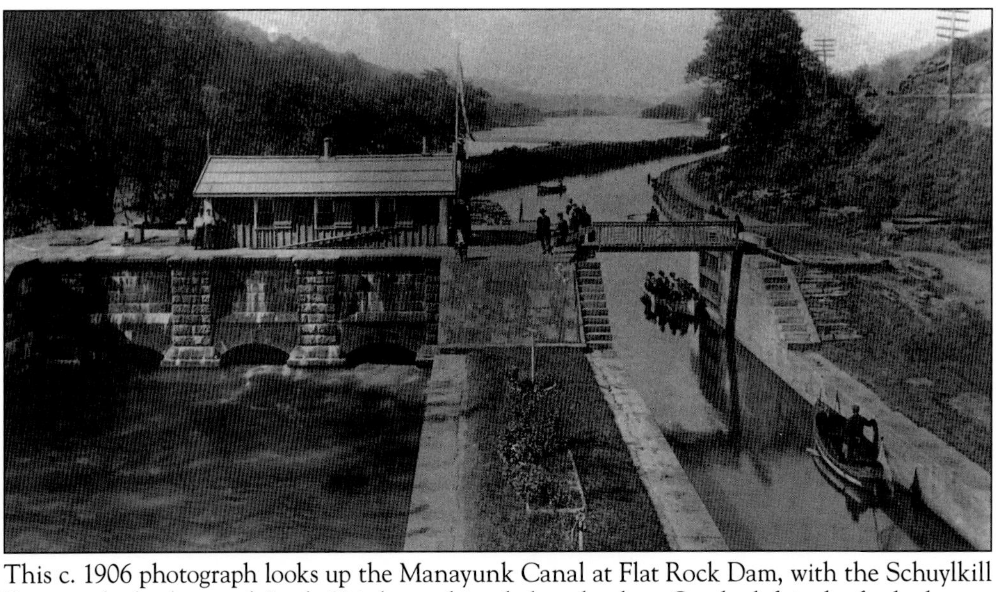

This c. 1906 photograph looks up the Manayunk Canal at Flat Rock Dam, with the Schuylkill River in the background. Lock 68 is located just below the dam. On the left is the feeder house, which was left standing when a newer one was built around it.

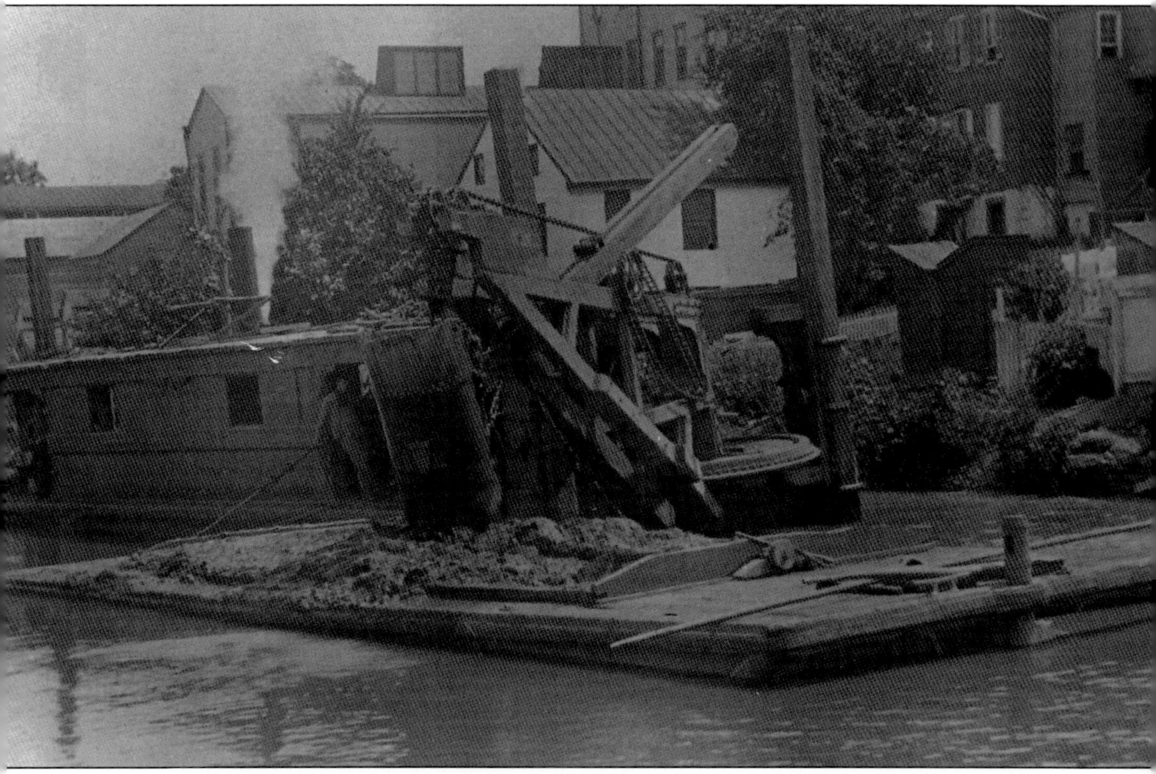

Here, the Schuylkill Navigation Company's dredge No. 2 is seen at the stop gate of the Vincent Canal in Spring City. This stretch of the Schuylkill Canal consisted of the Vincent Dam (Dam 25), Stoney Creek Aqueduct, and locks 58 and 59. Stop gates were built to help protect the canal downstream from floodwaters. They also divided long stretches of canal into smaller lengths as a precaution in the event of a break in the bank. The gates were closed while repairs were made, then reopened to allow water back into the drained area. The men on this dredge had the task of clearing coal silt and other sediment from the bed of the canal. The dredge operator would then place the removed material either on the canal bank or in scows for disposal elsewhere. The canal company operated several steam vessels on the canal for dredging and general repair work, and this typically occurred year-round, except when thick ice made the task impossible.

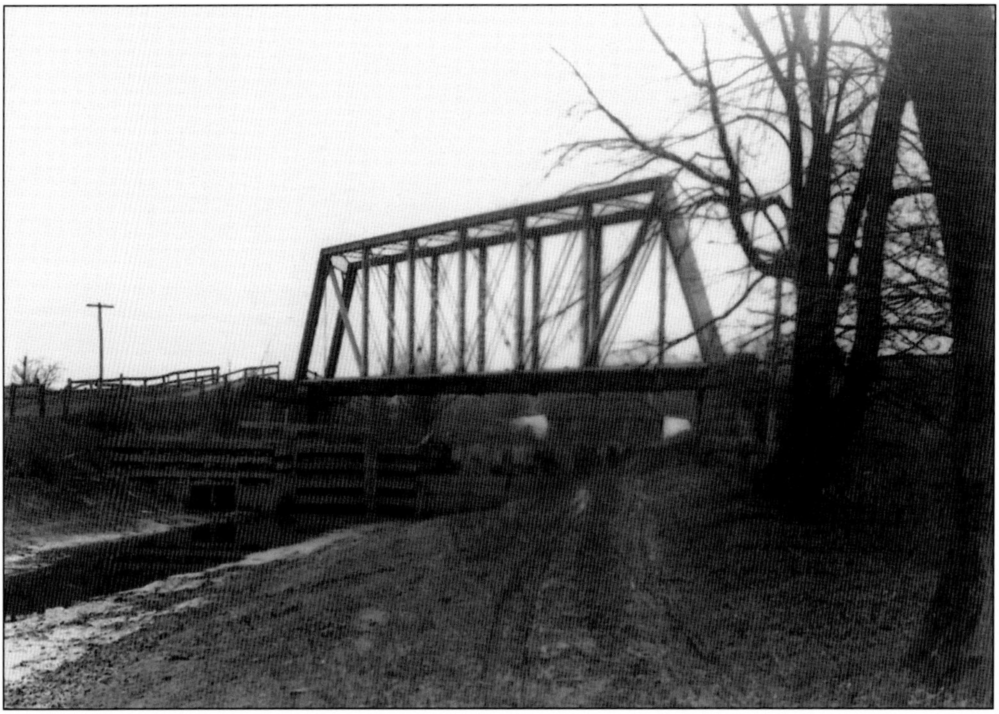

Here are two similar views of the stop gate on the Vincent Canal above Spring City, where the Pennsylvania Railroad crosses the canal. This bridge was located near the Pennhurst State School and Hospital, originally known as the Eastern Pennsylvania State Institution for the Feeble-Minded and Epileptic, which occupied roughly 120 acres of Crab Hill. It opened in 1908 and closed its doors in 1987, but it now opens seasonally as a haunted attraction. In 2009, it was proposed that the breached remains of Vincent Dam be removed and the eroded sections of the stream bank be stabilized; this took place a few years later.

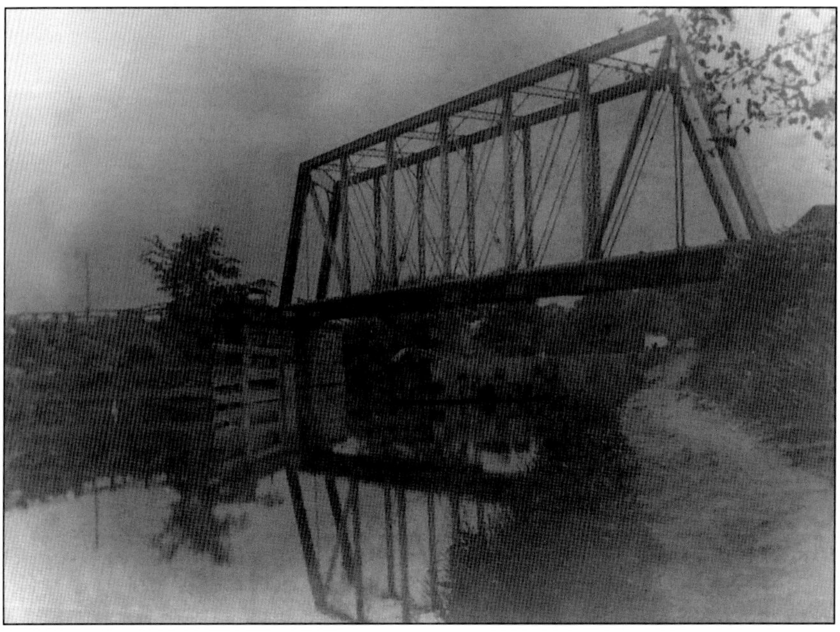

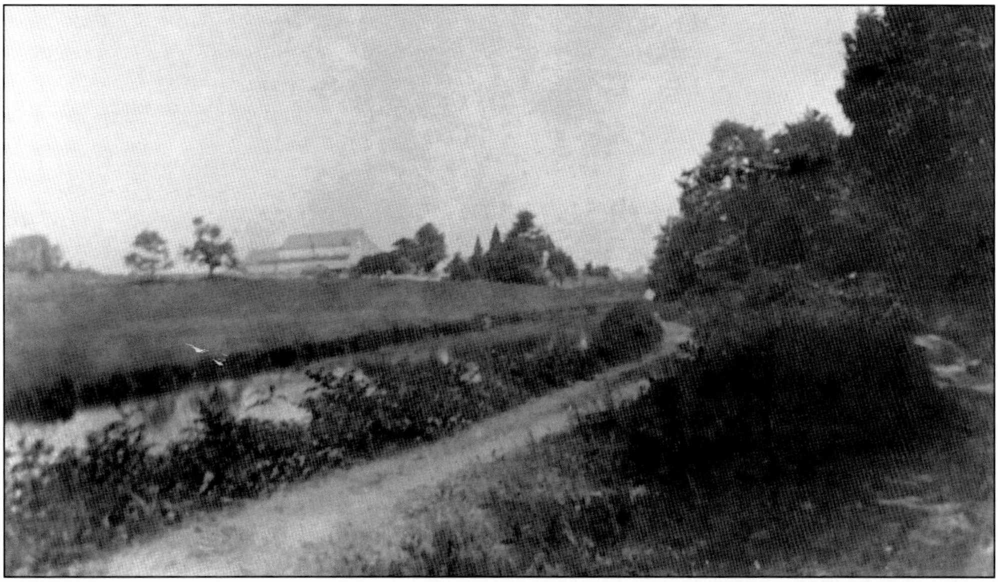

This undated photograph provides a bucolic view of the Vincent Canal above Spring City, with the towpath visible on the right. Towpaths were built alongside canals to allow the use of animals, mostly mules, for towing barges. These paths were typically 12 feet in width. Today, many sections of the towpath along the Schuylkill Canal are used recreationally.

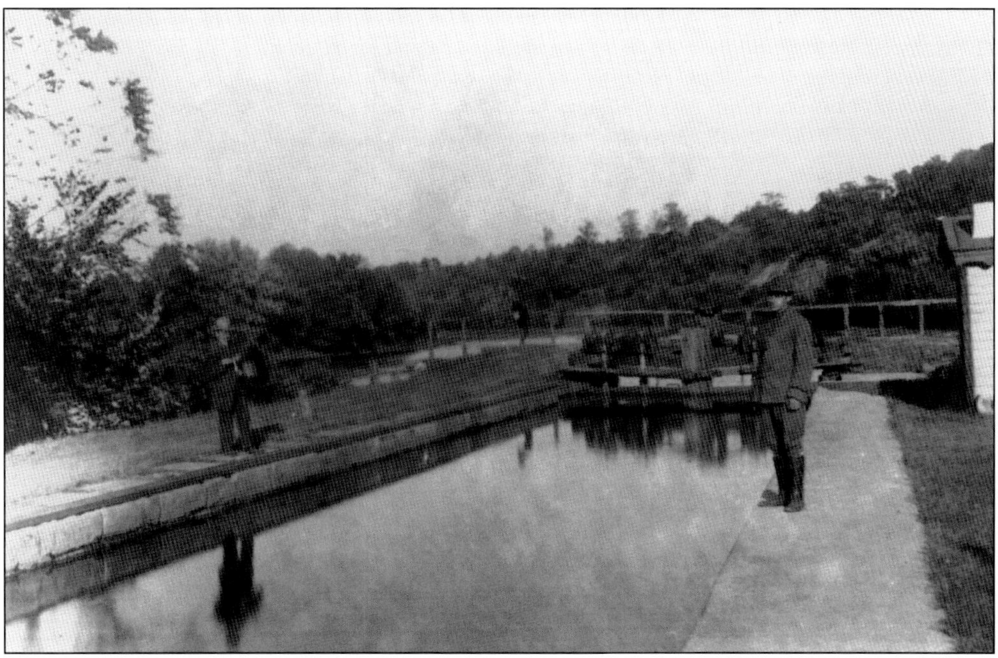

Canals have revealed themselves to be a good place to go fishing, as evidenced by the man (left) holding the fishing rod in this undated photograph at the upper gate at lock 57 in Parker Ford on the Girard Canal. Even today, the waters of the canal prove a worthy spot for catching catfish and bass.

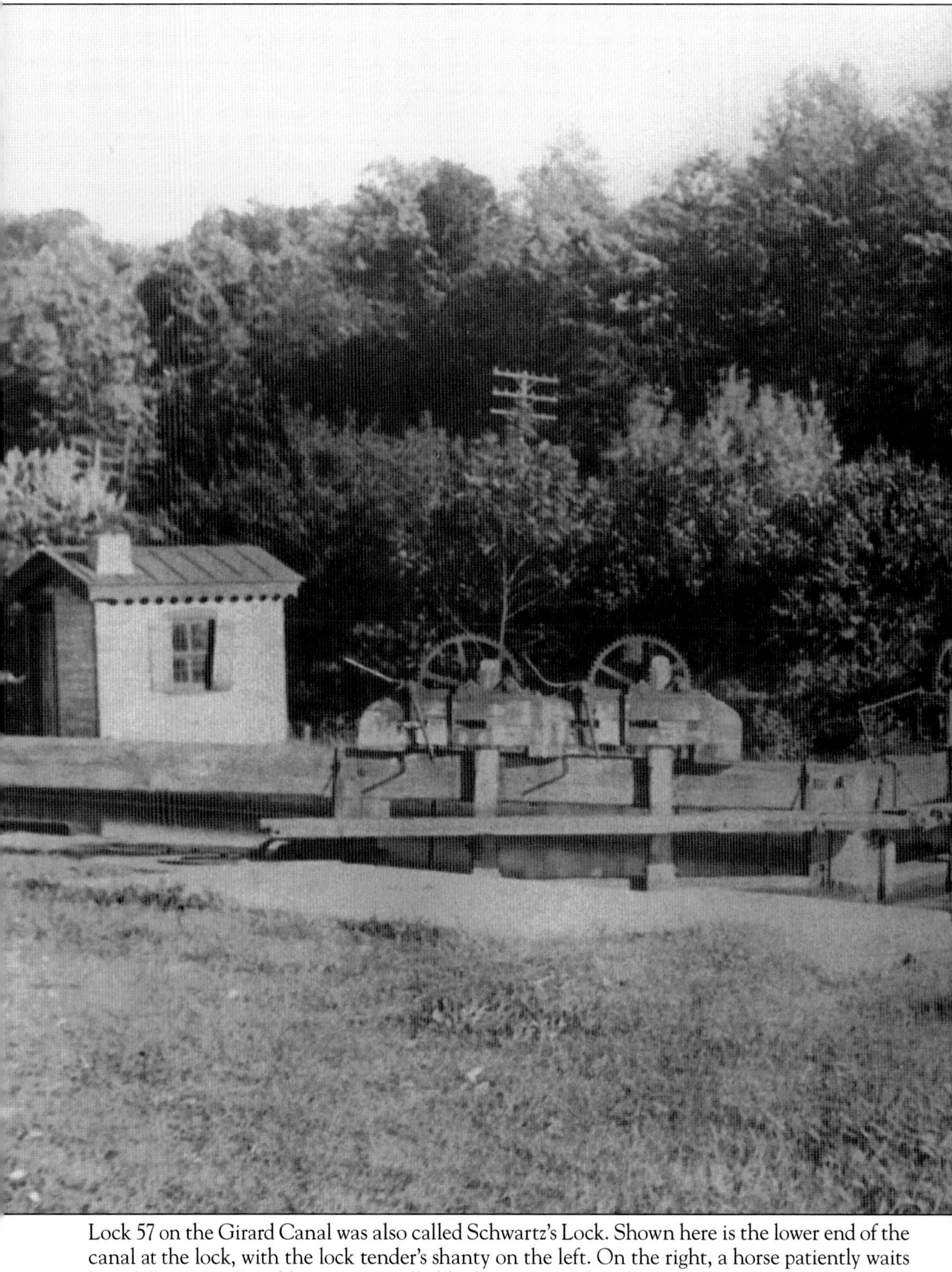

Lock 57 on the Girard Canal was also called Schwartz's Lock. Shown here is the lower end of the canal at the lock, with the lock tender's shanty on the left. On the right, a horse patiently waits by a full wagon. Canal boats were pulled by horses or mules; the latter were preferred, because

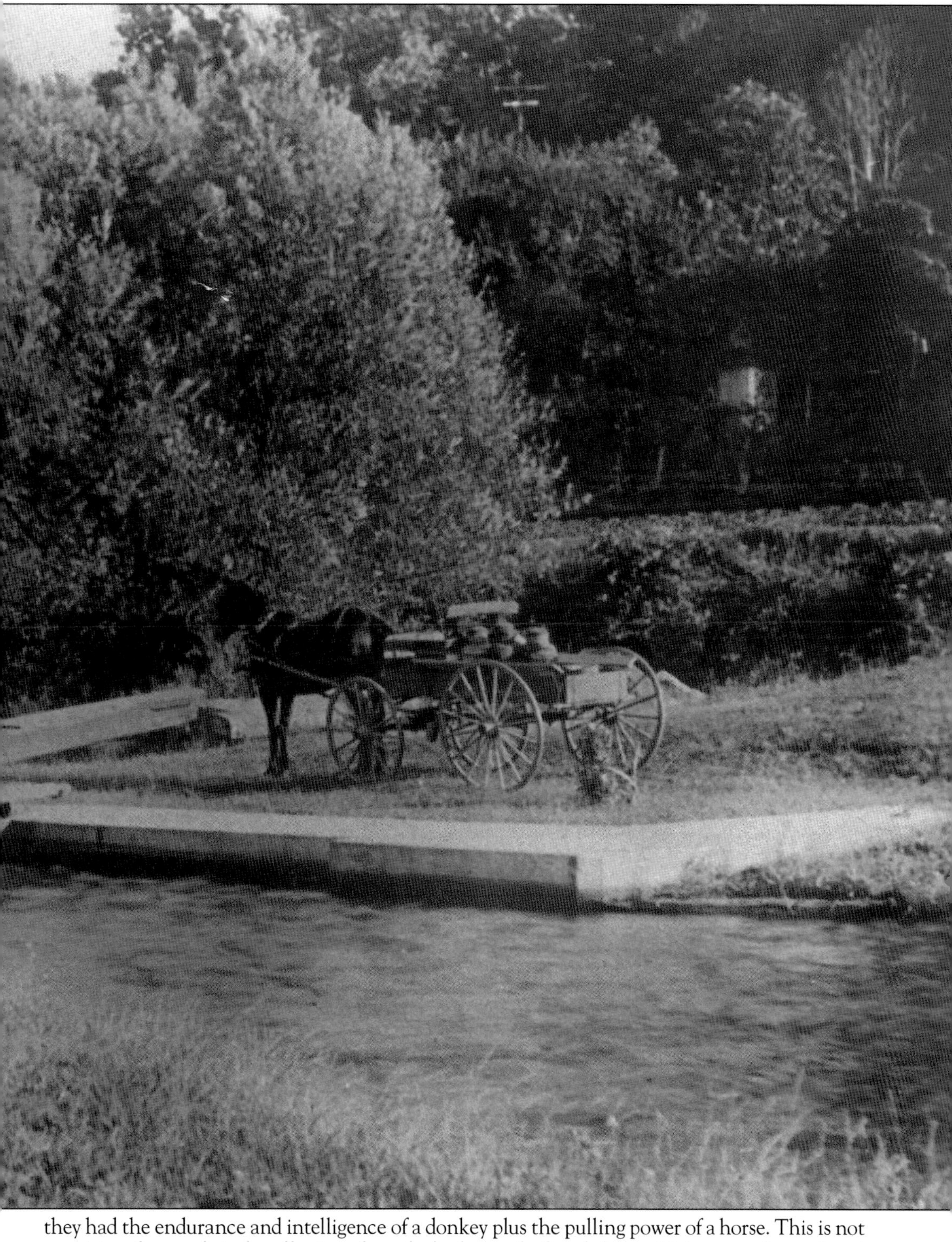

they had the endurance and intelligence of a donkey plus the pulling power of a horse. This is not surprising, for a mule is the offspring of a male donkey and a female horse. Mules were also preferred over horses for canal work because they drank less and were more sure-footed than horses.

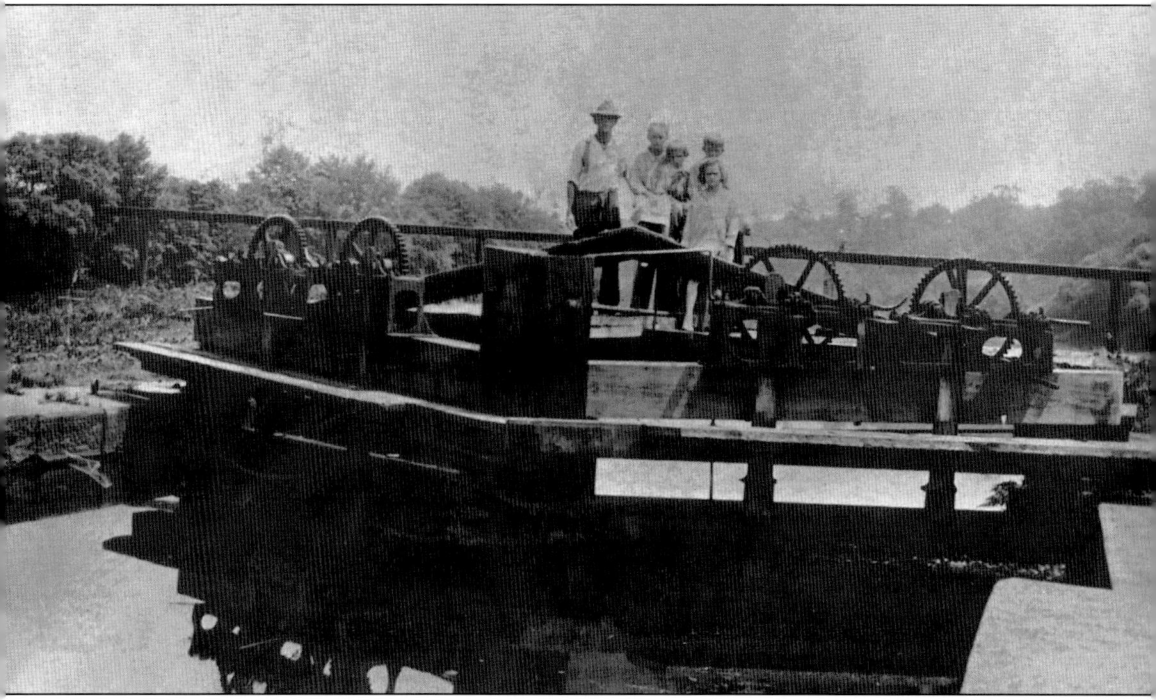

Charles Mull poses with his children at the lower gate at outlet lock 57 (known as Schwartz's Lock) in Parker Ford on the Girard Canal, which was roughly 22 miles long—the longest on the Schuylkill Navigation. Mull was lock tender here between 1913 and 1920. As such, he was in charge of opening and closing the lock gates to allow canal boats to move through the canal, as well as to maintain the water level. Traditionally, canal locks used miter gates with wickets, which are sluice gates, for regulating the amount of water in a canal or for emptying a lock. Lock tenders were usually stationed in small booths on bridges or near canal locks to watch for approaching vessels. It was also the lock tender's responsibility to monitor and inspect canal equipment for defects and to make minor repairs or adjustments as needed.

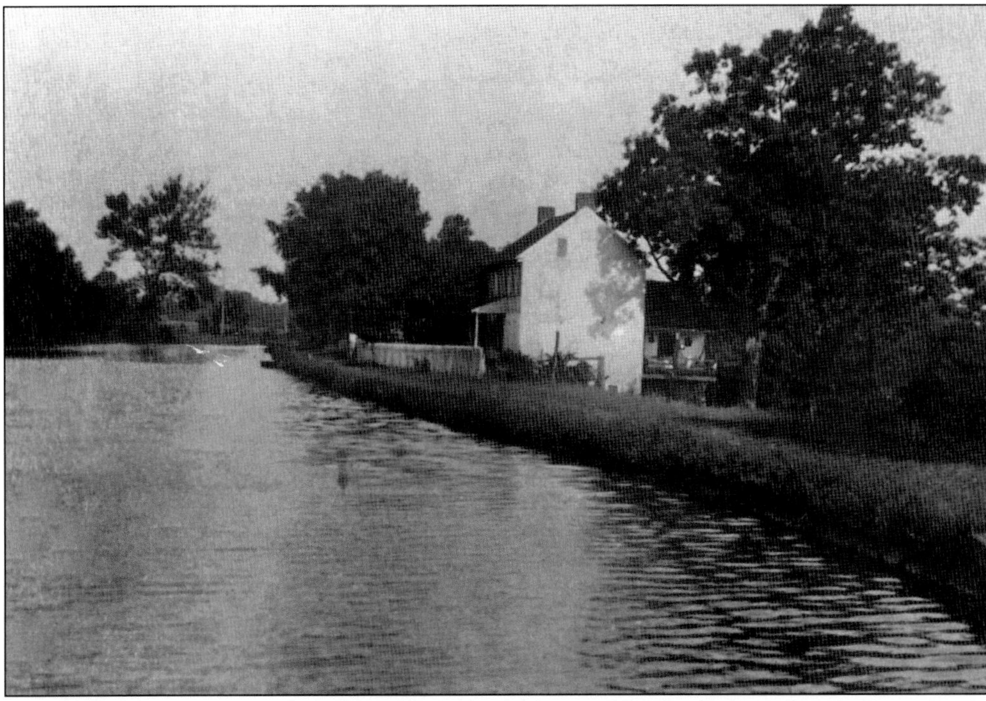

The Girard Canal is seen here from the outlet lock in 1913. The lock tender's house is on the right. The canal was named after Stephen Girard, a prominent man from Philadelphia who was heavily invested in the navigation project. Thomas Oakes was originally in charge of the canal's planning and construction, but Ephraim Beach took over upon his death.

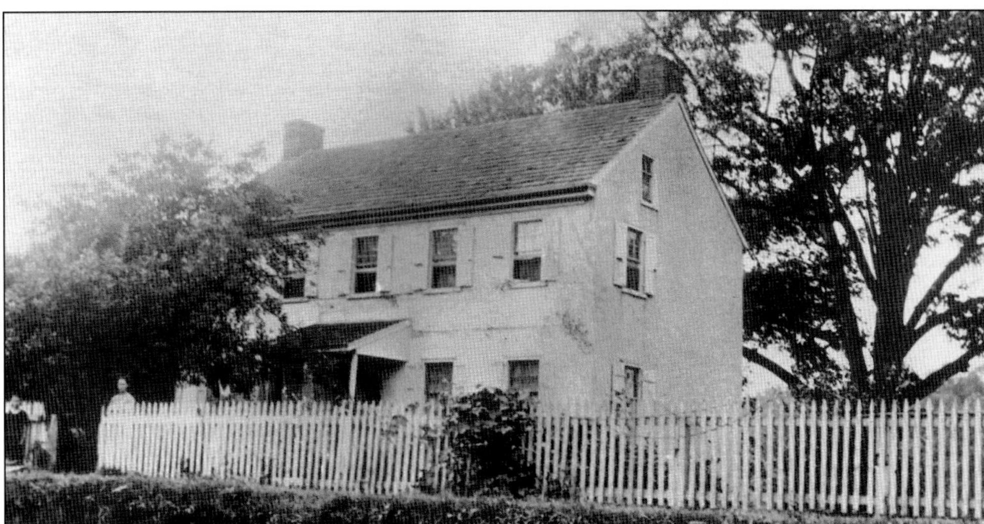

The lock tender's house at the outlet lock of the Girard Canal is seen here a few years earlier than the photograph above. The fieldstone lock tender's residence was built between 1822 and 1824, but it was later found to be too small, so an addition was built onto its west end.

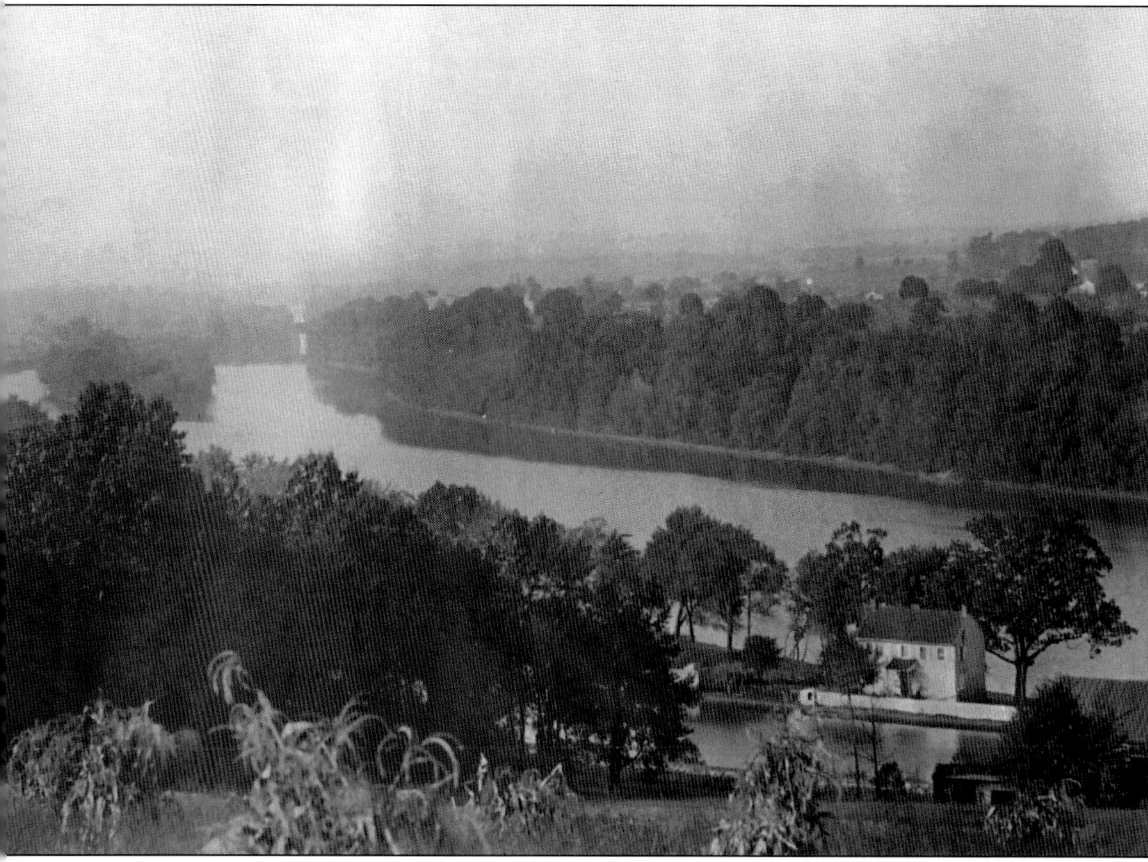

In this 1902 photograph, taken from Crab Hill, the Schuylkill River runs behind the lock tender's house, and the Girard Canal flows in front of it. The covered bridge between Parker Ford and Linfield can just be made out in the background. The island in the river (left background) was removed in the Schuylkill River Desilting Project of the 1950s, in which a team of engineers dredged the river to trap the coal sediment that had filled its bed and raised its floodplain. Unfortunately, the cleanup efforts also resulted in the destruction of many dams and locks along the canal. The Girard Canal was the longest segment on the Schuylkill Canal—roughly 22 miles in length—beginning at Lewis's Dam and ending at the Girard Outlet.

Two

Prime Time on the Schuylkill Canal

Once the Schuylkill Navigation System was up and running, it made inexpensive, long-distance transportation of goods a reality, and boats were transporting coal, iron, lumber, various merchandise, and produce along its 108-mile path. It also led to the rapid growth and industrialization of many towns along its banks. During the peak tonnage year of 1859, more than 1,400 boats were said to have traveled the canal, carrying a total of 1.7 million tons of goods, of which 1.4 million tons were anthracite coal. A steersman (usually the owner/captain) at the tiller (a part of the rudder that steered the canal boat), a bowman to tend the lines, and a driver on the towpath were all the crew needed to move 200 tons of coal to its destination. Drivers were usually young boys, who earned around $10 a month. Of course, life on the canal was not only about hard labor. Many also enjoyed the recreational opportunities of riding pleasure boats, fishing in the waterways, and paddling its channels in canoes.

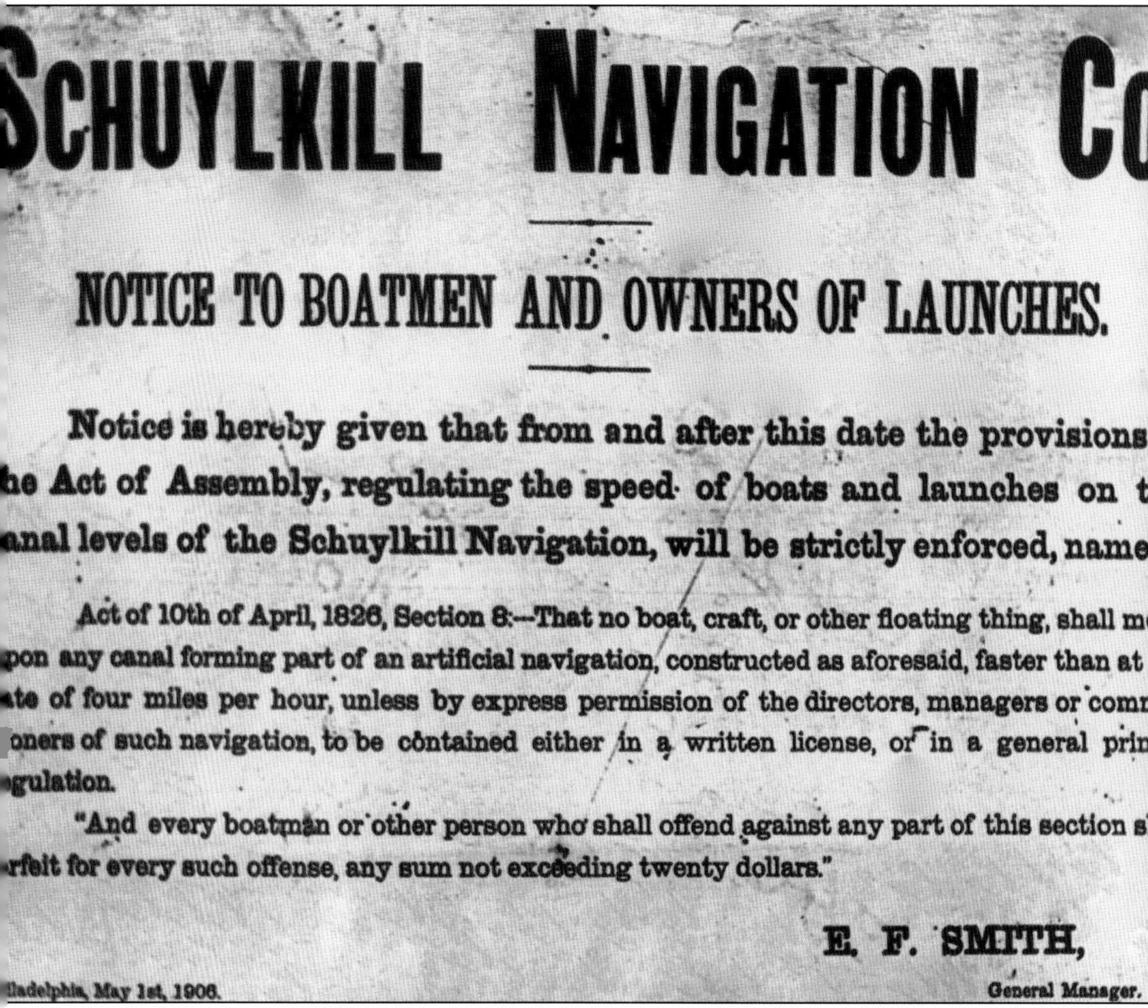
SCHUYLKILL NAVIGATION CO

NOTICE TO BOATMEN AND OWNERS OF LAUNCHES.

Notice is hereby given that from and after this date the provisions
he Act of Assembly, regulating the speed of boats and launches on t
anal levels of the Schuylkill Navigation, will be strictly enforced, name

Act of 10th of April, 1826, Section 8:—That no boat, craft, or other floating thing, shall m
pon any canal forming part of an artificial navigation, constructed as aforesaid, faster than at
ate of four miles per hour, unless by express permission of the directors, managers or comm
oners of such navigation, to be contained either in a written license, or in a general prin
gulation.

"And every boatman or other person who shall offend against any part of this section s
rfeit for every such offense, any sum not exceeding twenty dollars."

E. F. SMITH,
General Manager.

ladelphia, May 1st, 1906.

The life of boatmen and boat owners on the canal was quite enjoyable. These men only experienced occasional adversity—destruction caused by flooding, for example. However, those who traveled the Schuylkill Navigation, commonly but incorrectly referred to today as the Schuylkill Canal, whether for the Schuylkill Navigation Company or for their own purposes, had to abide by certain laws. For instance, boatmen using motor-powered boats—or launches—were not to exceed a designated speed. Such rules were often posted along the canal (pictured). Because the company owned the canal, it was entitled to govern the waterway's use. Edwin F. Smith, named in this notice, was the superintendent and engineer of the canals along the Schuylkill Navigation. In 1949, the Schuylkill Navigation Company was acquired by the Commonwealth of Pennsylvania.

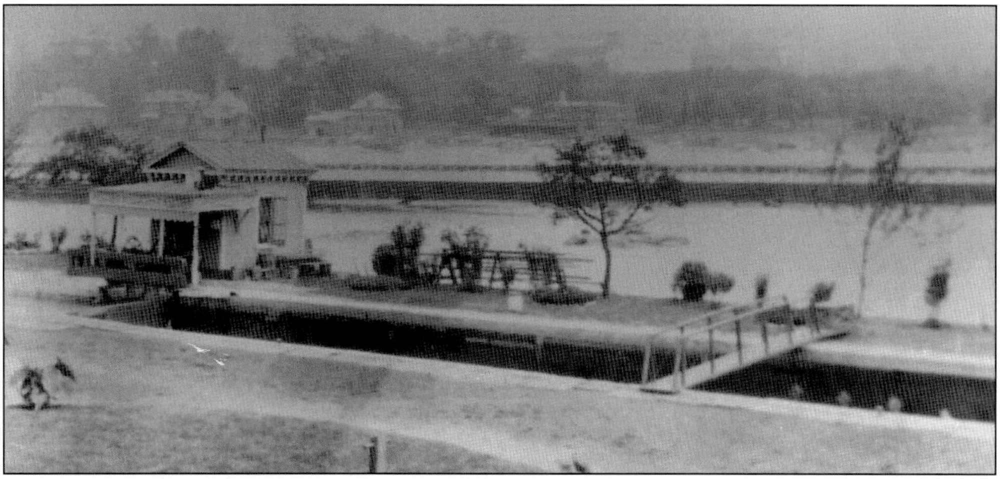

Originally, there were 72 locks on the Schuylkill Navigation; by the end of the canal's days, that number had dropped to 44. Seen here on August 18, 1909, are the lock tender's shanty (left) and lock 72 just in front of it (not visible). In the background is Fairmount Dam. (Photograph by H.C. Wilson.)

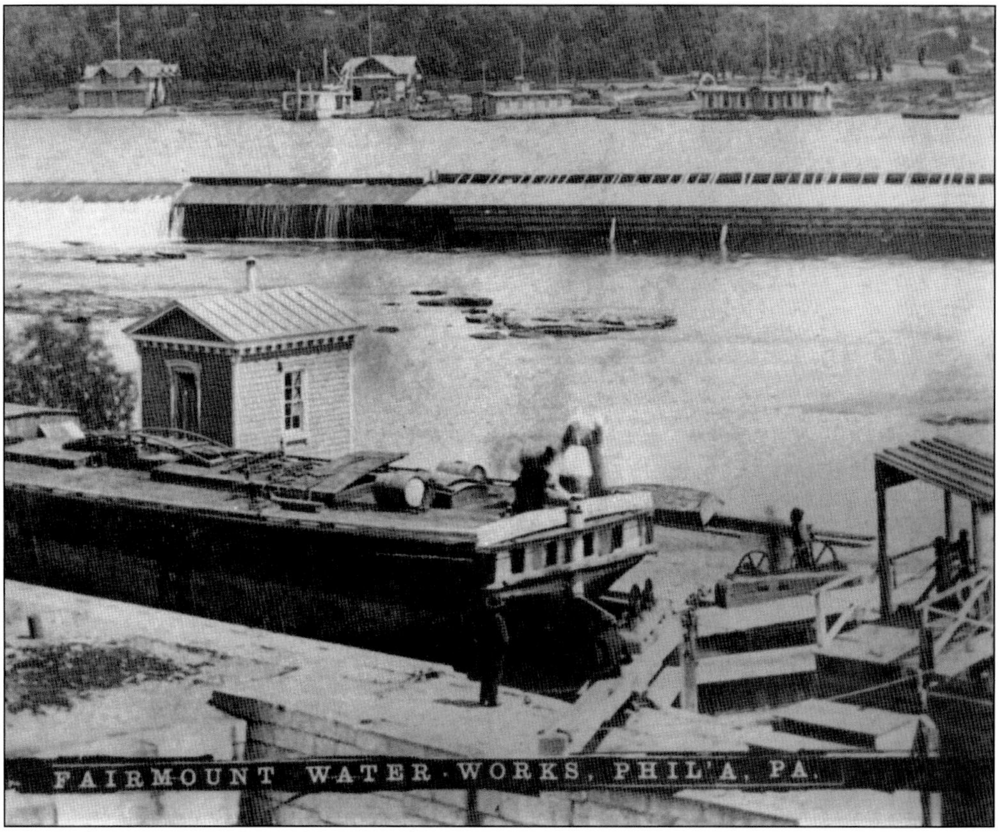

Shown here is a typical canal boat, built to transport anthracite, in a lift lock on the Schuylkill Canal. The Fairmount Dam is in the background. Lift refers to the height a boat is raised or lowered in a lock. A lift lock enables a boat to be raised from one level to another by allowing water to flow into or out of it.

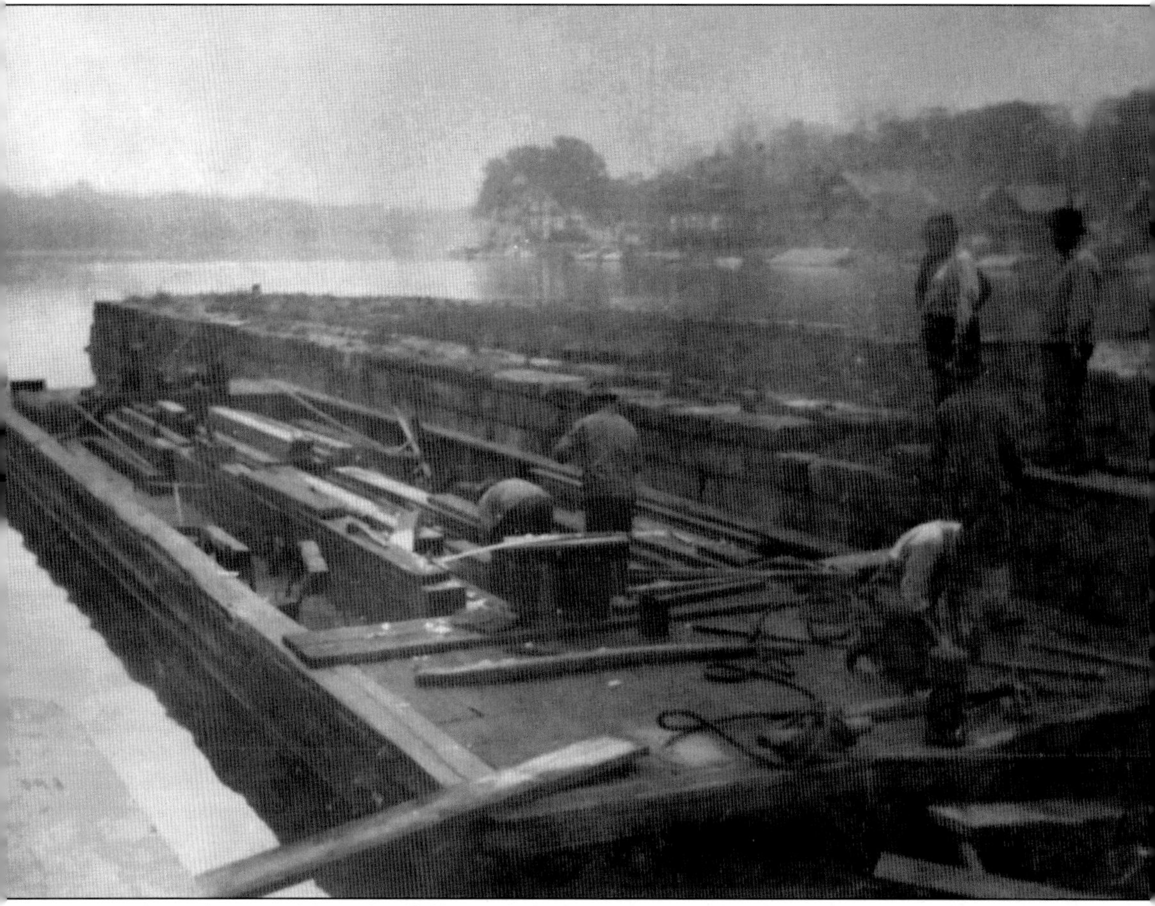

In the early years of the Schuylkill Canal, the boats that traveled the waterway were relatively small and often towed by men, referred to as bow haulers, walking at the end of a line. Once towpaths were completed, boatmen used mules to tow their boats. Scows, like the timber scow shown in this August 1926 photograph at lock 71 in Fairmount, were short, steerable canal workboats used to haul sand, gravel, coal, and the sort. Note that both the bow and stern of the boat are square. This is a typical feature of scows. At lower left is a wooden gangplank. These were used to allow passage between the canal boat and the shore. In the background on the right are the houses on the east bank of the Schuylkill River that make up Boathouse Row.

In 1815, the Schuylkill Navigation Company was hired to build a series of dams and canals—known collectively as the Schuylkill Navigation, or simply the Schuylkill Canal today—along the Schuylkill River. It completed this project in 1827 and saw its best year of business in 1859, but the opening of the Philadelphia & Reading Railroad and several floods put a strain on its finances. The company leased the canal to the railroad in 1870 and eventually closed its doors in 1917. These 1915 photographs show partial views of the Schuylkill Navigation Company's building at 415-417 Walnut Street in Philadelphia.

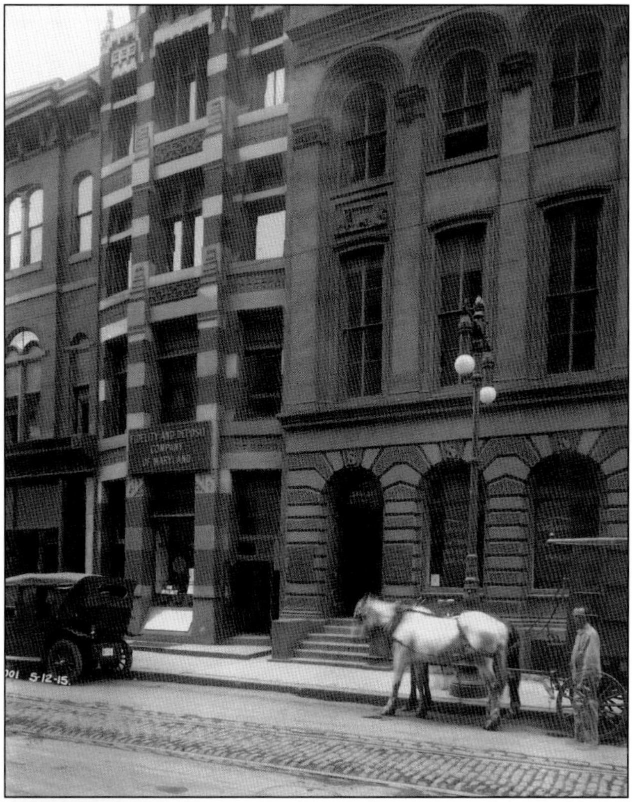

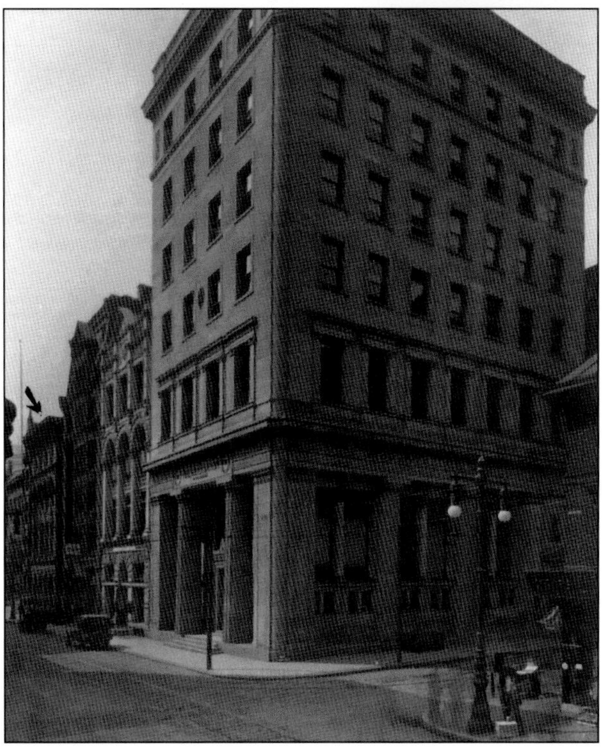

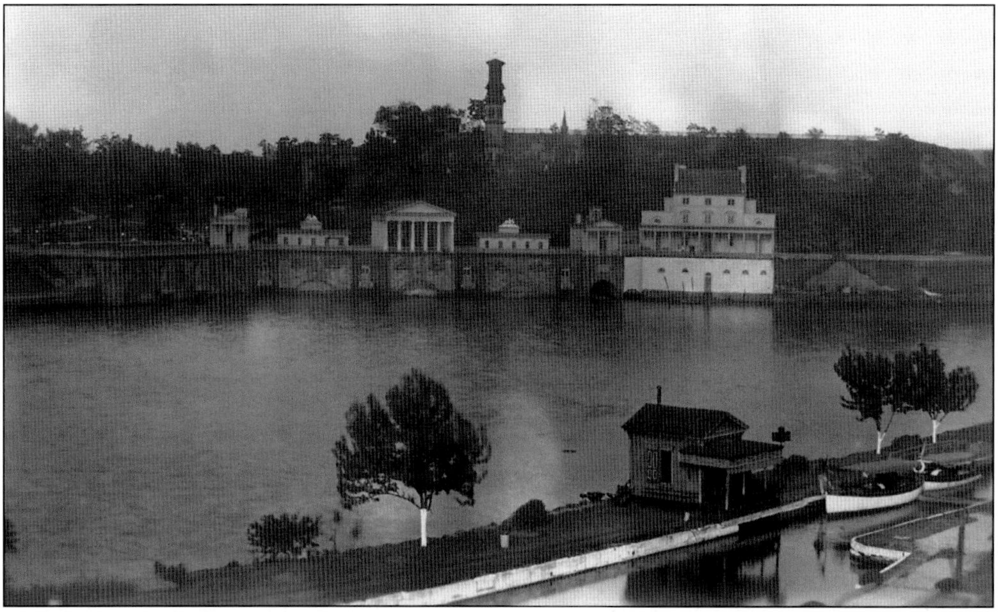

Fredrick Graff was the chief engineer of the Fairmount Water Works. The facility's earliest building was erected in 1812 to meet the water needs of the growing city of Philadelphia. This 1910 photograph shows the waterworks buildings along the Schuylkill River. The canal runs in the foreground at lower right.

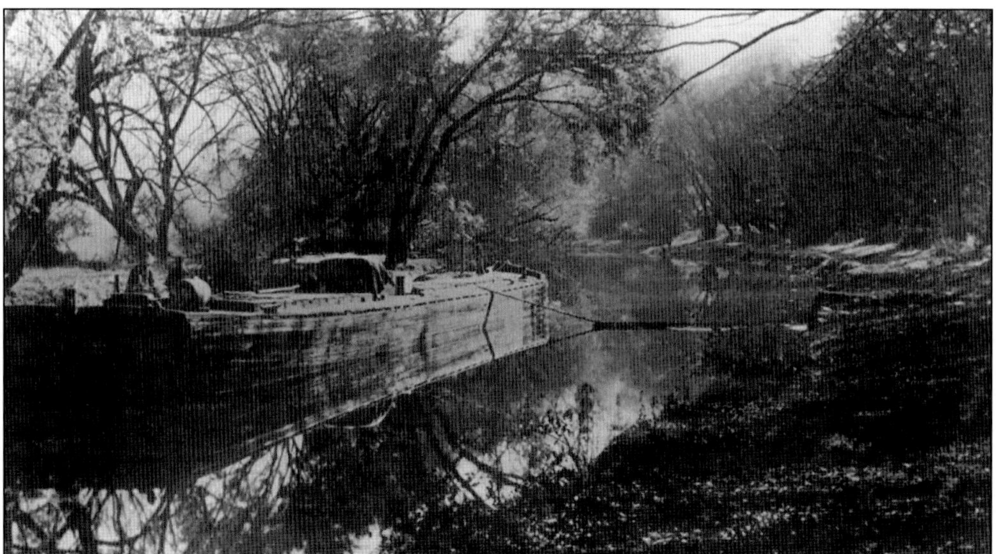

Men are seen on a canal boat in the channel between Peter's Island and the west bank of the Schuylkill River in Fairmount Park, Philadelphia. The island still exists today and is immediately north of the concrete Columbia Railroad Bridge—also known as Columbia Bridge. Built in 1920, the bridge crosses the river, as well as Kelly Drive and Dr. Martin Luther King Jr. Drive.

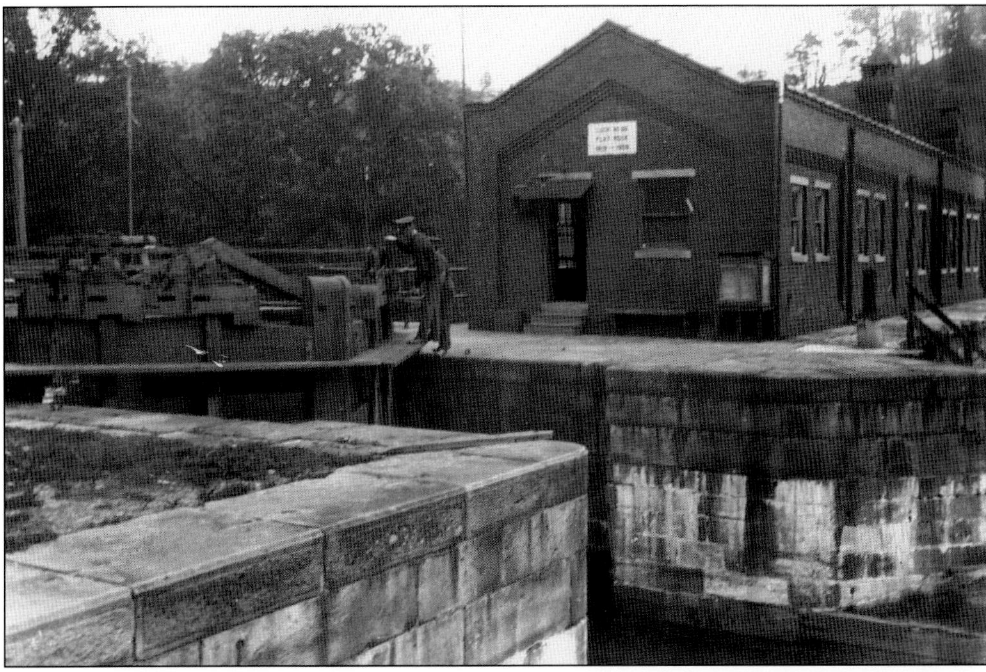

This is the Flat Rock feeder building at lock 68 on the Manayunk Canal. This building housed the mechanisms that controlled the water flow in the canal. The man pictured is operating the wicket bar, or lock wrench, which is a crank handle that opens the wicket of the lock gate.

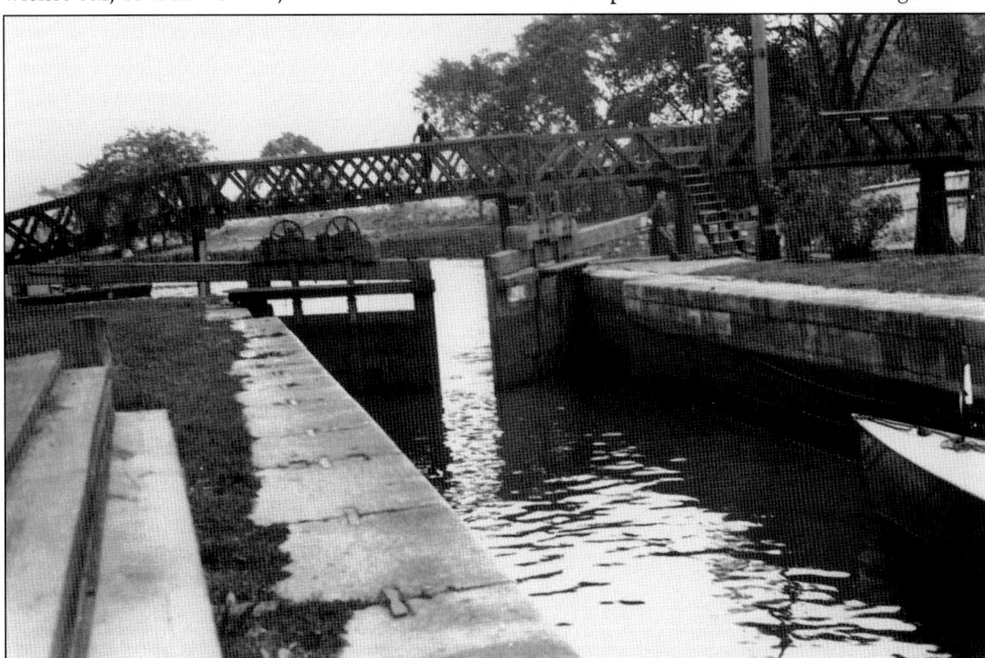

The Manayunk Canal originally passed through the Flat Rock Dam structure at lock 68, seen here in 1919. An observer on the bridge watches as the man below opens the outlet gate for a waiting boat. Lock 68 has been plated off, and the area above it was filled in. This section of the canal forms the northern side of what is known as Venice Island.

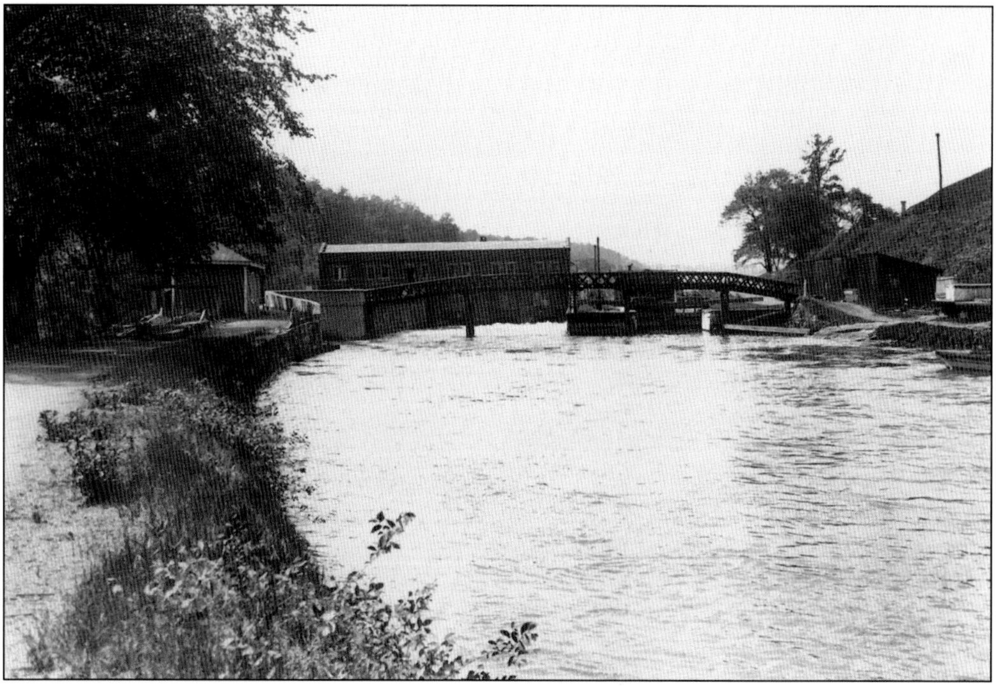

The above photograph looks up the Manayunk Canal toward lock 68, which served as a guard lock, as well as the feeder house (center) at Flat Rock Dam (Dam 31). Several maintenance buildings can be seen on the right. The lock and feeder house are seen in the below photograph from a different perspective. The people seem to be aware of the photographer, including the man waving at upper right. The Manayunk Canal was purchased by the City of Philadelphia and was improved for use as a recreation area. It is now considered a part of the Fairmount Park system.

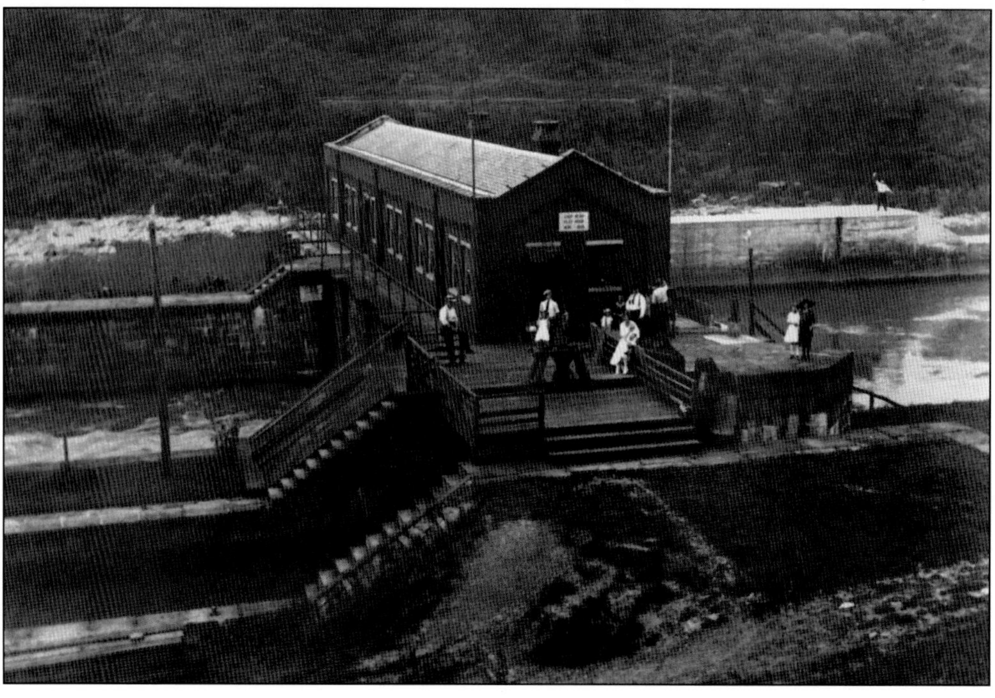

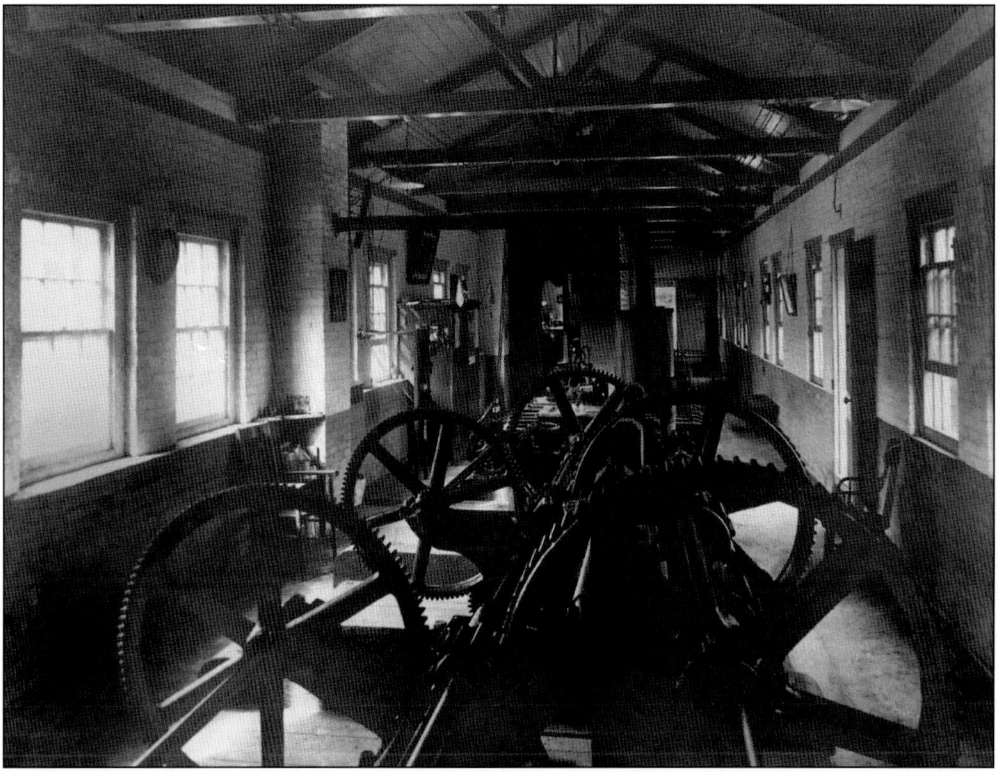

Here are two slightly different views of the interior of the Flat Rock feeder house at lock 68, showing new and old feeders. The feeder was completed and rebuilt in 1909. The man in the below photograph is said to be William Bostick, who put in 27 years of service to the canal company. On October 18, 1818, the Manayunk section of the Schuylkill Canal opened, and, between 1840 and 1854, the city experienced rapid growth and industrialization. The Friends of the Manayunk Canal is a not-for-profit watershed organization, established in 1996, dedicated to the protection, restoration, and preservation of the natural and historical resources of the canal and towpath.

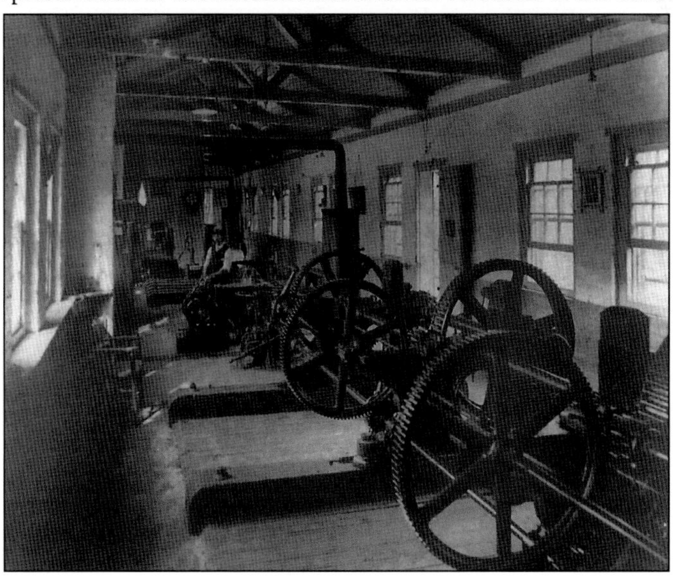

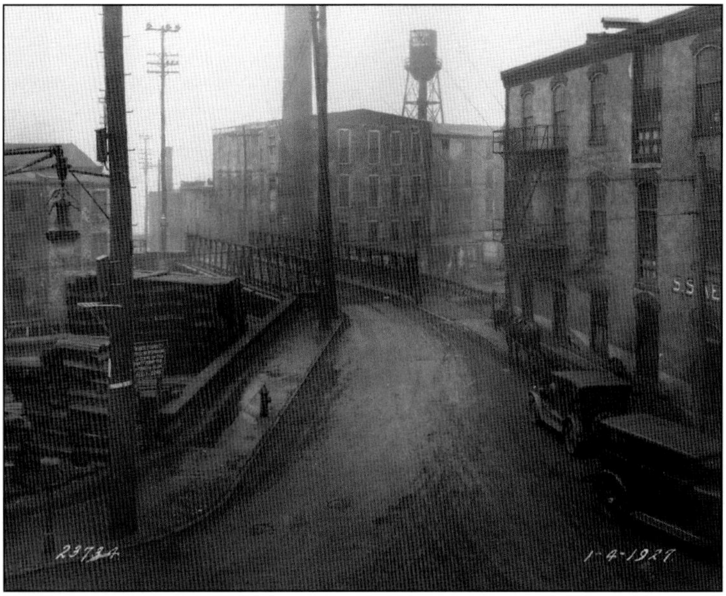

The Leverington Avenue Bridge in Manayunk is seen from the north end of Main Street. Out of sight beneath the bridge runs the Manayunk Canal, which, by 1929, was almost completely out of use. The three-story S.S. Keely planing mill is at right. In 2005, the former lumberyard behind the mill was developed and is now a multilevel condominium building along the canal.

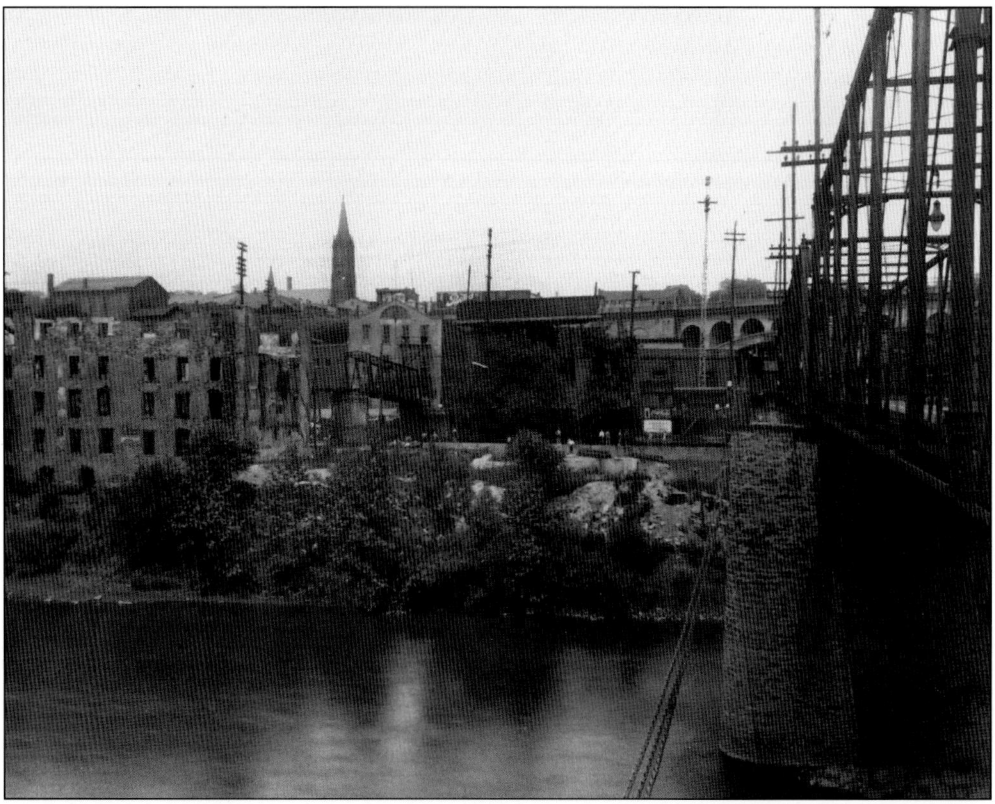

Manayunk is seen here across the upstream side of the Green Lane Bridge in 1926. The canal is just beyond the wall that the boys across the river are standing on. To the left are the ruined factory buildings that were part of the Sevill Schofield, Son & Company Eagle Mill, which produced cotton and wool.

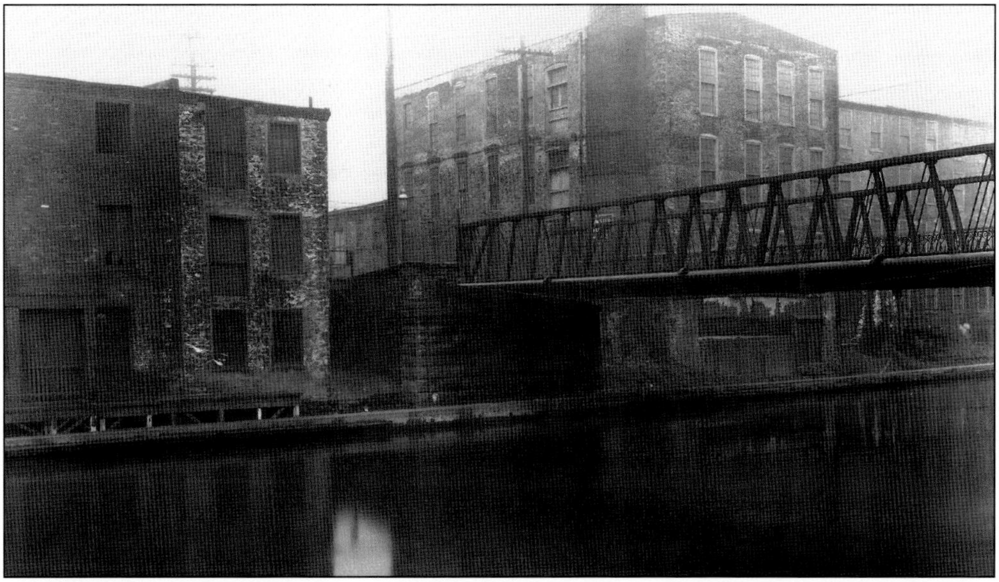

Another view of the old Sevill Schofield, Son & Company Eagle Mill buildings, this time showing the Manayunk Canal beneath the iron bridge that gave workers access to the buildings. Manayunk emerged as a major world textile center during the Civil War. The mill's operations came to a halt around 1906.

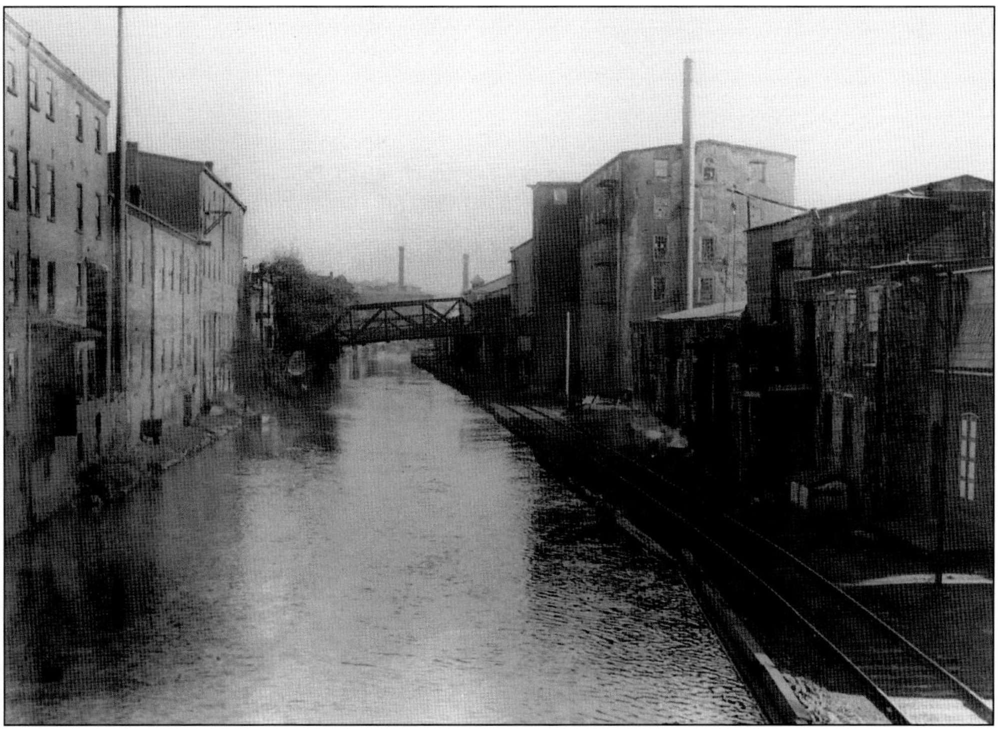

The original towpath along the Manayunk Canal was used by mules as they pulled canal boats through the water. In 1889, the railway covered the towpath. At one time, various mills lined either side of the canal, and small bridges like the one pictured here were common. Workers used them to cross over the canal to get to work.

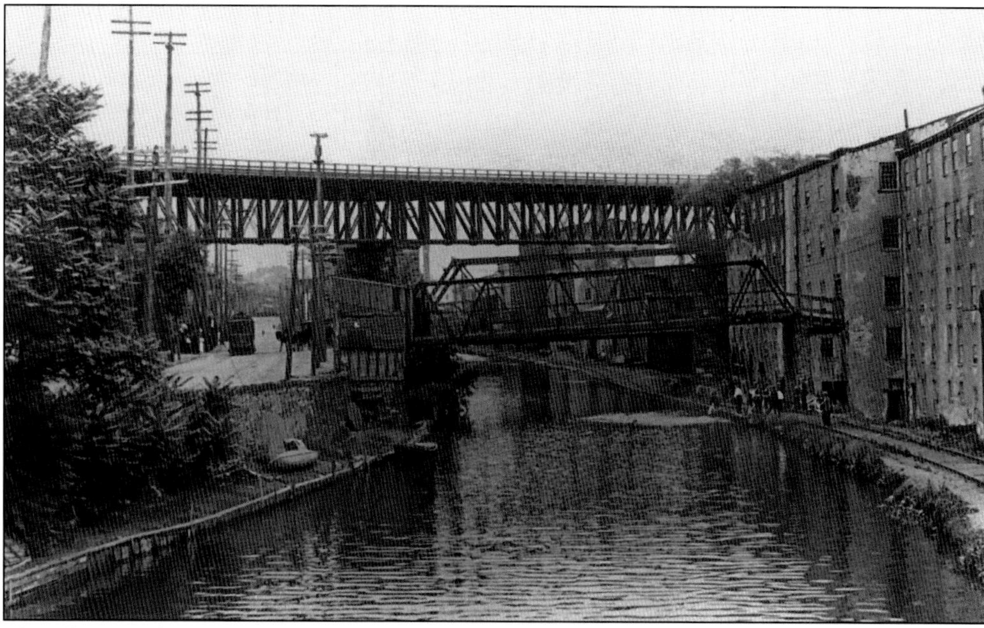

This photograph, taken from the Green Lane Bridge, looks down the Manayunk Canal. At left, a trolley car is visible. The trolley line ran between Philadelphia and Manayunk. At right, children play in the canal. The high steel bridge above was built by the former Schuylkill Valley Division of the Pennsylvania Railroad.

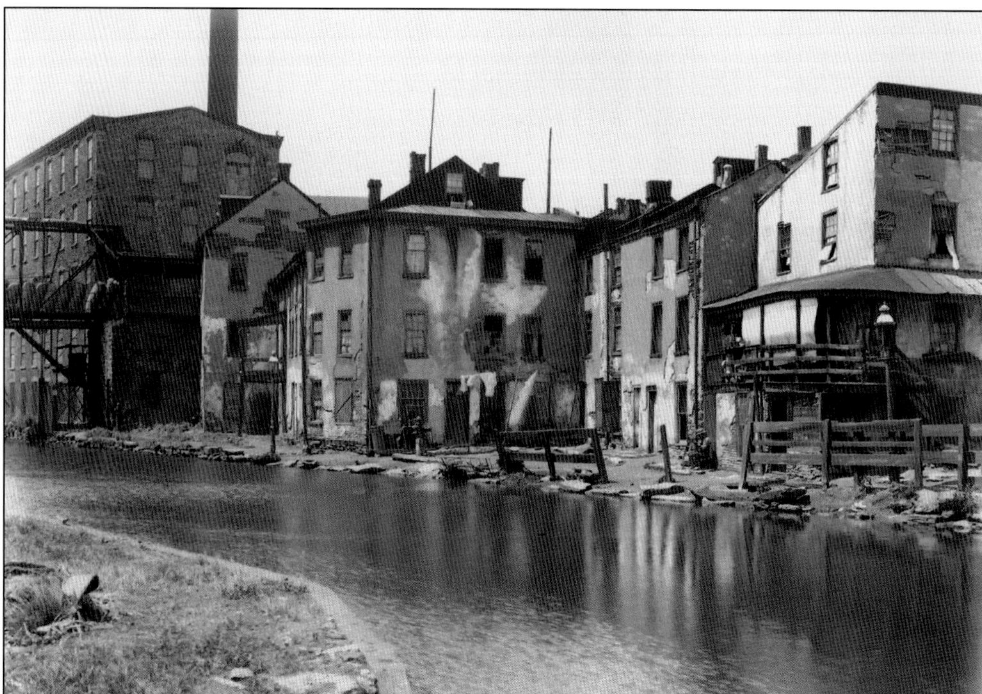

This 1932 photograph, taken just above the outlet locks on the Manayunk Canal, paints a bleak picture; the waterway's heyday has passed. The 1920s marked the end of the area's reign as a major textile center. Paper mills, however, were still profitable at the time and continued operation.

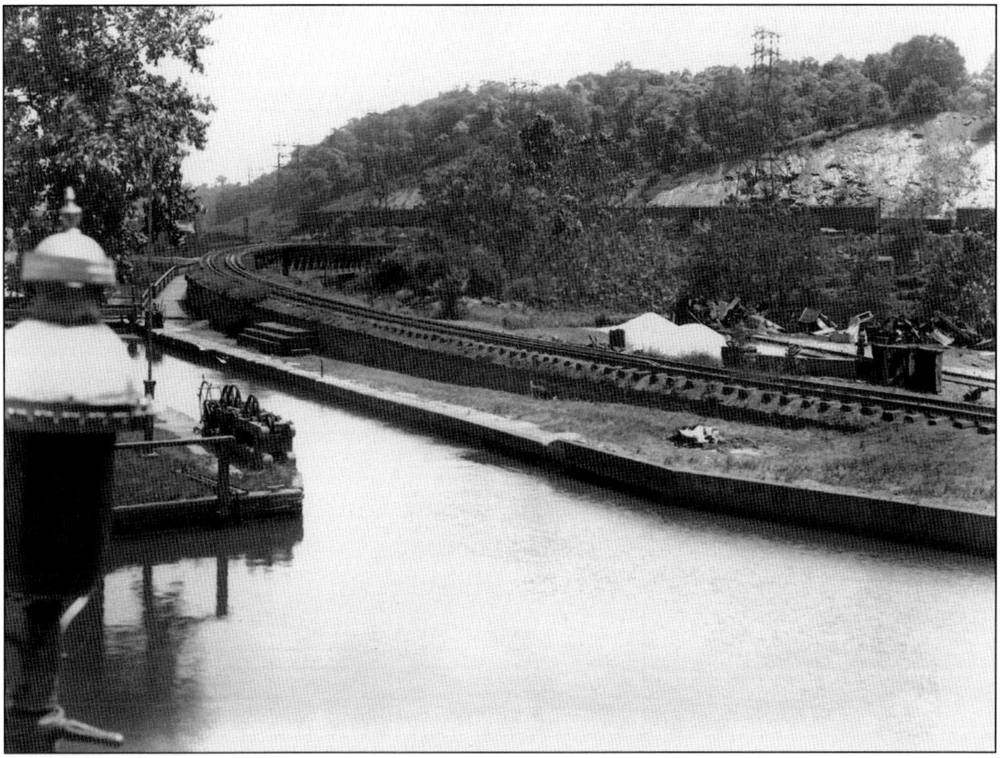

A chamber, formerly called a cistern, is the body of a lock between the upstream and downstream gates. These photographs, taken on June 3, 1932, offer a view through the upper chamber of the outlet locks on the Manayunk Canal. Shown in the above photograph is the railroad across the canal, with freight train cars lined up above it. The below photograph offers a wider perspective, showing less of the railway but revealing the lock tender's shanty (the small dark building to the left of the tracks), which often served as an office or sleeping quarters for the lock tender.

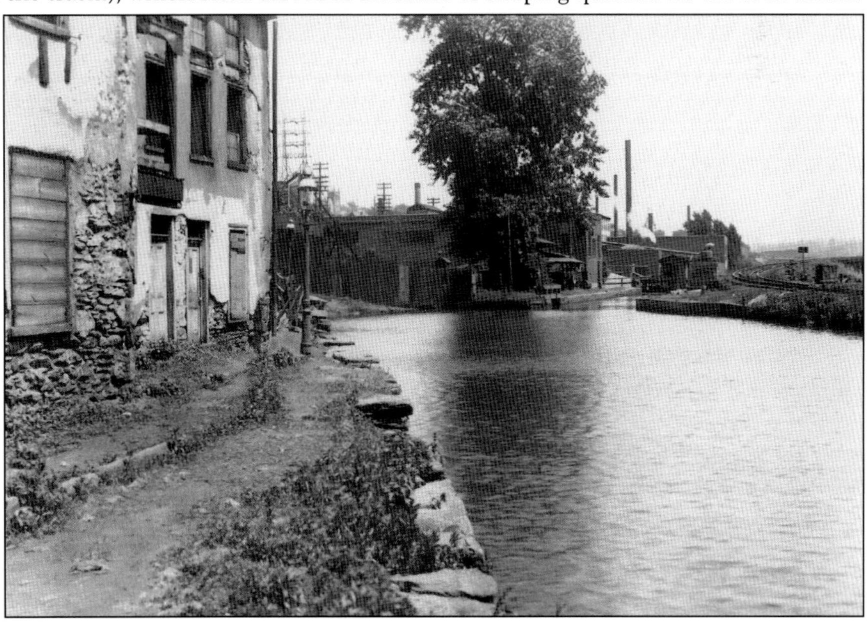

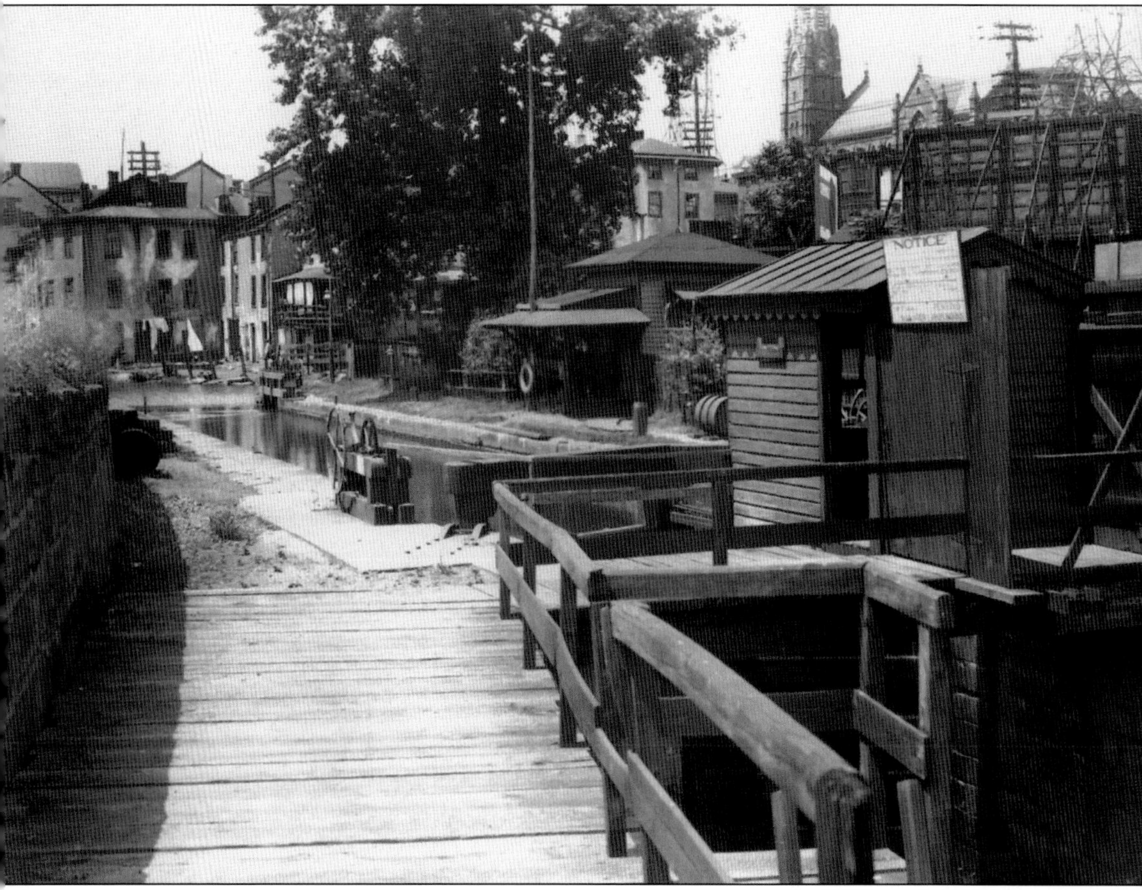

From this view, both outlet locks of the Manayunk Canal are visible. This section of the Schuylkill Navigation consisted of Dam 31 (Flat Rock Dam), lock 68 (in Shawmont) and locks 69 and 70 (seen here at Lock Street). Today, the canal has been gradually reconstructed, with proposals to renovate the locks at both ends. Here, a notice is posted by the office and bears the name of Pencoyd Iron Works, which was started by the Roberts family in 1852 on 50 acres along the Schuylkill River. The company became a major steel supplier. A sign at lower right cautions canoers in the canal to keep back. The clock tower of St. John the Baptist Church is visible in the background. The church was designed by New York architect Patrick Charles Keely and dedicated on April 1, 1894.

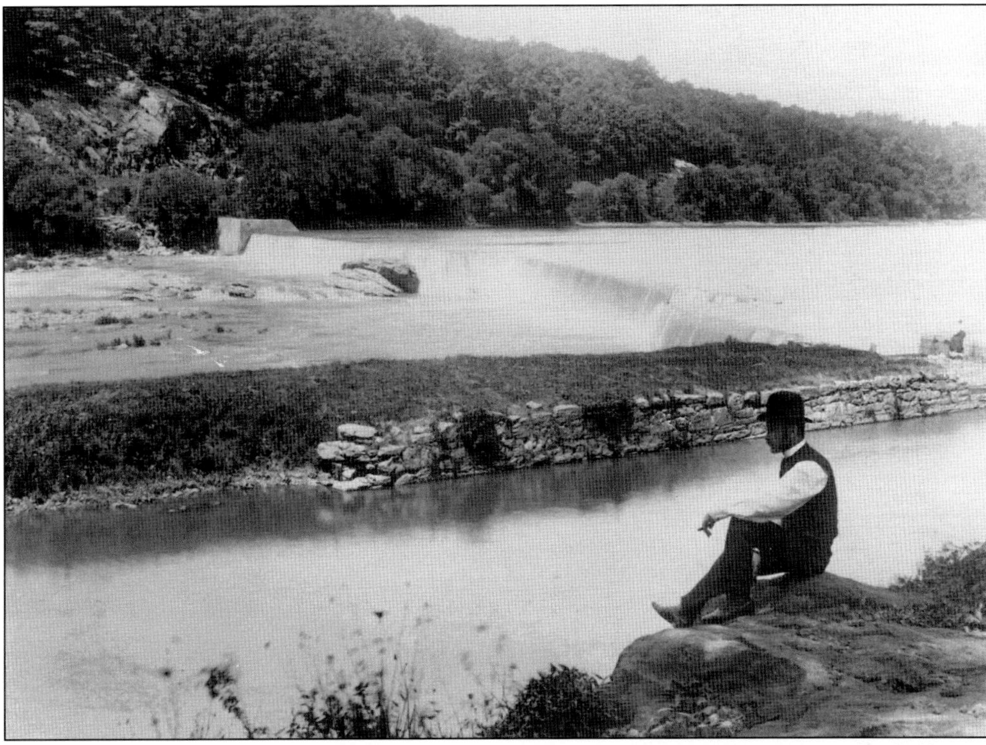

This 1897 photograph displays Flat Rock Dam, which is the highest dam on the Schuylkill River south of Reading. The Commonwealth of Pennsylvania now owns the dam and completely rebuilt it in 1977 using concrete. The entrance to the Manayunk Canal, which begins on the eastern side of the dam, is in the foreground.

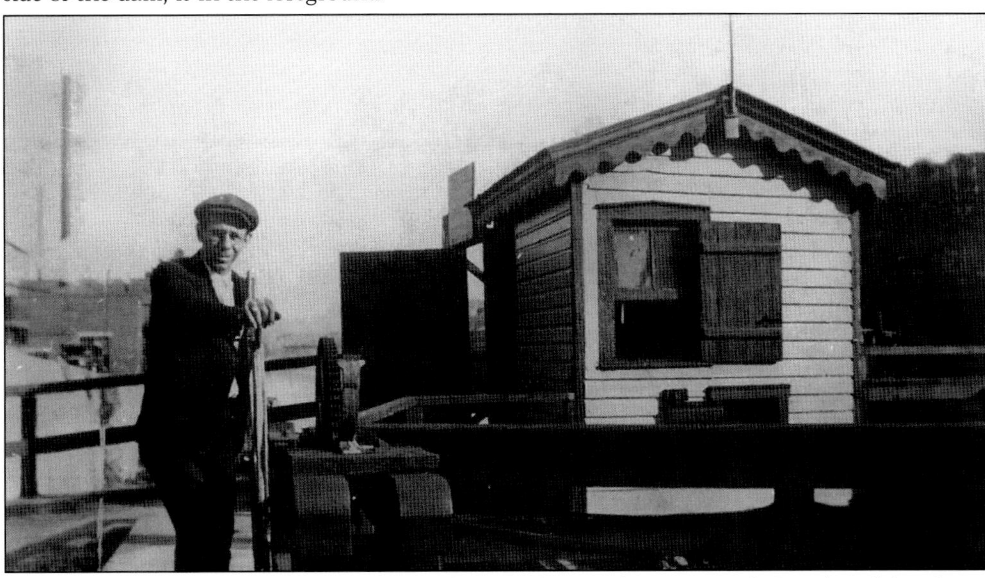

Lock tender John Wright operates outlet locks 69 and 70 on the Manayunk Canal, with his shanty behind him. During the active canal era, the lock tender and his family were as self-sufficient as possible, and any products they could grow or make themselves could be sold to or bartered with the workers on the passing boats.

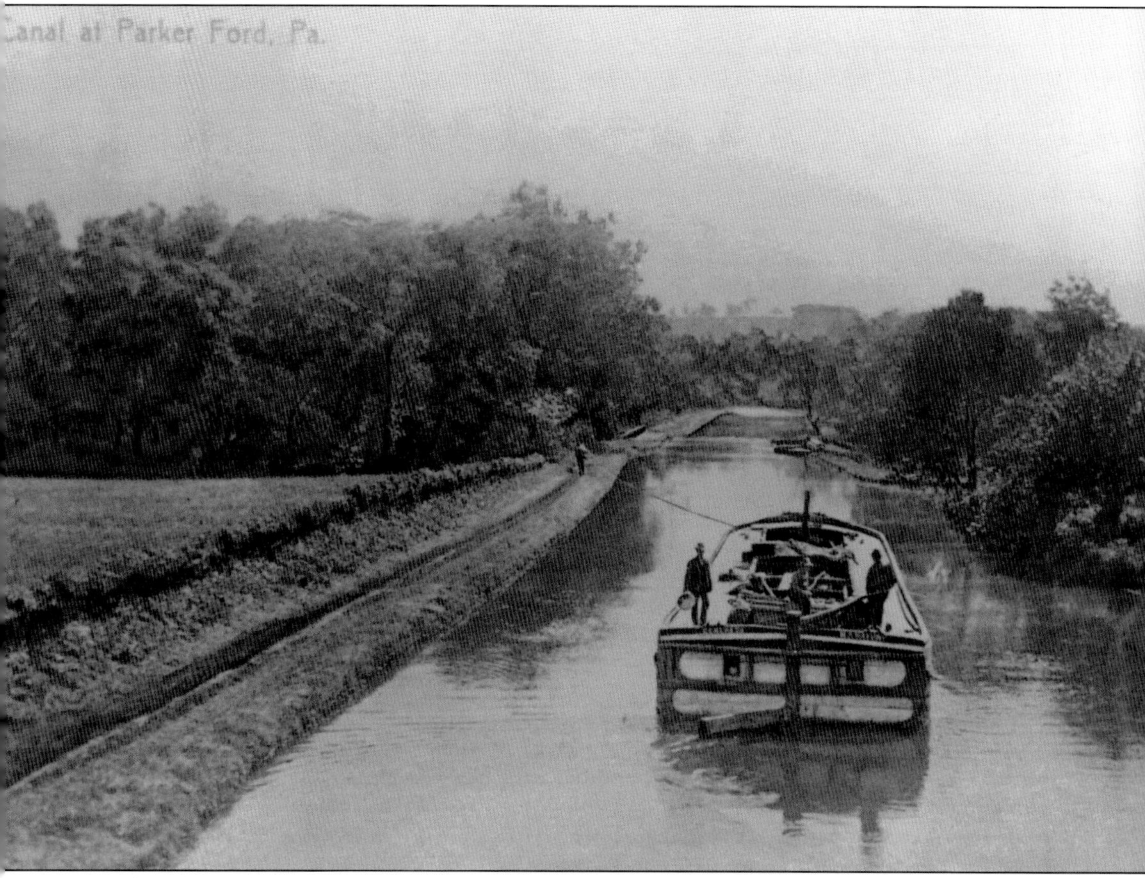

Taken from the Linfield Road canal bridge just below lock 56 in Parker Ford, this photograph shows the canal boat *Congress of Manayunk* descending the Girard Canal, with the Pigeon Creek aqueduct in the distance (seen as a narrowing of the canal). This aqueduct is one of 17 stone arch structures that carried the canal over tributary streams. Before proper towpaths were constructed, men would have to tow canal boats, as seen in this picture, by pushing against a sturdy stick tied to the towrope as a crossbar. In 1826, a towpath made the route serviceable for horses and mules. In 1827, a guidebook, the *Schuylkill Canal Navigator*, gave boatmen instructions on how to avoid running aground or getting caught on stumps or rocks. The Girard Canal reenters the Schuylkill River at the Girard Outlet, which is one and one-quarter miles above the town of Spring City.

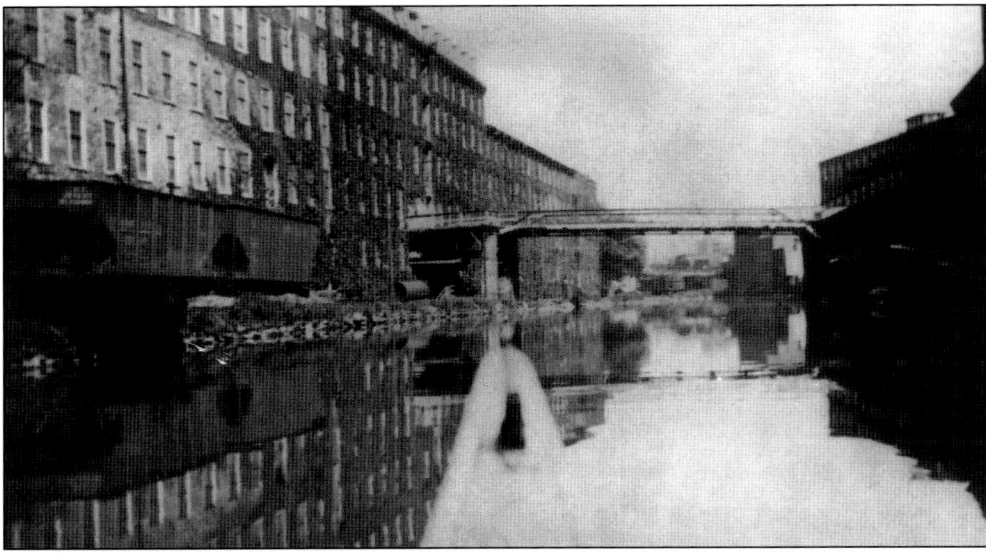

Many of the stone buildings along the towpath were once part of a large textile manufacturing center that produced cotton blankets for the Union army during the Civil War, among other things. The below photograph, taken in 1919, looks west from the Umbria Street Bridge. In the distance, the Fountain Street Bridge can be seen, and on the right is the lumberyard belonging to the S.S. Keely Planing Mill. In the water on the left, two people in a canoe enjoy the recreational benefits of the canal. The above photograph provides a unique view from the bow of a boat.

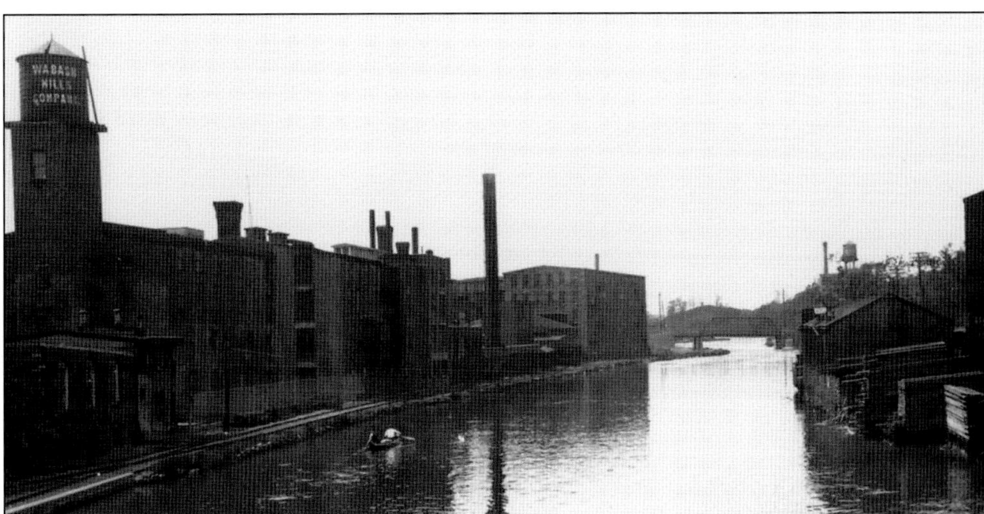

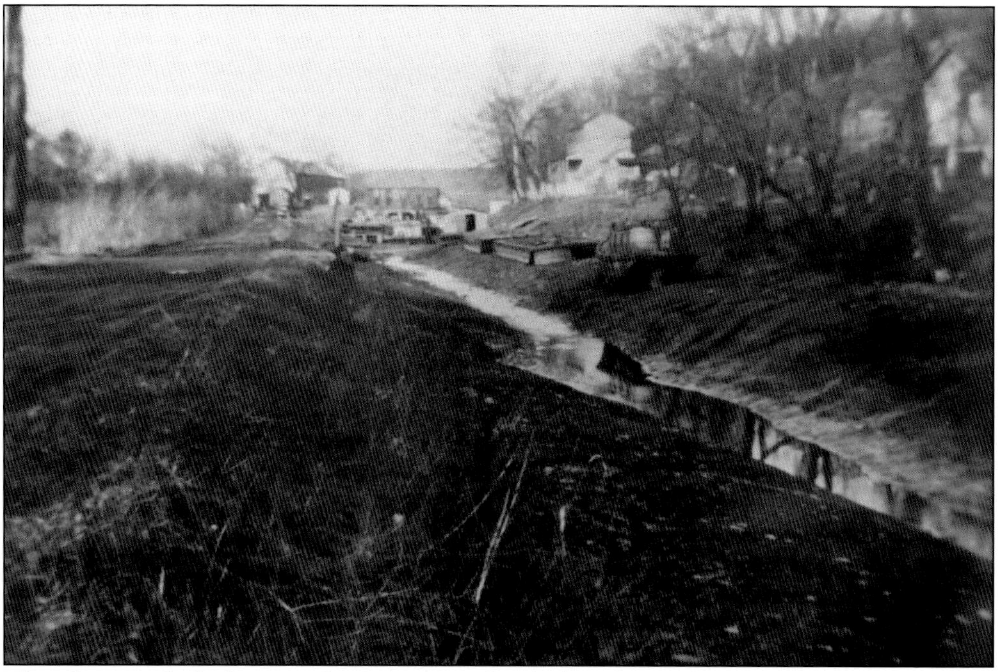

This photograph, looking up the Oakes Canal at lock 60, was taken during the winter, when the canal was dewatered. In the area in front of the locks is an assortment of equipment (dredge, scows, and barges). The lock tender's house is visible on the bank at the right.

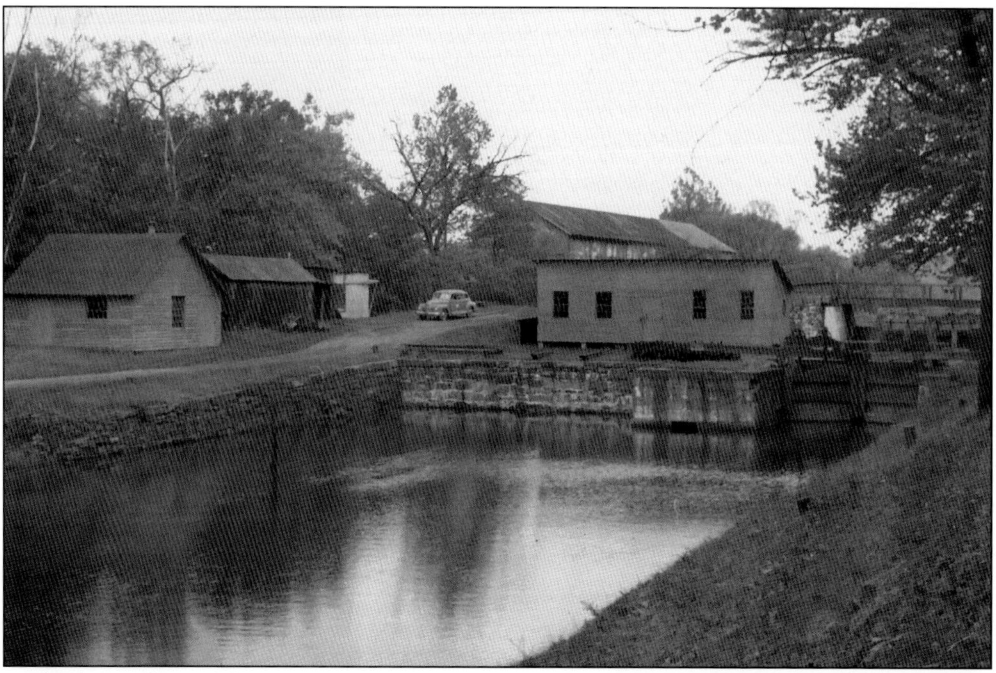

In the latter days of the canal, after the closing of the navigation shops in Reading, floating maintenance equipment like those seen in the photograph above were stored over the winter months here at lock 60 on the Oakes Canal. This 1948 view of the downstream side of the lock shows the various lock buildings, with the exception of the lock tender's house.

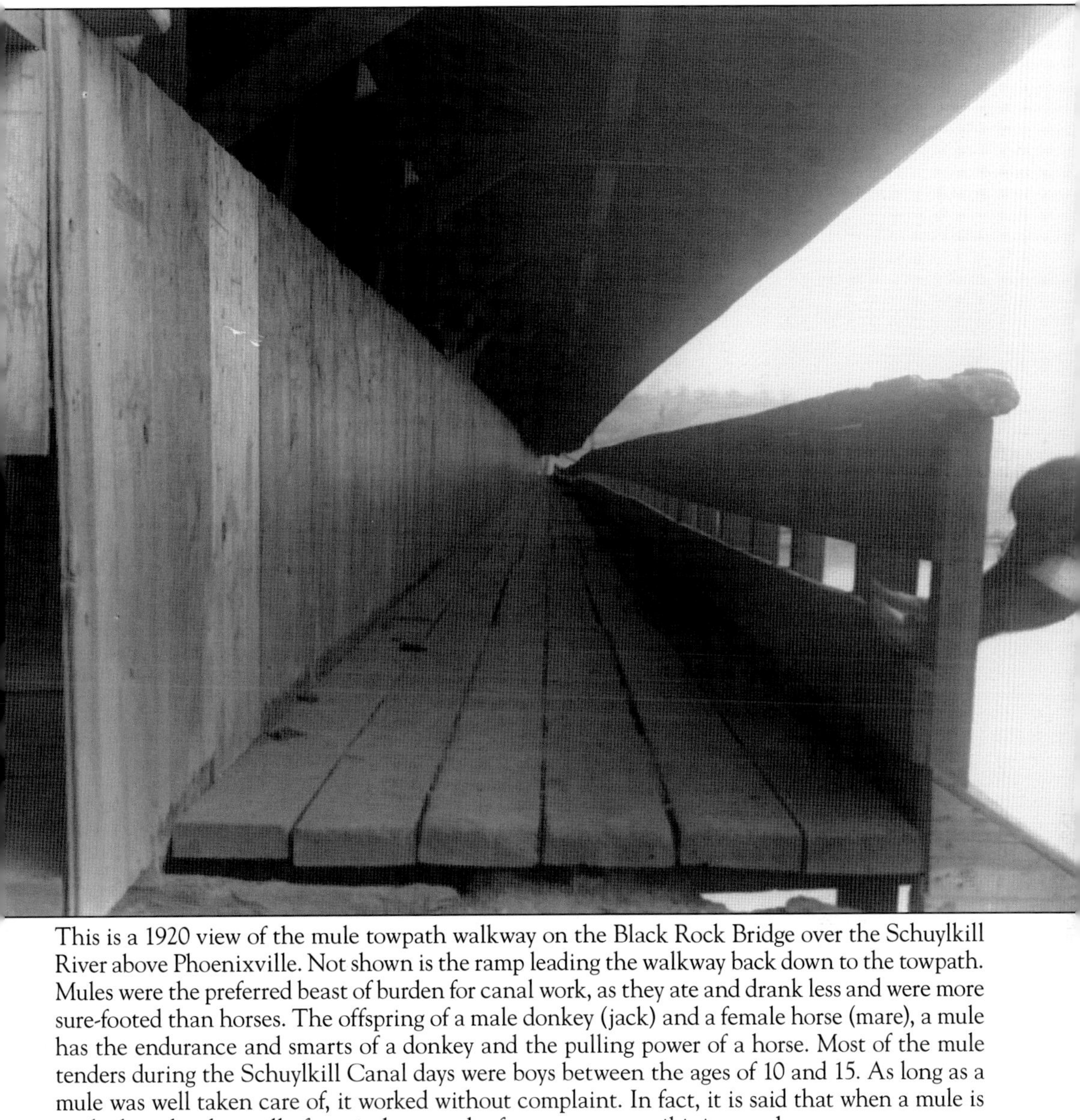

This is a 1920 view of the mule towpath walkway on the Black Rock Bridge over the Schuylkill River above Phoenixville. Not shown is the ramp leading the walkway back down to the towpath. Mules were the preferred beast of burden for canal work, as they ate and drank less and were more sure-footed than horses. The offspring of a male donkey (jack) and a female horse (mare), a mule has the endurance and smarts of a donkey and the pulling power of a horse. Most of the mule tenders during the Schuylkill Canal days were boys between the ages of 10 and 15. As long as a mule was well taken care of, it worked without complaint. In fact, it is said that when a mule is worked too hard, it will often sit down and refuse to move until it is rested.

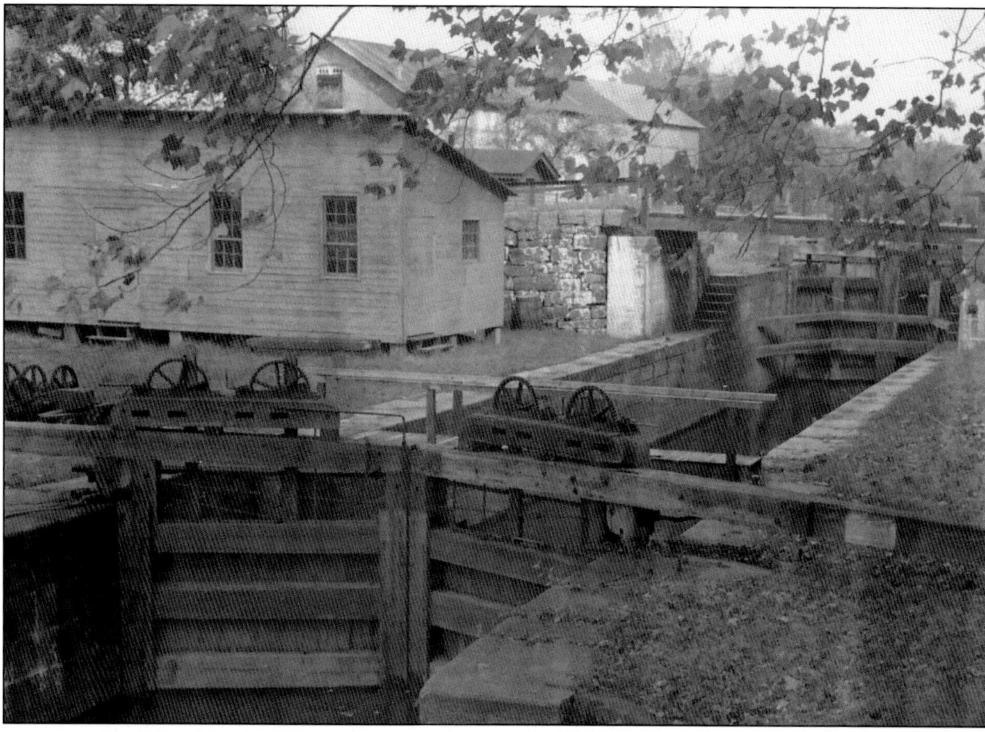

The guard lock outlet gate of lock 60 at Black Rock Dam is shown from two different perspectives. The Chester County section of the Schuylkill Canal, built in 1829, flowed from the Black Rock Dam to Phoenixville. Waterpower from the dams created by the canal company was a power source for local mills, and the company received rental revenue from this operation. In fact, power from the dam was used to operate George Thompson's Phoenix Nail Works (now a part of the Phoenixville Historic District, a National Register of Historic Places site), which produced iron nails, as well as a cotton factory constructed in 1828 by Edward Garrigues.

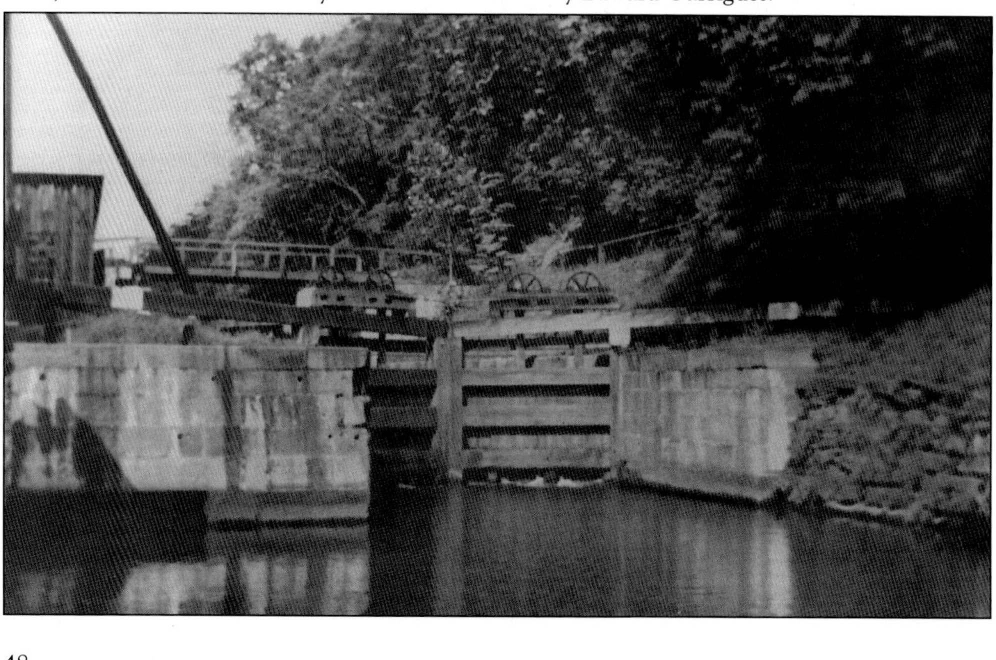

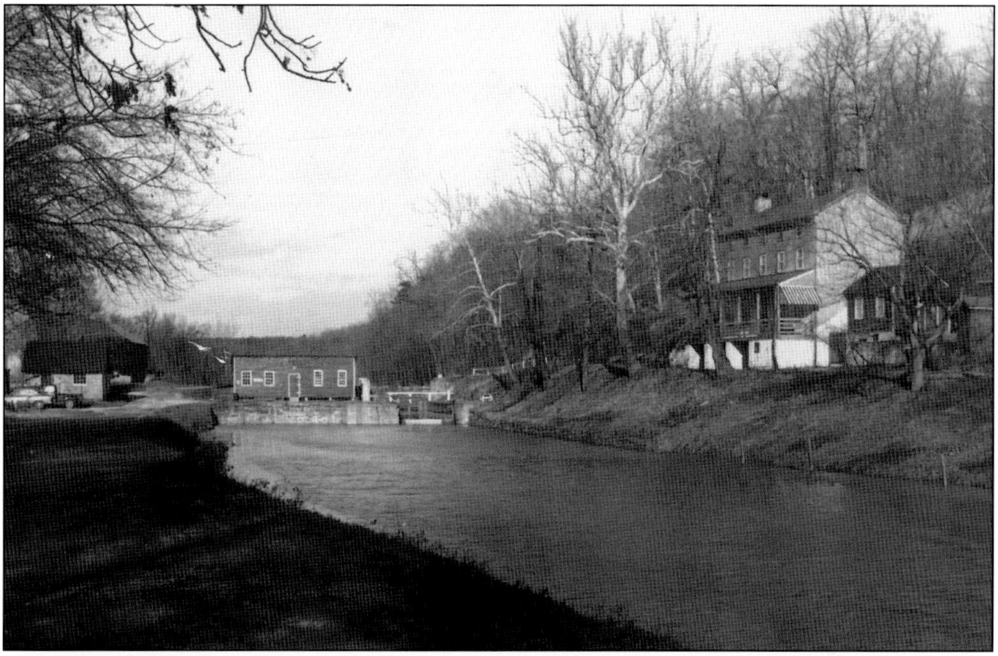

This photograph, also shown on the cover, was taken from the towpath in 1958. Lock 60 (center) was added to the Black Rock Dam in 1828. The lock tender's house stands on the berm side (opposite the towpath) of the Oakes Canal on the right. This section of the Schuylkill Canal was damaged by a flood in 1869.

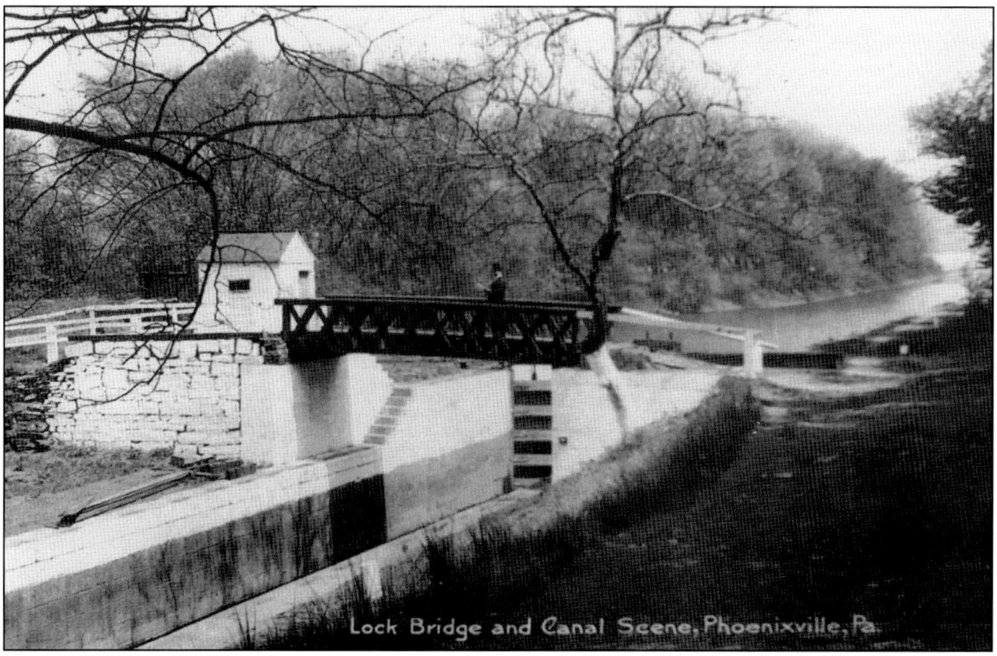

An enlarged lock was built in 1846 and measured 100 feet long by 18 feet wide. A small truss bridge crosses the Oakes Canal. In the canal's prime, mule drivers would lead their animals across this bridge to stay on the towpath. Along the way, they would stop at the small shanty at the end of the bridge to pay the toll.

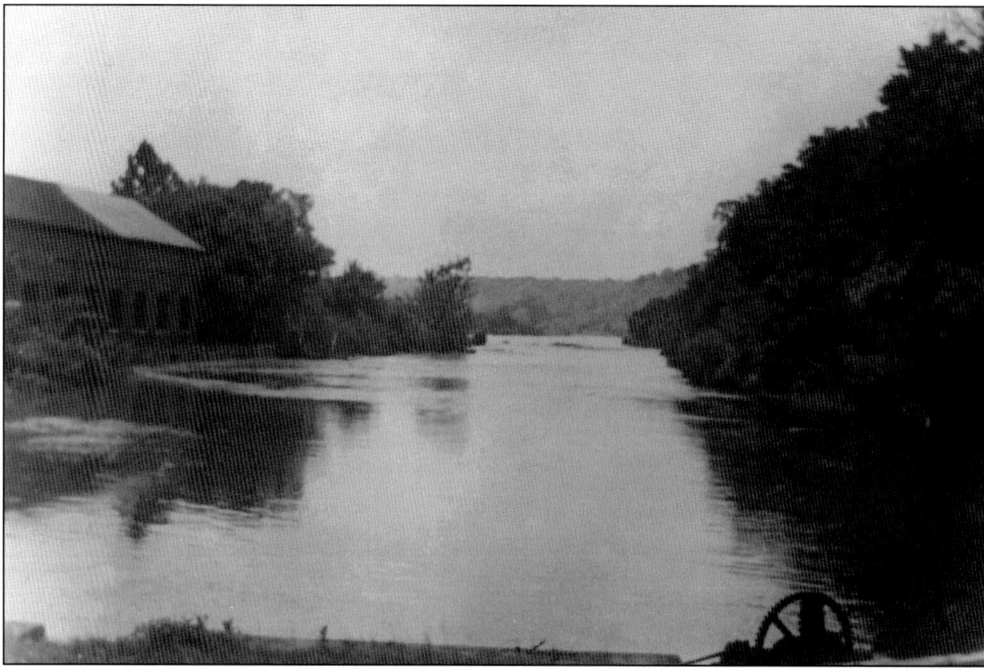

The Reading Traction Company was an interurban railroad in and around Reading. Pictured during high water in May 1942 is the hydroelectric generating station (left) that the company built at Black Rock Dam on the Schuylkill River to provide electric power for the Norristown-Reading trolley line. The generating station contained three turbines.

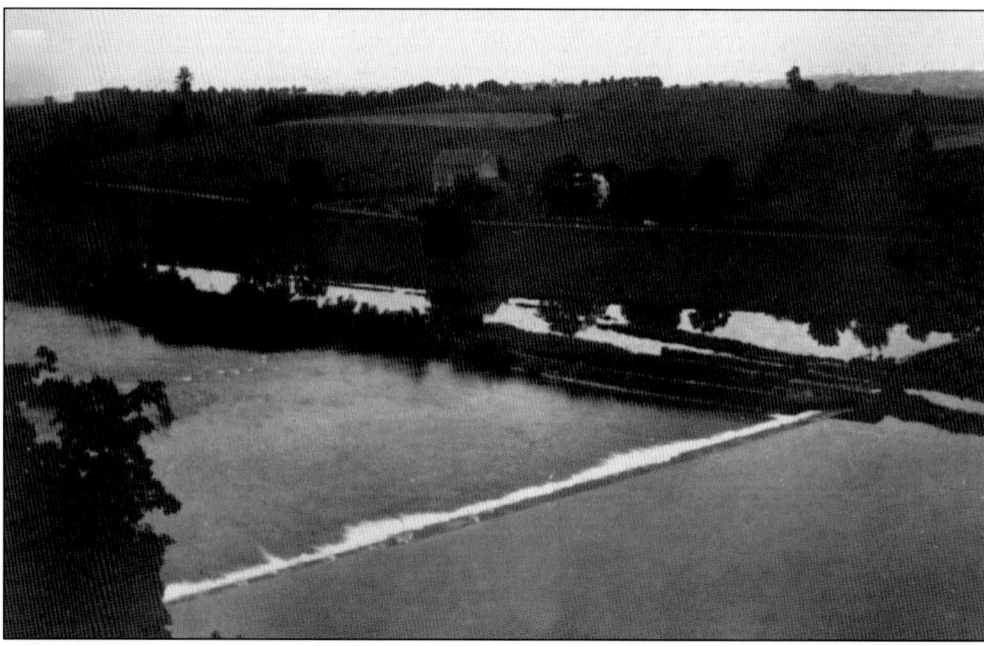

The Chester County Canal, also known as the Phoenixville Branch Canal, connected the slackwater pool of the Schuylkill Canal above the Black Rock Dam to Phoenixville. This view looks downstream over Black Rock Dam. A wall built of massive, finely carved stone juts out of the river, marking the beginning, or forebay, of the canal.

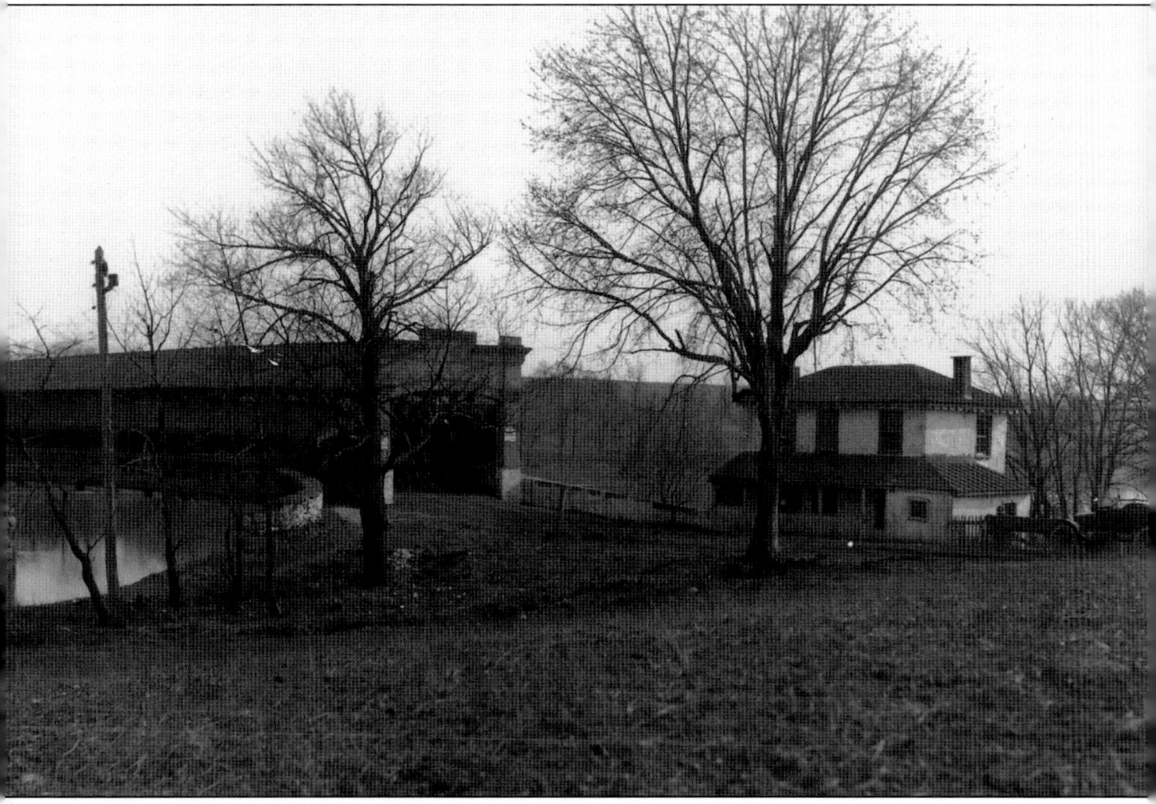

A mule walk located on the outside of the covered bridge on Black Rock Road in Phoenixville allowed mules to pull boats across the Schuylkill River where the canal towpath switched from the Montgomery County side of the river to the Chester County side. In this 1920 photograph is the toll collector's house (right), which sat on the Montgomery County side of the river and bridge. This structure is no longer in existence. The covered bridge is also a thing of the past. It is now the site of the Route 113 bridge. Only 15 covered bridges remain in the county. The Phoenixville Branch Canal was built on the Chester County side of the river to provide waterpower to the Phoenix Iron Company and to move goods to the larger canal system on the other side of the Schuylkill River.

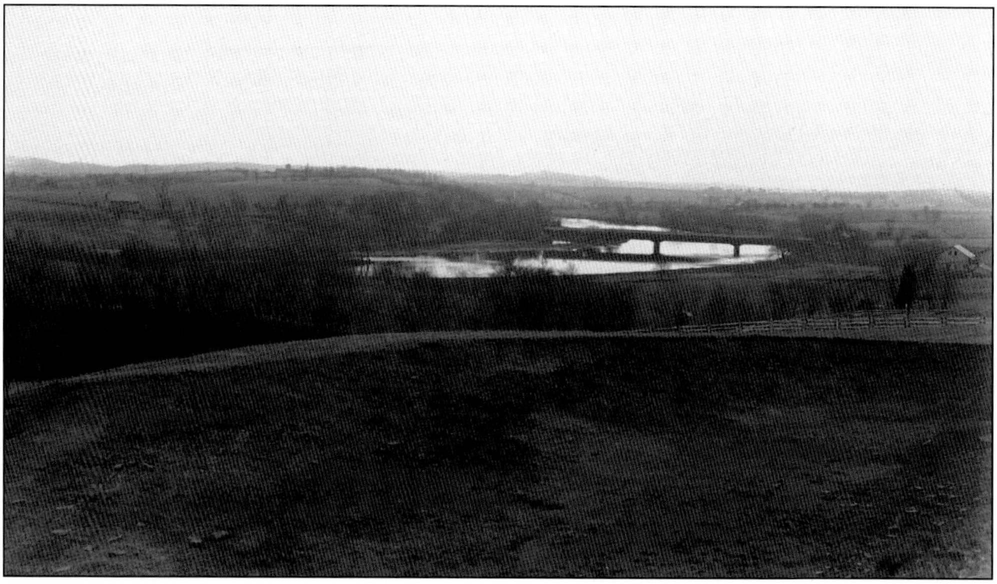

The above photograph, taken on March 28, 1920, offers a distant view of the covered bridge at Black Rock Road above the Schuylkill River, revealing the surrounding farmland. A closer view of the bridge is seen below on August 8, 1919. The toll collector's house appears at left in Montgomery County. The covered bridge was an important transportation resource; according to county records, Chester County once had 85 covered bridges, 21 of which were shared with other counties. The earliest recorded covered bridge in Chester County was built in 1807.

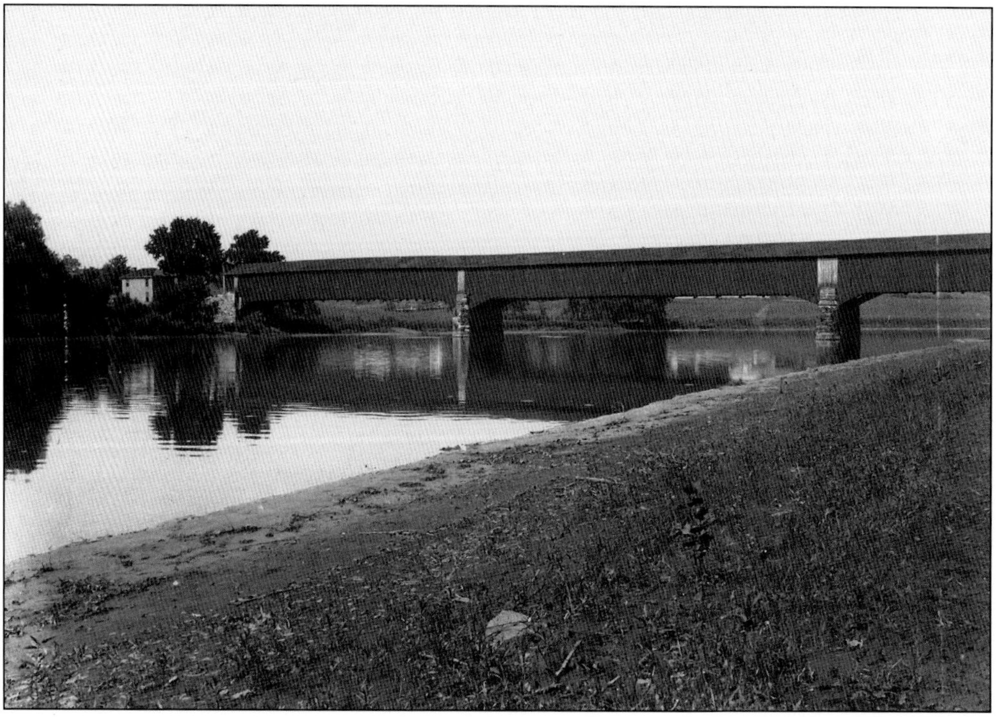

This switchboard is seen inside the Reading Traction Company's hydroelectric generating station (referred to by locals as the power plant), located on the Schuylkill River near Black Rock Dam. The three turbines housed in this building could generate more than 2,000 kilowatts of power. Hydroelectricity is the term for electricity generated through the use of the gravitational force of falling or flowing water.

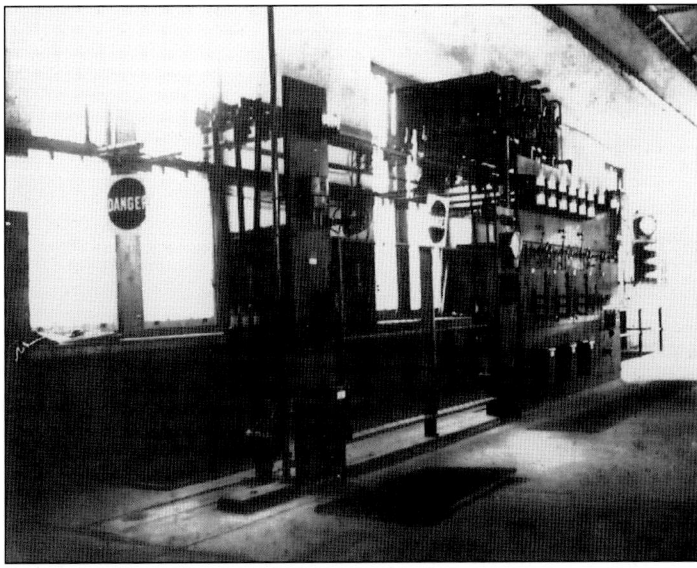

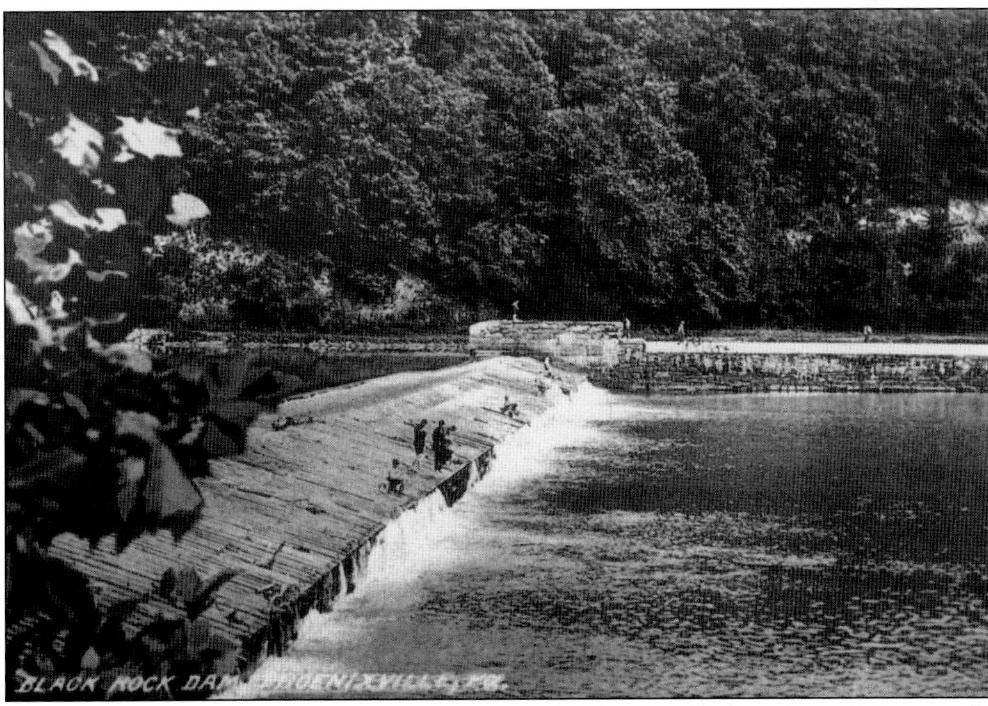

People play on and around Black Rock Dam, a low-head, stone-filled, timber crib dam on the Schuylkill River between Phoenixville and Mont Clare. Dams diverted water into canals that were built to navigate around more treacherous stretches of water that were difficult for larger boats to pass through.

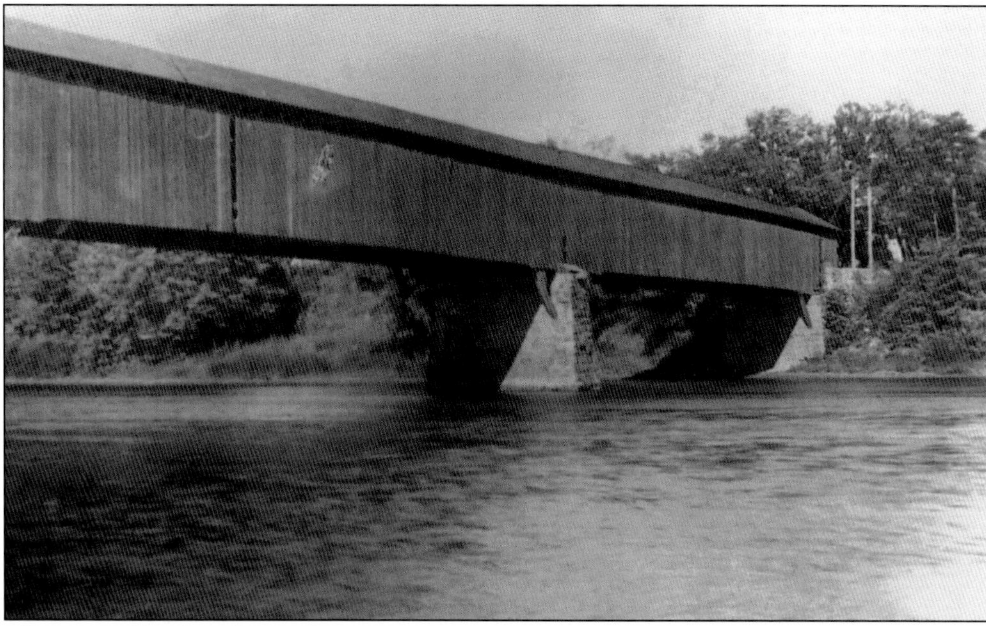

This covered bridge is believed to be the Lawrenceville Bridge, which linked Linfield and Parker Ford across the Schuylkill River in Chester County. This view shows the Linfield end of the bridge. The Laws of the General Assembly of the Commonwealth of Pennsylvania, passed at the Session of 1848, specified that this bridge be so constructed as to admit any load not exceeding four tons and not drawn by more than six horses or oxen at all times.

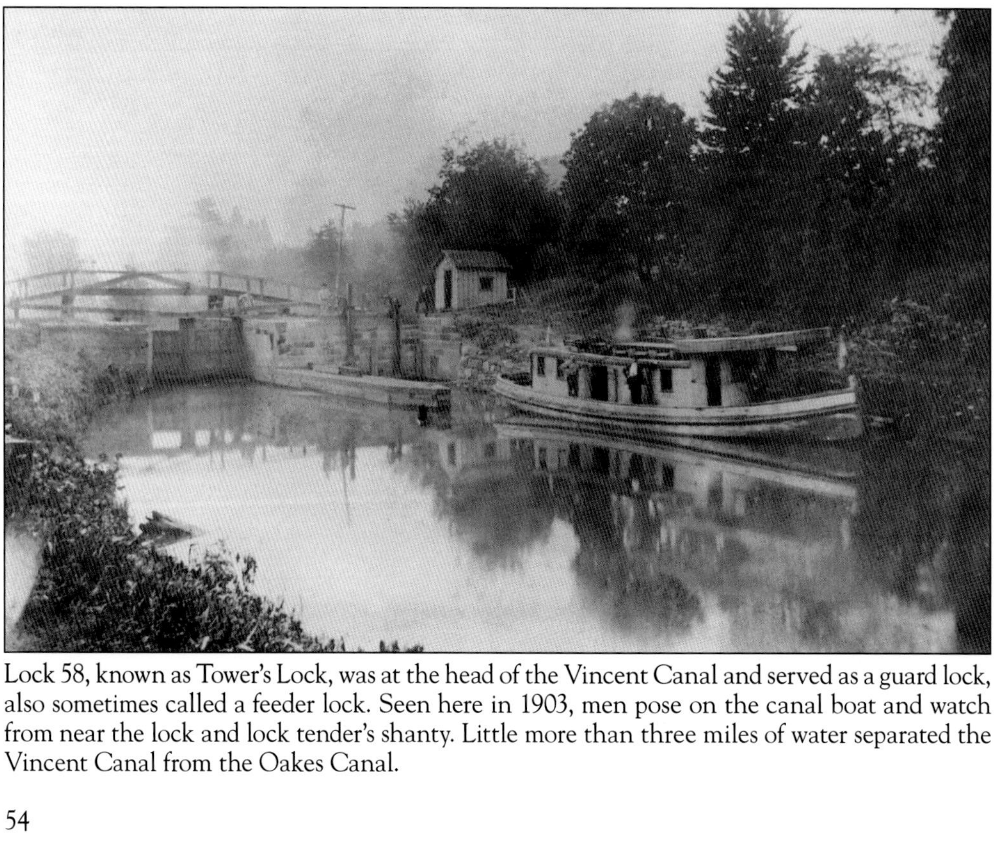

Lock 58, known as Tower's Lock, was at the head of the Vincent Canal and served as a guard lock, also sometimes called a feeder lock. Seen here in 1903, men pose on the canal boat and watch from near the lock and lock tender's shanty. Little more than three miles of water separated the Vincent Canal from the Oakes Canal.

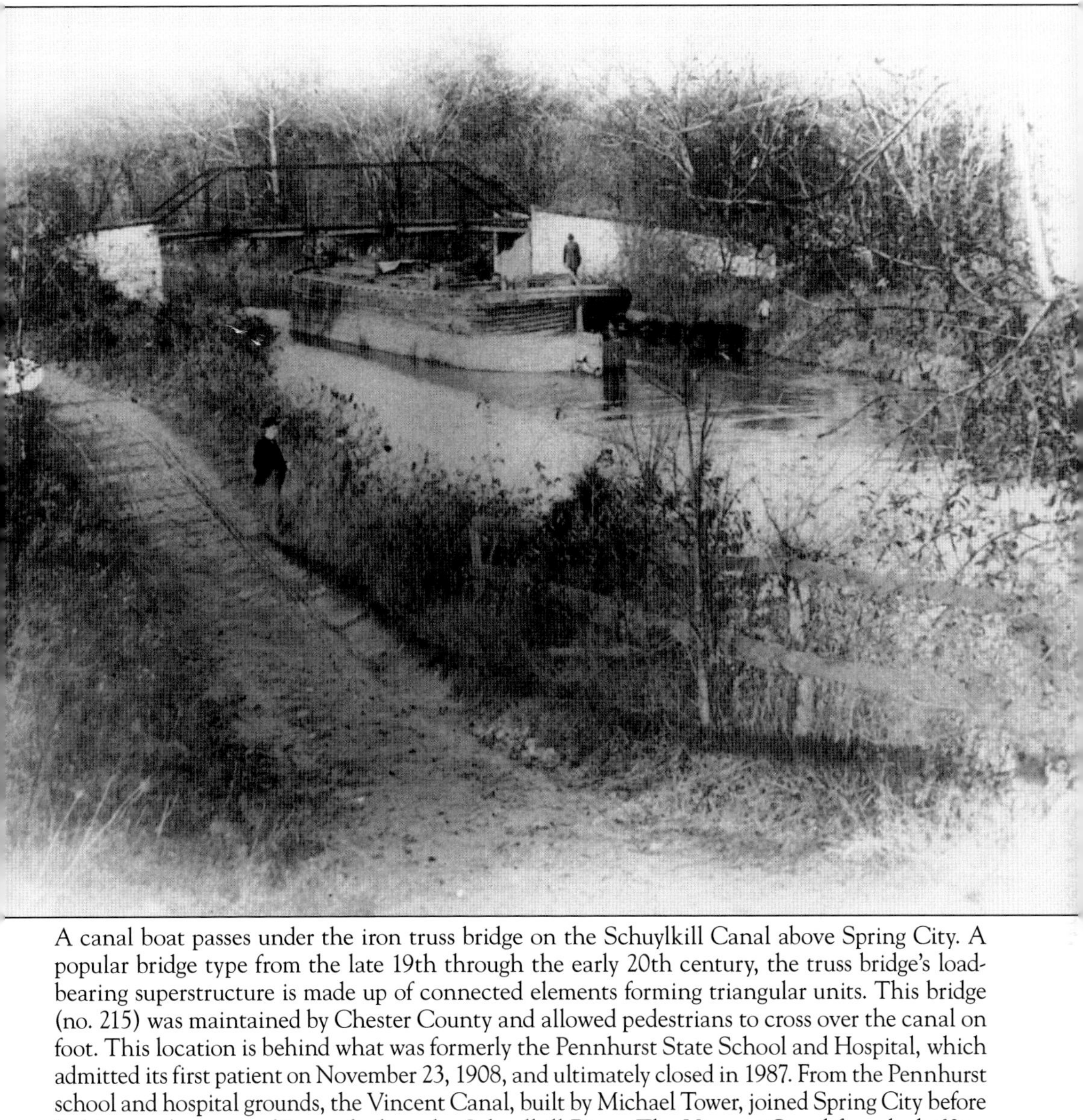

A canal boat passes under the iron truss bridge on the Schuylkill Canal above Spring City. A popular bridge type from the late 19th through the early 20th century, the truss bridge's load-bearing superstructure is made up of connected elements forming triangular units. This bridge (no. 215) was maintained by Chester County and allowed pedestrians to cross over the canal on foot. This location is behind what was formerly the Pennhurst State School and Hospital, which admitted its first patient on November 23, 1908, and ultimately closed in 1987. From the Pennhurst school and hospital grounds, the Vincent Canal, built by Michael Tower, joined Spring City before linking to the town of Royersford on the Schuylkill River. The Vincent Canal from lock 60 to lock 57 (Schwartz's Lock) makes up the sixth reach of the Schuylkill Navigation System.

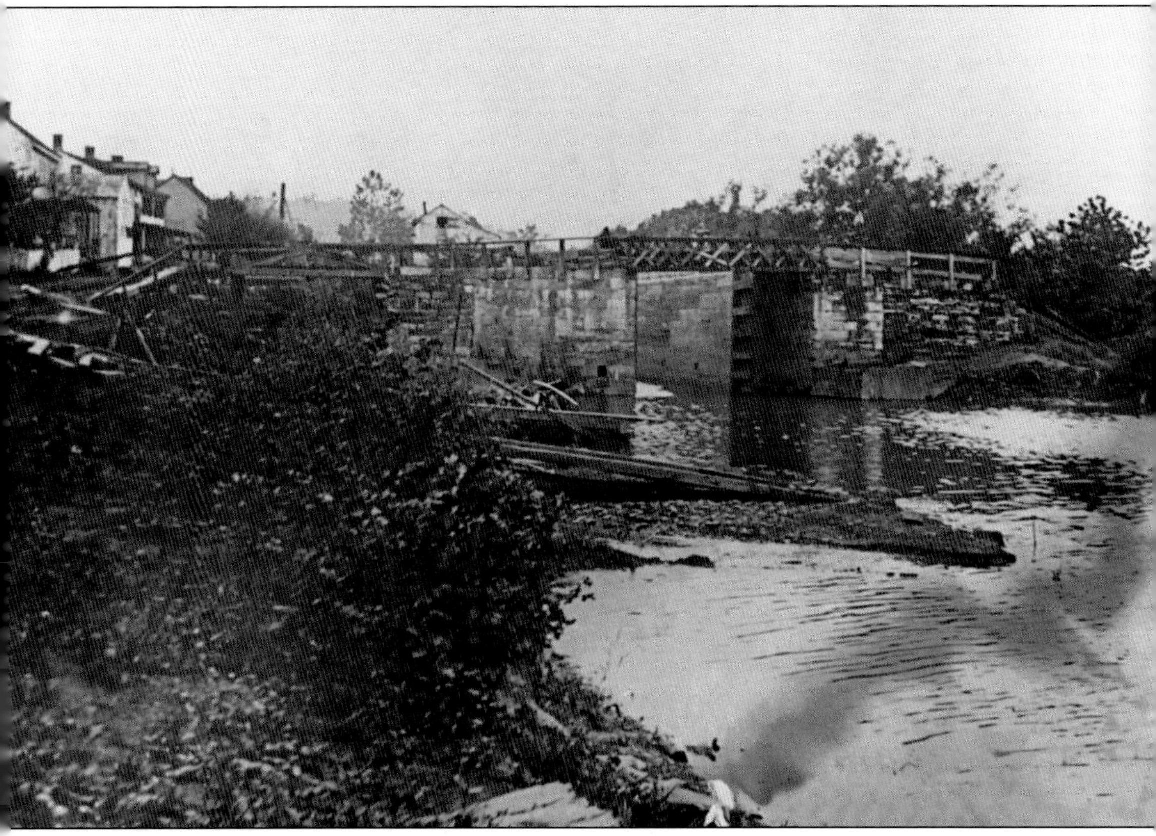

This photograph shows an earlier, smaller lock (left) and the large main lock (right) on the Vincent Canal in an area called Cromby. The lock tender's house is visible on the far left. The lock tender's shanty can also be seen at center. At one point, canal traffic became very heavy, and boats sometimes had to wait to pass through the locks at different points. Because of this, a second lock was sometimes built next to the original one for simultaneous two-way traffic. Between 1825 and 1931, the majority of boats that navigated the canal measured about 60 feet long by 7 feet wide. Below lock 59 (Wissamer's Lock) was the Phoenixville Municipal Water Works' pump house. Above the lock was the Stoney Creek aqueduct, which is a bridge that carried the canal and towpath across the Schuylkill River.

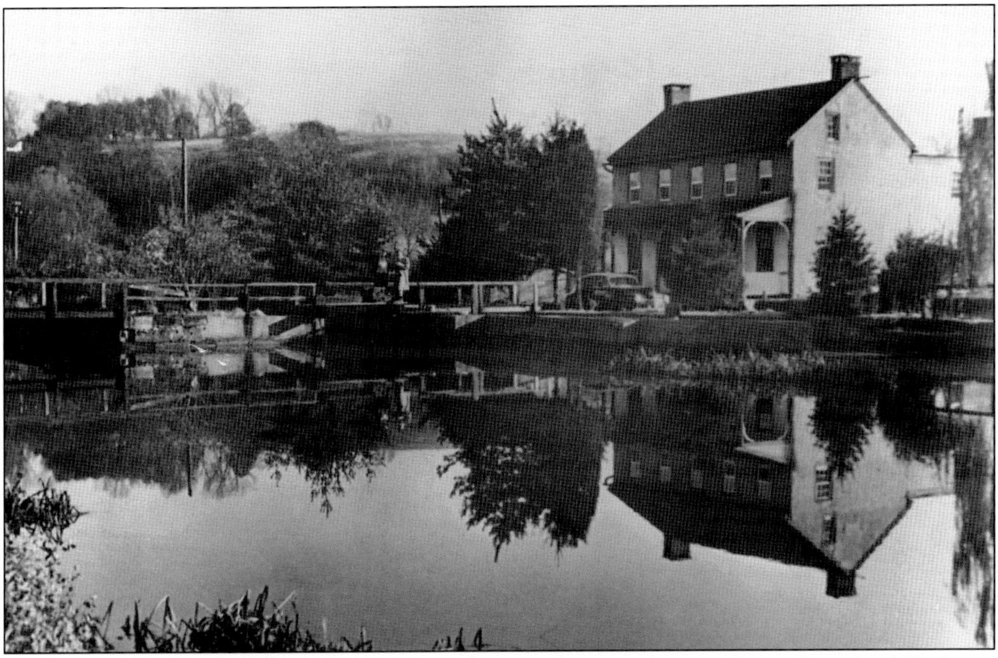

The above photograph, taken by a local newspaper photographer on November 19, 1947, shows a reporter interviewing Richard L. Turner, the last lock tender here. Seen from across the canal, the men stand at the upper gates of lock 59. A closer look of the lock tender's house and garage is shown below. Cromby is an unincorporated community in East Coventry Township, Chester County. The name is now popularly recognized locally for its association with the Cromby trailhead of the Schuylkill River Trail, a multiuse trail planned to be almost 130 miles in length when completed.

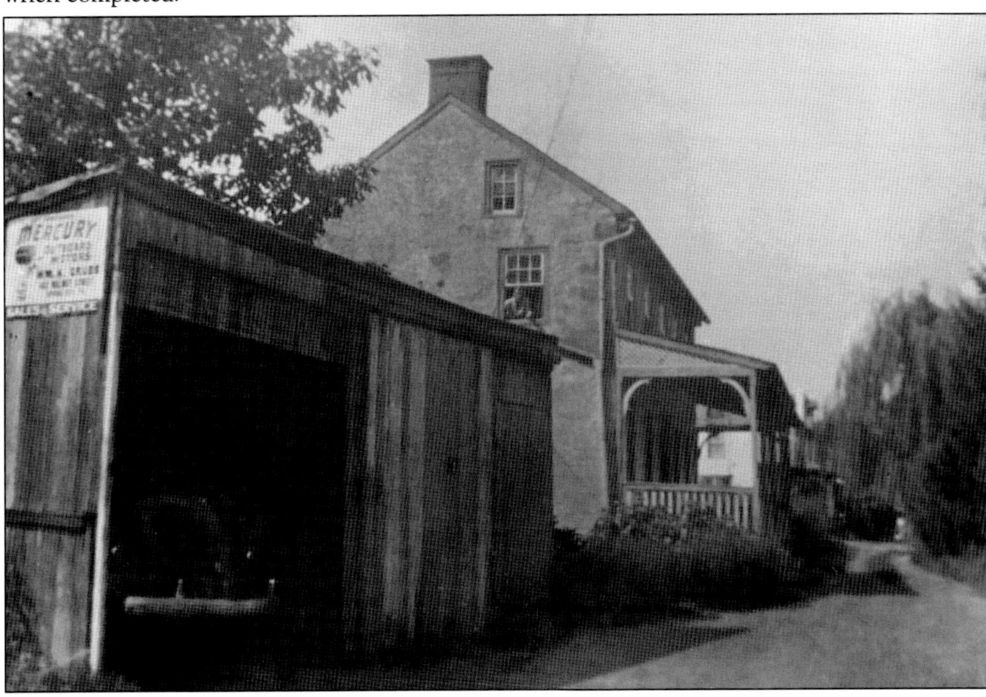

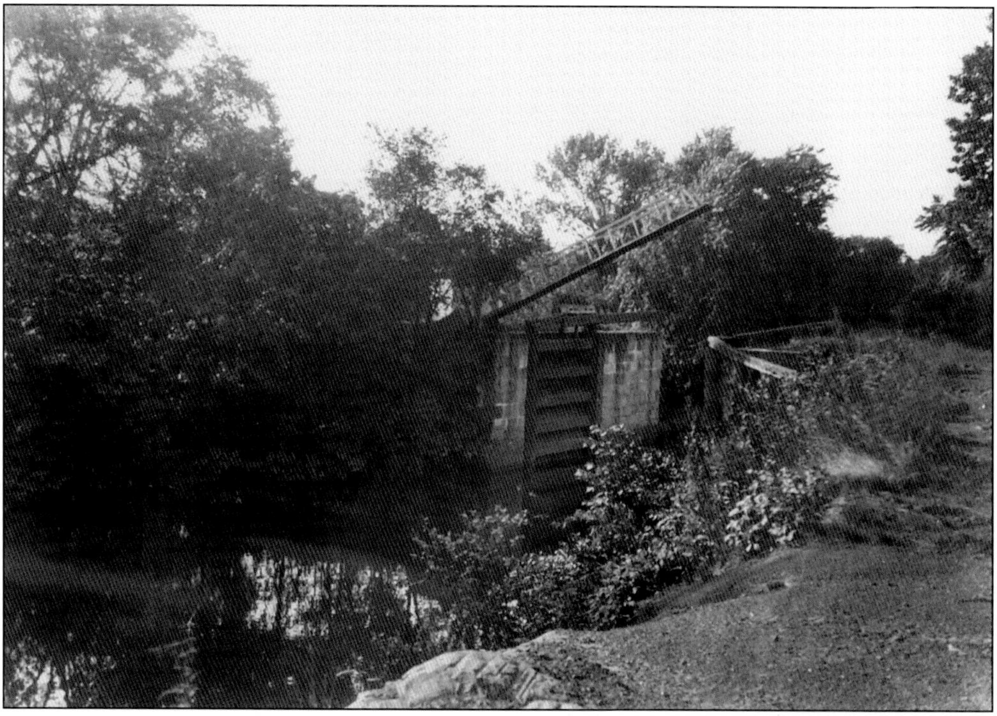

Above, the stop gate at Vincent Dam, also called the Yankee Dam, is in view on the Vincent Canal near Spring City and Royersford in 1919. The truss bridge above it has been raised to allow the passage of a large canal boat through the gate. This wooden dam washed away at some point in the past, leaving behind little evidence of its existence. Towers' Lock is shown below. This lock was located below Vincent Dam on the canal. In 1932, all boat traffic utilizing the Schuylkill Canal had officially ceased.

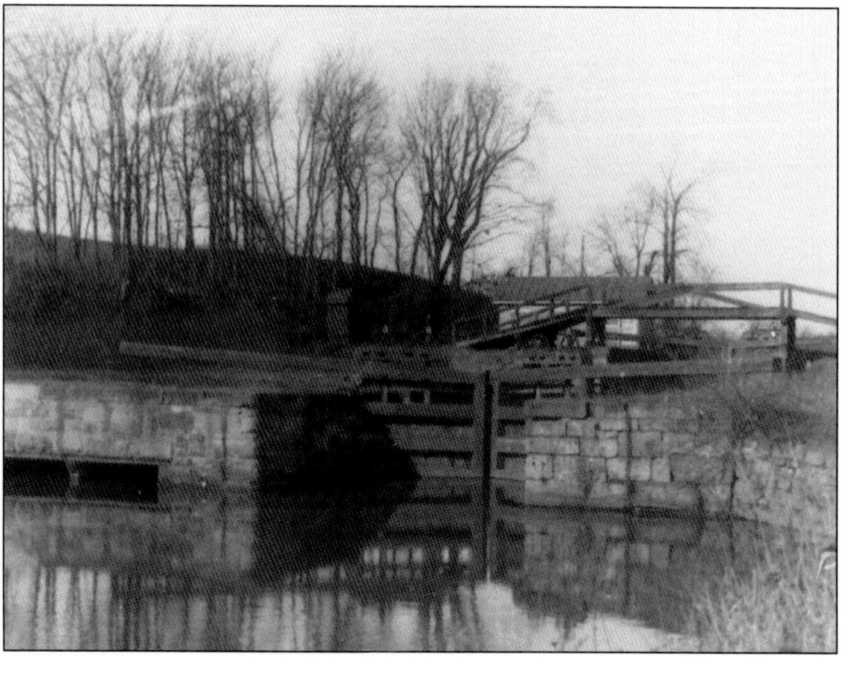

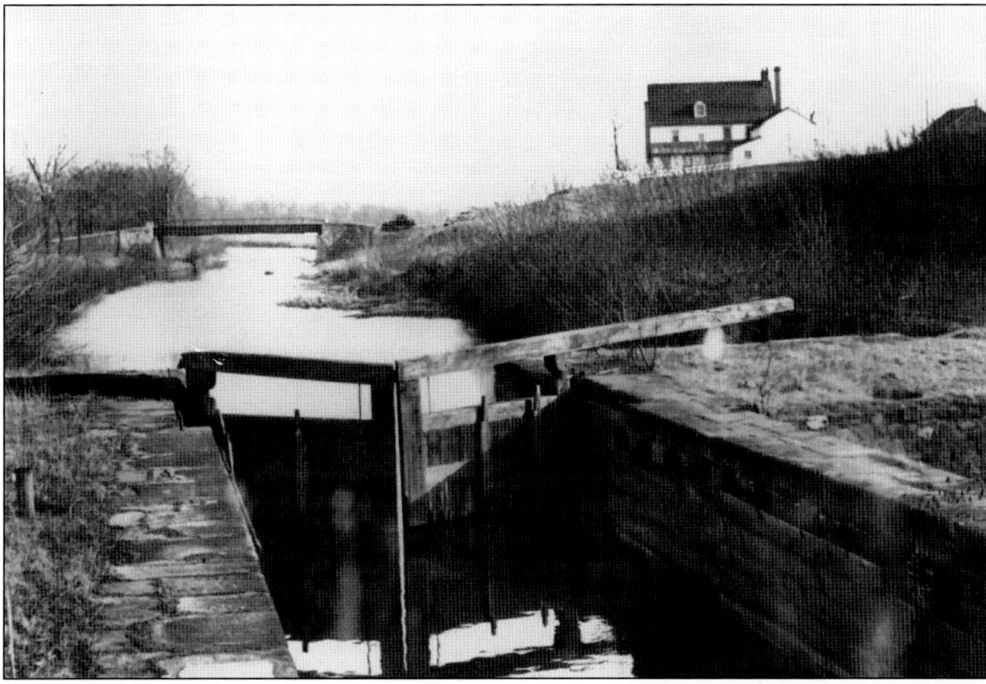

Michael Towers, born on September 24, 1800, in Upper Providence Township, Montgomery County, purchased his homestead farm in East Vincent Township. The property is shown above at right in 1824. The photograph looks down the Vincent Canal from Towers' Lock. Downstream is a bridge leading to the Michael Towers Farm, which eventually became part of what was formerly Pennhurst State School and Hospital. A carpenter by trade, Towers was hired by the Schuylkill Navigation Company in 1827. After several years away from the canal work, he returned in 1845 to help with its enlargement. Around this time, he also built the Vincent Dam. A closer look at Towers' Lock is shown below.

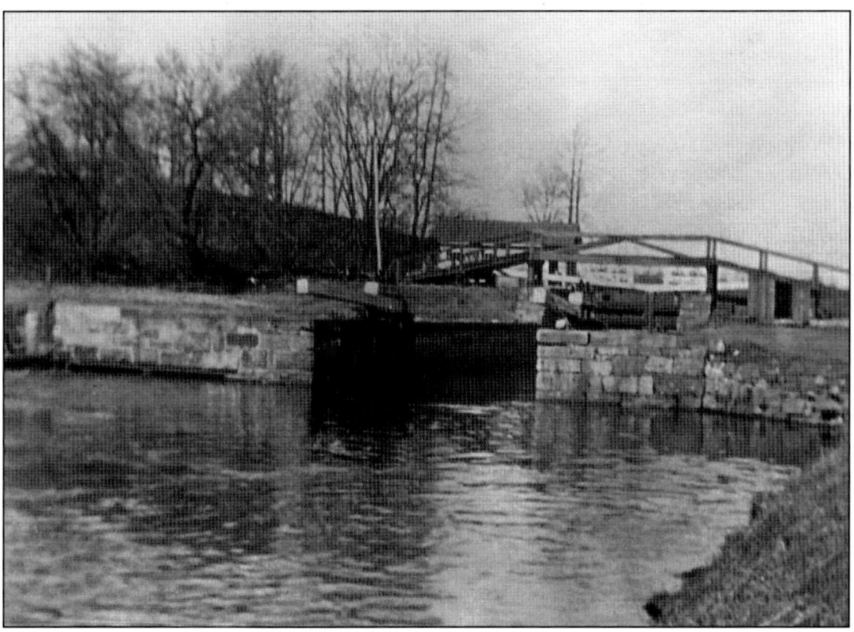

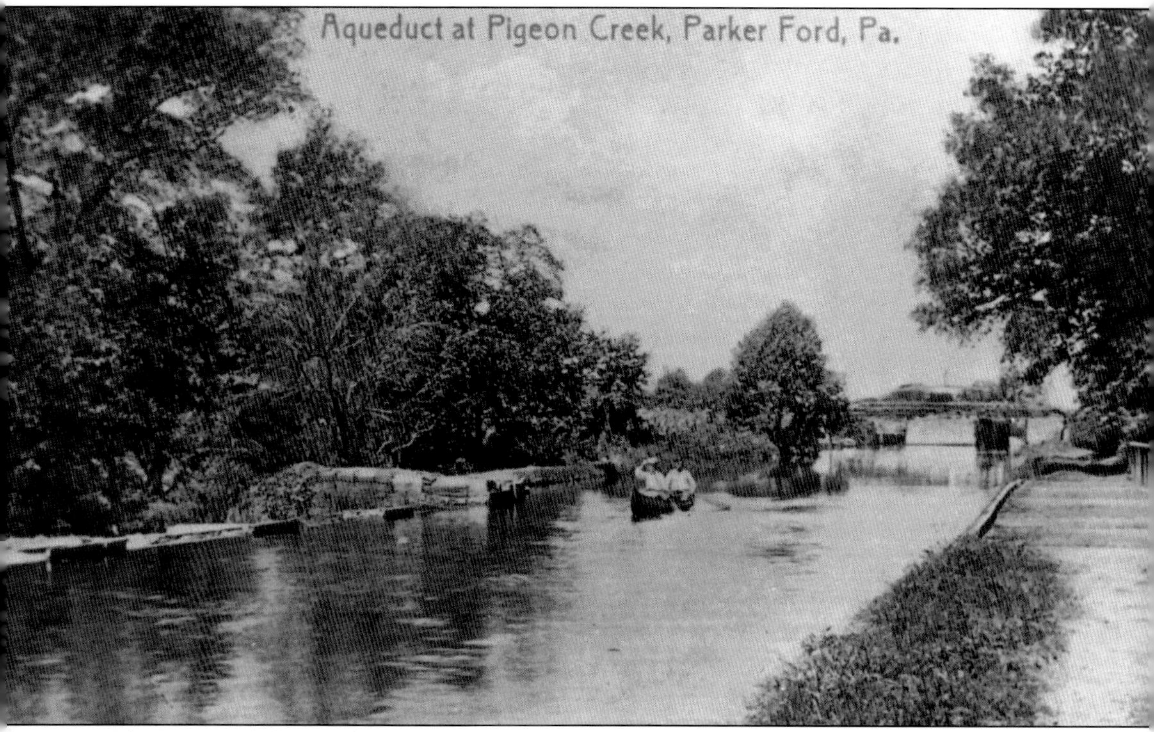

This postcard shows the Girard Canal over the Pigeon Creek aqueduct, which was located downstream from lock 56 in Parker Ford. The longest aqueduct on the Schuylkill Canal was the Hay Creek aqueduct in Birdsboro near lock 51, located on the south side of Route 724. The flood of 1955 caused so much damage to the structure that it was removed. Lock 56, also called the Lawrenceville Lock or the Lock at Pigeon Creek, was two miles below Frick's Locks (locks 54 and 55). In front of lock 56 was Chester County Bridge No. 217 over the canal. Parker Ford is another unincorporated community in East Coventry Township, Chester County, near Linfield in Limerick Township, Montgomery County. The head of the Girard Canal was at Dam 24 (also called Lewis's Dam or Big Reading Dam), constructed between 1820 and 1824 and located in Cumru Township, Berks County.

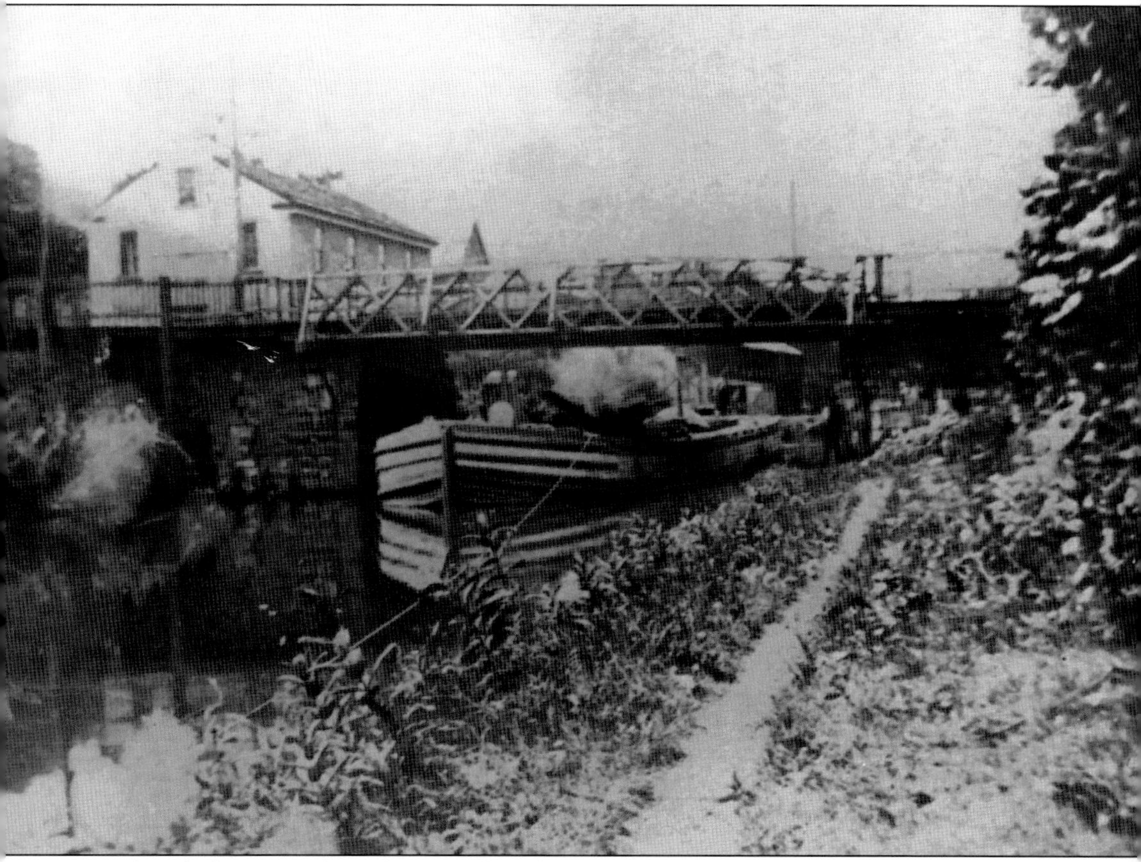

An unidentified man stands on the towpath under the bridge as a barge passes through the canal. In 1824, the first bridge connecting Spring City to Royersford across the Schuylkill Canal was completed. When the area was settled, it had become known as Pump Town, because of a local pump that many locals and visitors frequented. However, some people in town liked the name Jamestown, while others thought the natural springs in the area was a good reason to choose the name Springville, and so they did—temporarily. Unfortunately, Pennsylvania already had a town with this name, so, in 1872, the name was changed to Spring City. The building at left of the bridge was the Inter-Borough Press building of Spring City. Lt. F. LeRoy Moser was the former publisher of the *Inter-Borough Press*. He died of pneumonia in 1918. (Photograph by Wilbert Amster.)

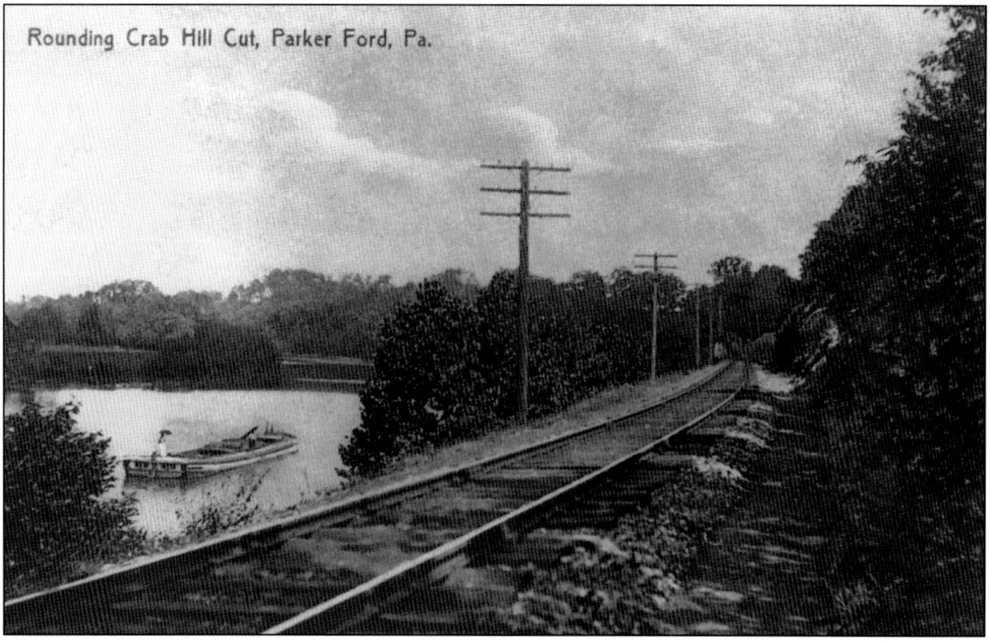

This photograph, taken from the tracks of the Pennsylvania Railroad, shows a canal boat floating in the slackwater behind Vincent Dam. Technically speaking, the Schuylkill Canal was a navigational system consisting of a succession of dams and canals. The dams created an area of slackwater for boats in the river, while the canals provided passage around changes in water levels.

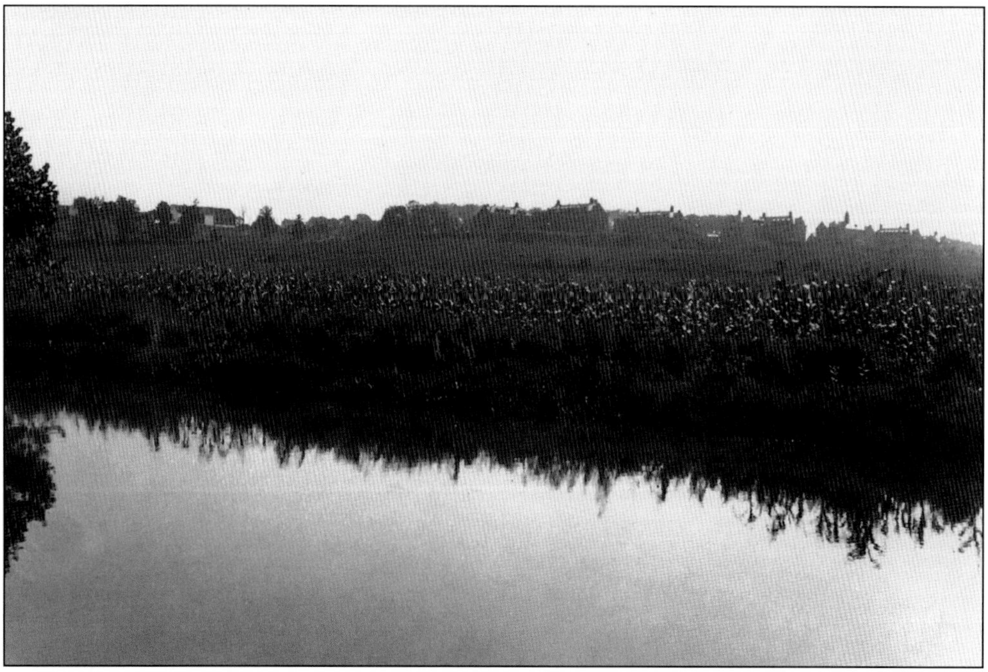

The Pennhurst buildings can be seen from the Vincent Canal towpath above Spring City on August 9, 1919. In 1824, a paper mill, a stove foundry, a canal store, a gristmill, and several houses formed the town formerly called Springville, for the natural springs in the area.

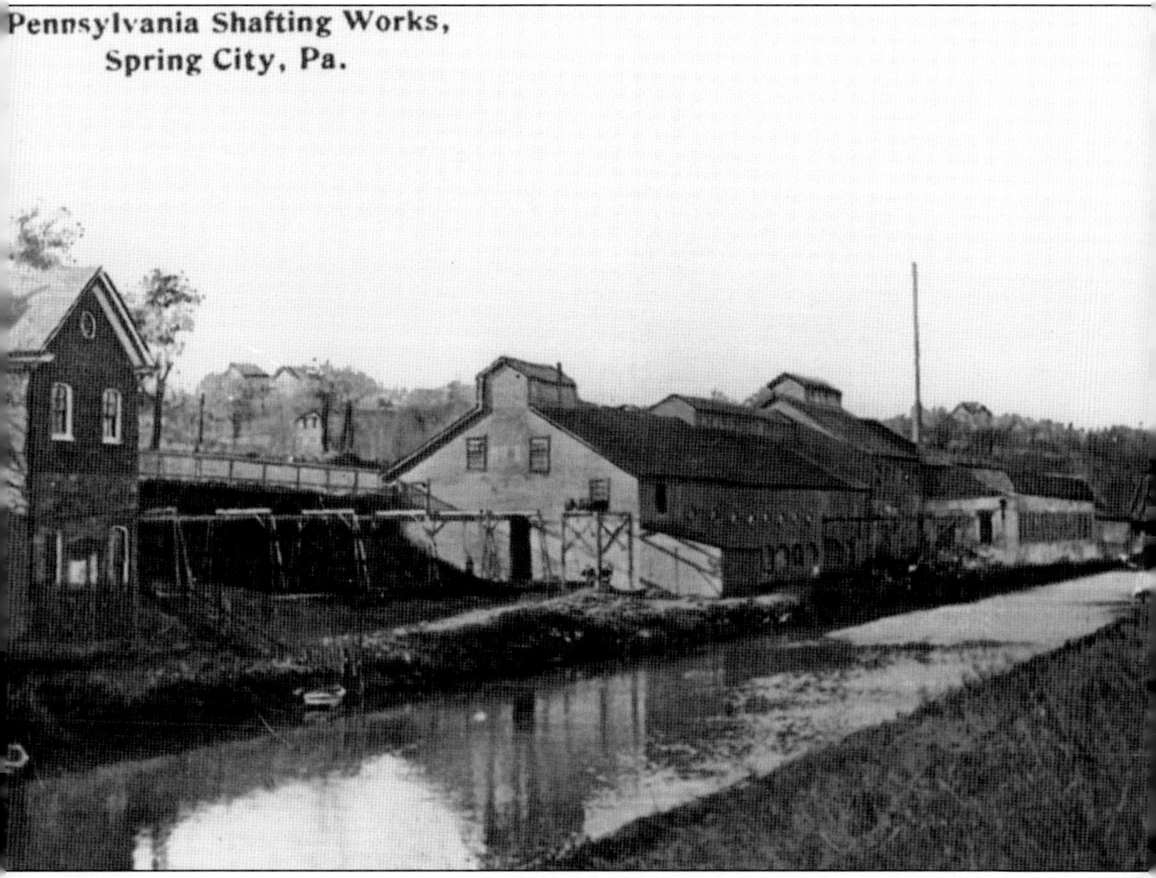

By the 1850s, canal-born industries, such as the American Paper Company and the Spring City Stove Company, were in full swing, attracting new people to the town. Soon after, houses, churches, schools, and local government were erected and organized. Glass-making and knitting mills, as well as multiple brickworks, eventually joined the fold. The building at center is the Pennsylvania Shafting Works in Spring City, seen here around 1904. The business manufactured iron stem shafts and cold-pressed metal parts. Previously, the building belonged to the American Wood Paper Company; after the days of the Shafting Works, it became the Keystone Drawn Steel Company. Now, the area is home to the A.C. Miller Concrete Company, which supplies a wide variety of precast concrete products to utility, electric, telephone, transportation, and gas companies.

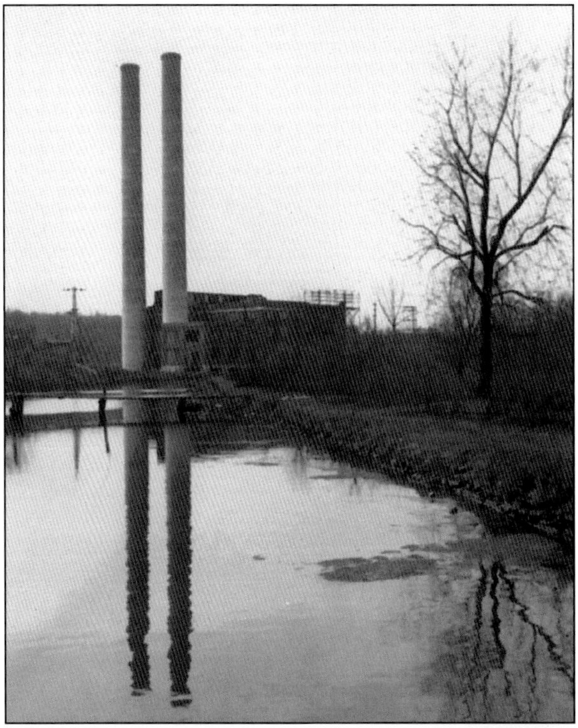

Spring City photographer Harold W. Amster aimed his camera down the Vincent Canal at the old Philadelphia Electric Company power station at Cromby. This station had its first generator installed in 1918, and it was shut down in 1929. In 1951, it was torn down to make way for a newer power plant, no longer in operation.

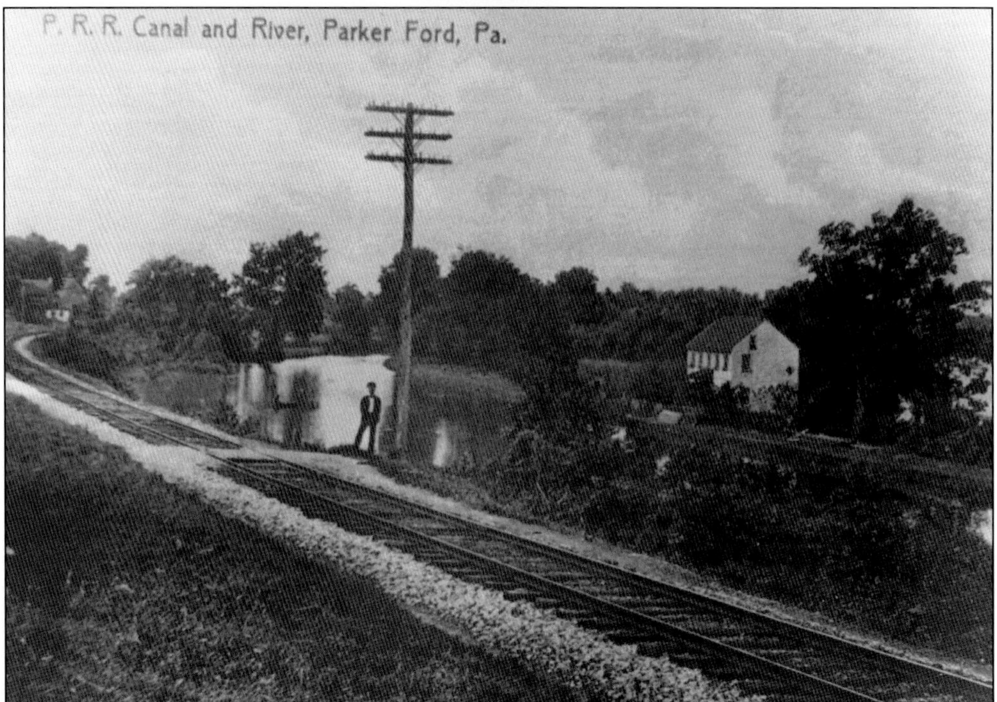

This photograph, taken beside the tracks of the Pennsylvania Railroad, looks up the Girard Canal from outlet lock 57 in Parker Ford. Across the canal sits the quaint lock tender's house. Settled in the early 18th century, the community was the site of both a gristmill and a sawmill.

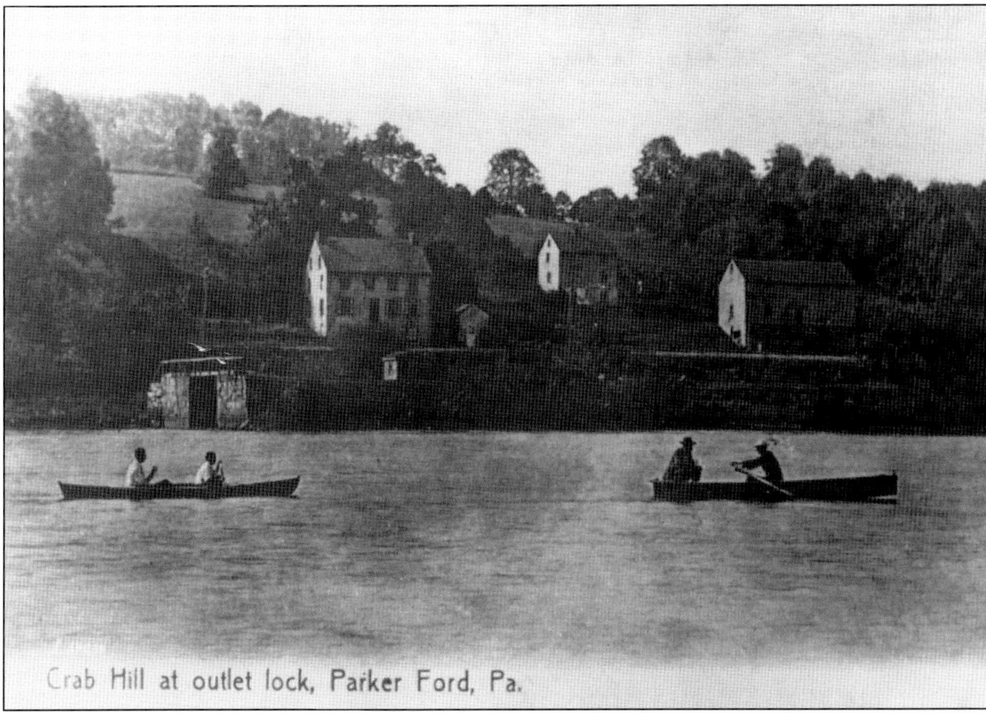

These photographs provide additional views of the Girard Canal. In the above photograph, taken from Crab Hill at outlet lock 57, people enjoy a recreational opportunity to canoe in the water. In 1869, the chamber walls of lock 57, the Girard Outlet, were bulging into the chamber and had to be rebuilt. It was located on the property of a small water company at the end of Shady Lane. Below, people take a pleasure ride in boats equipped with awnings to provide shade from the sun. In both photographs, the lock tender's house can be seen across the canal.

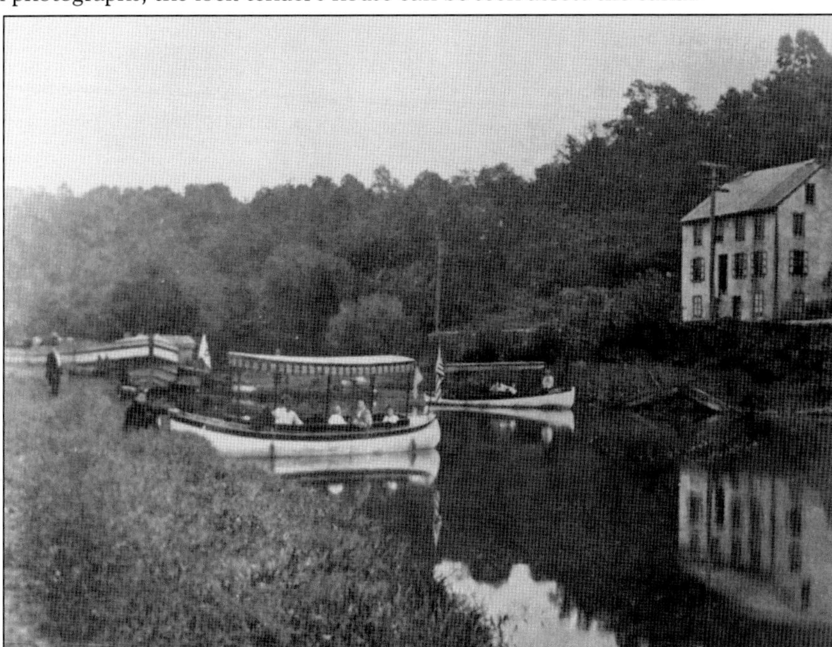

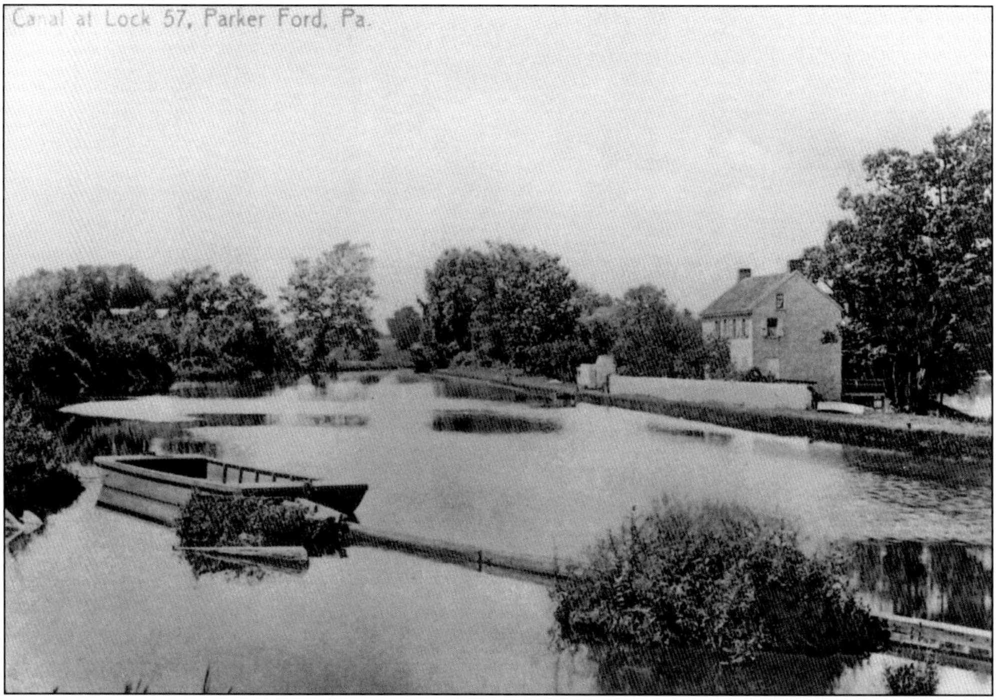

In this serene scene on the Girard Canal above lock 57, or Schwartz's Lock, a wall stands in front of the lock tender's house (right), located in Parker Ford. Behind the house, but not visible, coursed the Schuylkill River. Apparently, there was quite a trade along the canal in all sorts of items and commodities, including fresh oysters.

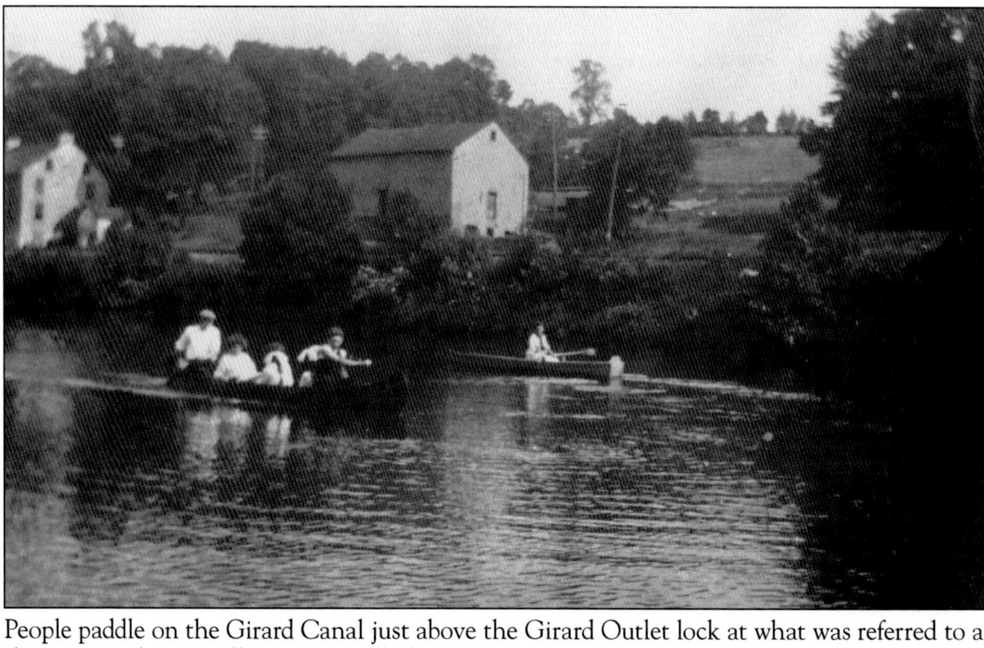

People paddle on the Girard Canal just above the Girard Outlet lock at what was referred to as the waterworks, a small company called Citizens Water Resources. Located at the end of Shady Lane in Parker Ford, the building is now Pennsylvania American Water's Shady Lane Treatment Plant, serving roughly 15,000 customers in Montgomery and Chester Counties.

Three

A Time to Rebuild

Maintenance efforts are an accepted reality for many aspects of life. Running a business—even if that business involves water transportation—is no different. Both natural and man-made structures experience wear and tear, which, if not caught and addressed, can end up becoming dangerous. The Schuylkill Navigation Company had to inspect and repair bridges and all other wooden and stone structures along its length. Damaged lock gates had to be replaced immediately, and dams required periodic attention. Each section of the canal had a maintenance scow and crew. Even lock tenders were responsible for keeping an eye on the lock systems of which they were in charge. Additionally, the canal company operated several steam vessels on the canal for dredging and general repair work. At one time, five dredges were operating more or less continuously, particularly on the upper sections of the canal. Aside from maintaining and repairing boats, bridges, locks, and the like, canal workers were no strangers to repairing and rebuilding as a result of unexpected damage—from floods, for example. In fact, the navigation system weathered quite a few rough patches—floods, droughts, competition, and war—but always seemed to come through. That is, until the late 1940s. The canal's heyday was over, and to add insult to injury, a massive river cleanup took place to remove the tons of silt from the Schuylkill River. In the process, much of the remaining canal was destroyed. Dams were removed, locks gutted of their gates and/or filled, and towpath bridges were pulled down.

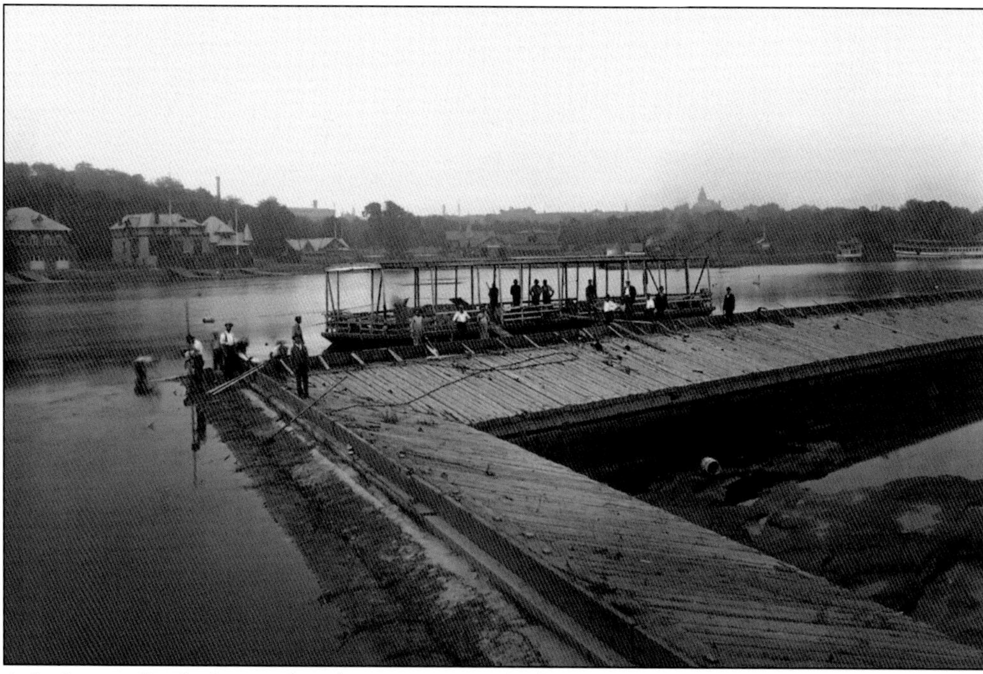

A freshet is a flood of a river from heavy rain or melted snow, and structures on the Schuylkill River and Schuylkill Navigation System were affected—more than once—by such events. Fairmount Dam was originally built in 1822 as a straight-drop, cribbed dam to provide water for the city and to form a slackwater pool for navigation in conjunction with river locks. Above, workers labor in August 1896 to make repairs at the bend in the Fairmount Dam at the west abutment near the locks after a freshet in February of that year. Another break in the dam caused by flooding and melting ice is seen below in May 1904.

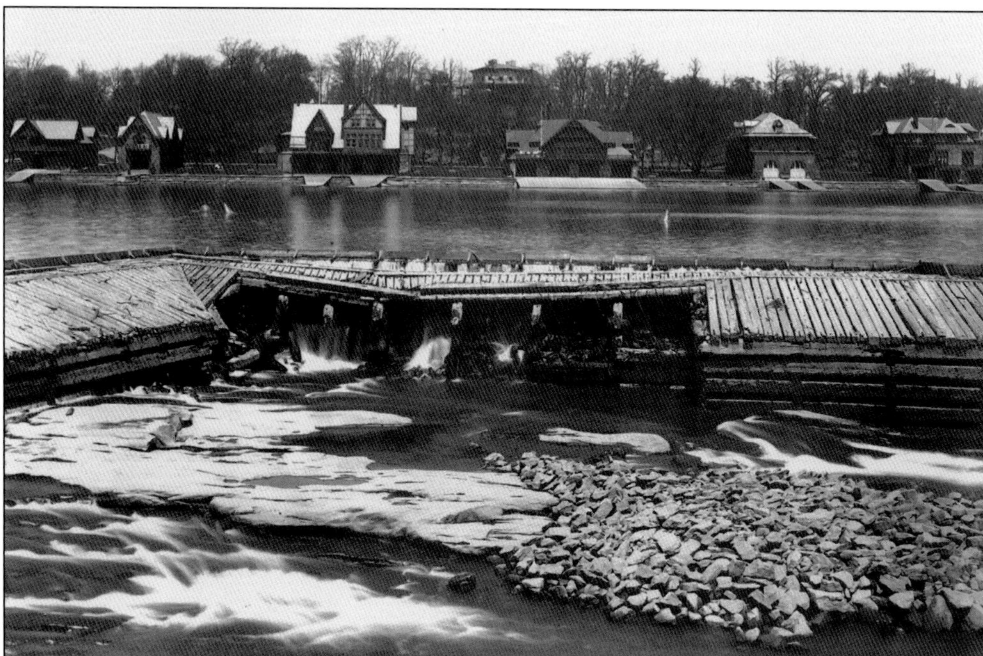

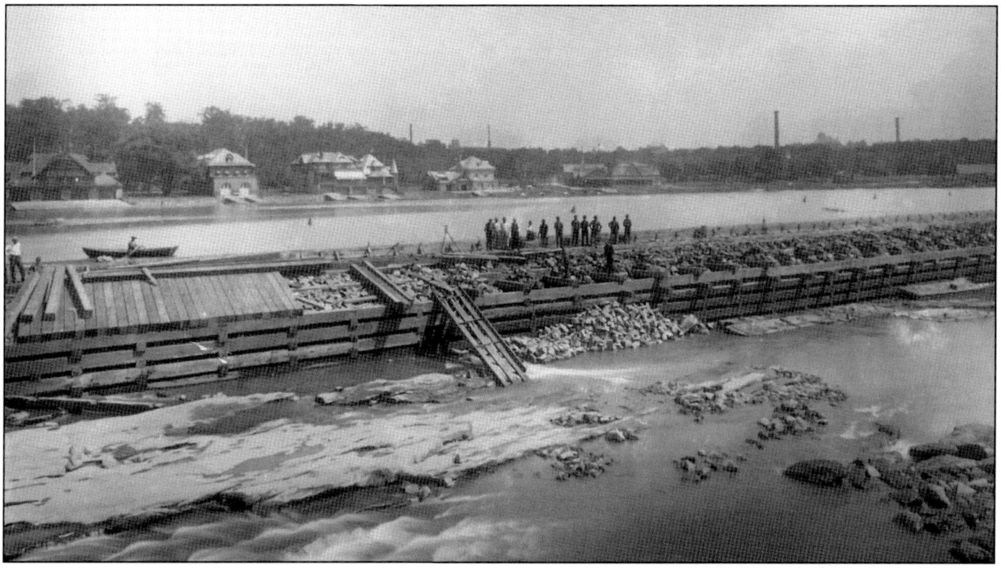

Above, men work to repair breaks in another section of the Fairmount Dam on August 29, 1904. On the shore across from them, the houses that form Boathouse Row line the Schuylkill River. The dam was originally built from wooden crates filled with rocks, but over the years, it was repaired, rebuilt, and expanded, resulting in its over-fall moving 38 feet beyond its original line. Below, construction efforts take place on the dam near the Fairmount Water Works on May 26, 1924. In 1926, the addition of a concrete mound stabilized the crib dam.

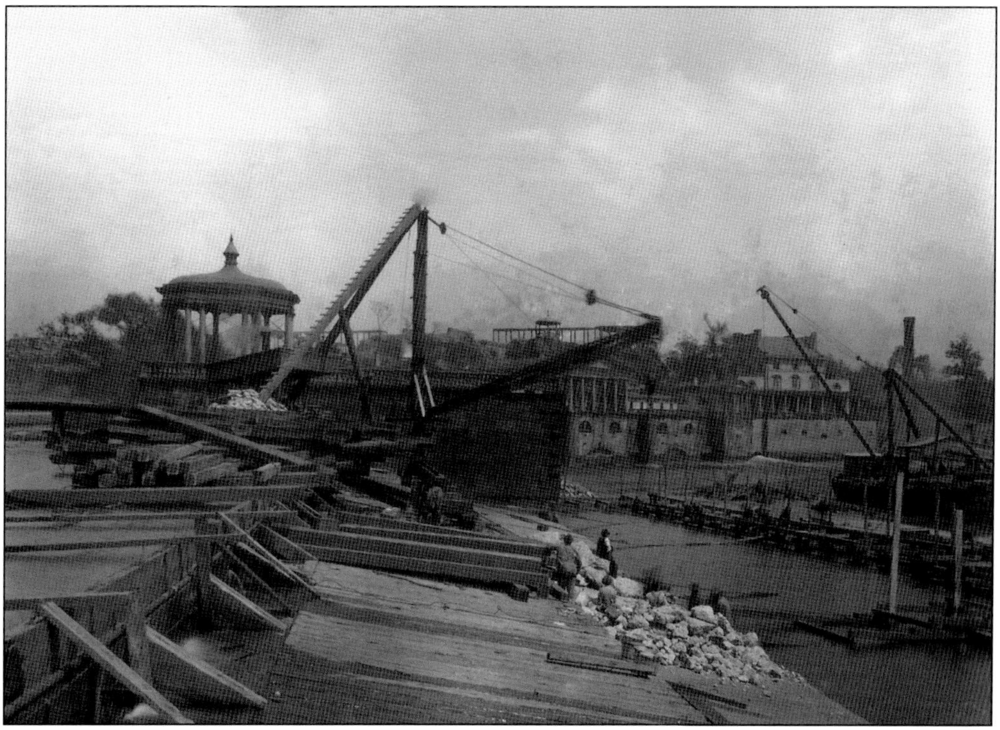

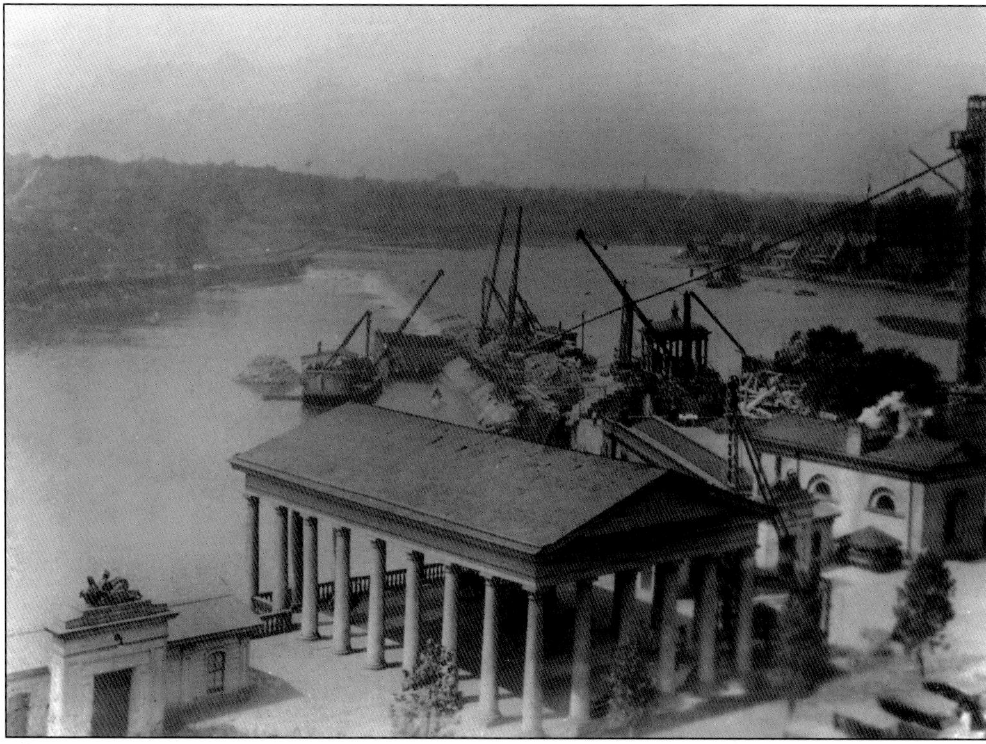

The Fairmount Dam on the Schuylkill River is seen here in 1925. Presumably taken from atop a building belonging to the Fairmount Water Works, the photograph shows construction of the concrete dam, which was undertaken by the US Army Corps of Engineers, which had taken over care of the dam.

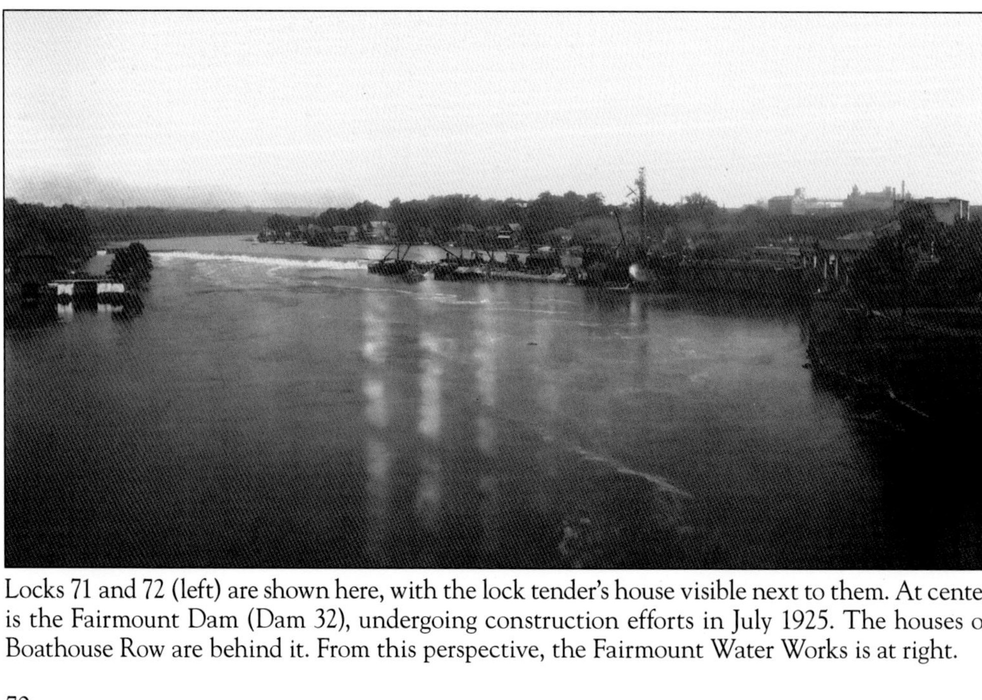

Locks 71 and 72 (left) are shown here, with the lock tender's house visible next to them. At center is the Fairmount Dam (Dam 32), undergoing construction efforts in July 1925. The houses of Boathouse Row are behind it. From this perspective, the Fairmount Water Works is at right.

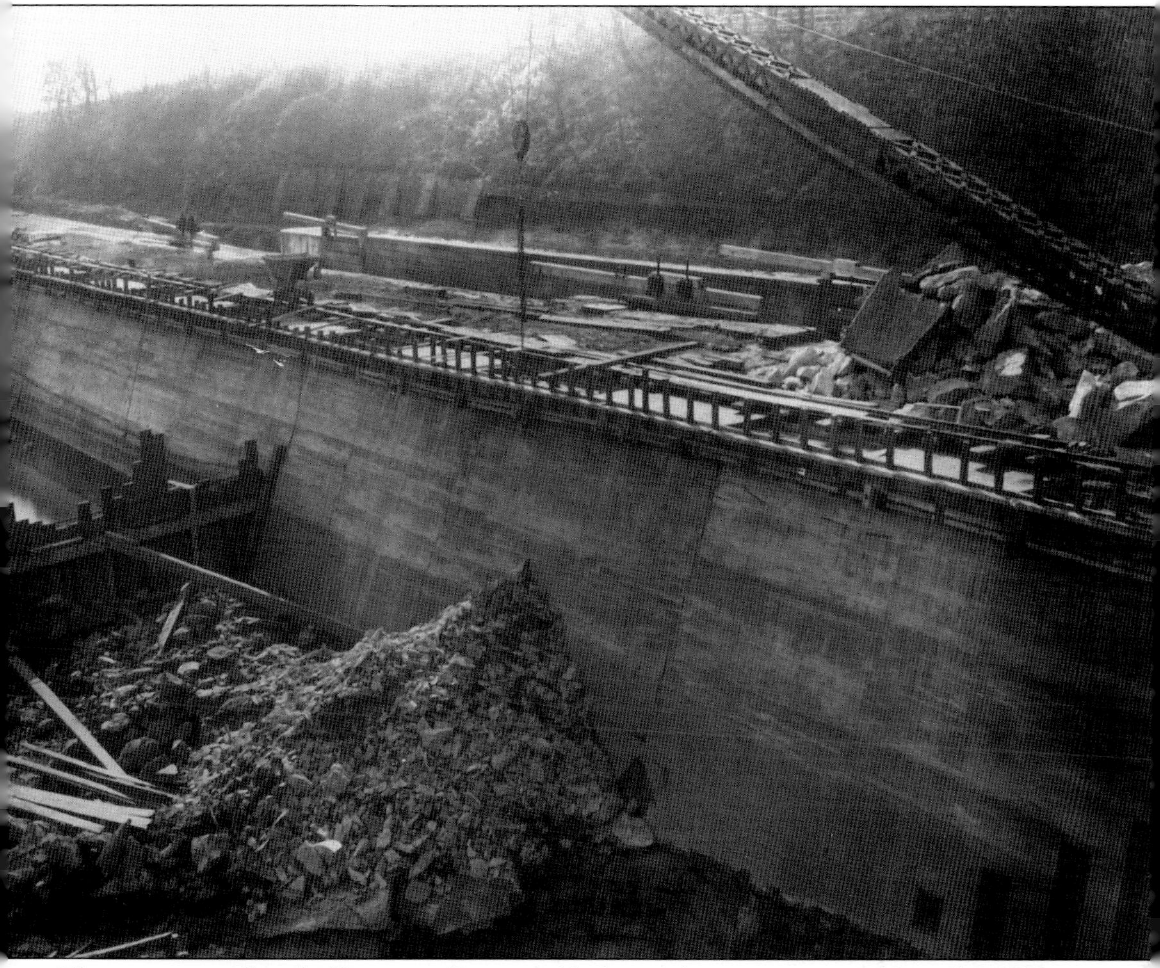

The retaining wall at the Fairmount Dam guard lock is under construction in November 1926. The dam, located roughly 8.5 miles upstream from the Schuylkill River's confluence with the Delaware River, is the uppermost reach of the river that is influenced by fluctuations in the tide. The Schuylkill River itself, which runs through several counties, is an estimated 123 miles long from its confluence with the Delaware River in Philadelphia to its headwaters in Pottsville. In the 1990s, the Philadelphia Water Department raised the Fairmount Dam along the lower fish pier area, and in 2008, the Fairmount fish ladder was built at the dam site to provide a stairway to the river, whose main stem and tributaries are the shad's native habitat. The fish are now once again migrating up the river to spawn, indicating improved ecological conditions.

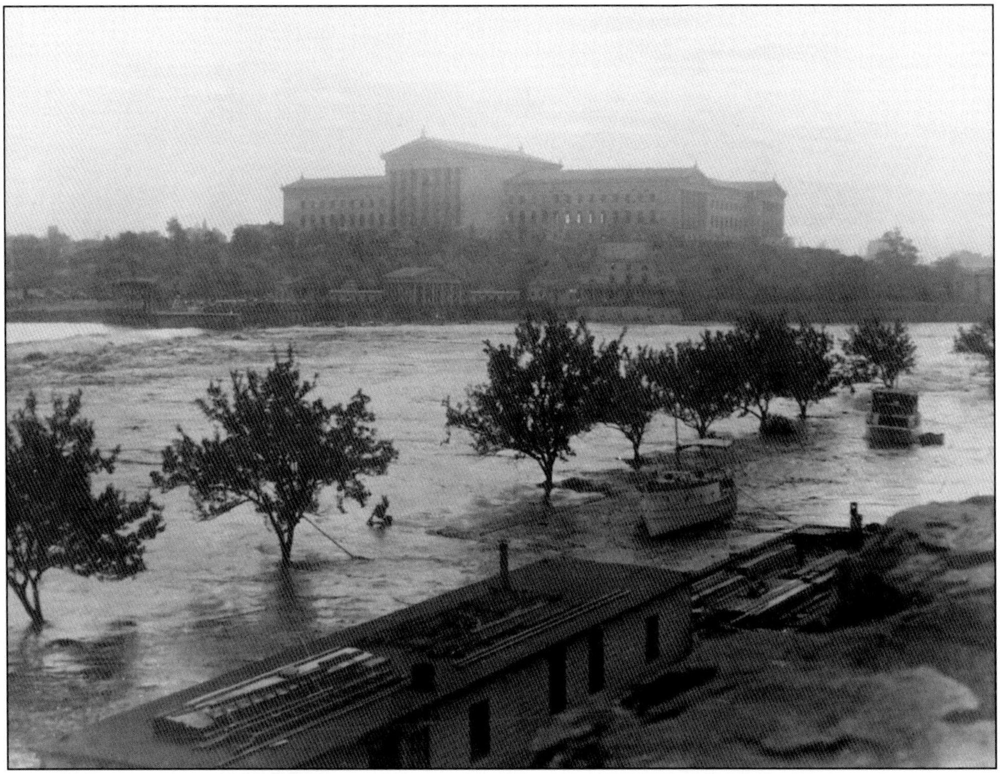

In 1933, the Chesapeake-Potomac hurricane, known as the Great Hurricane of 1933, was among the most damaging storms in the mid-Atlantic states. It was reported that the Schuylkill River crested 21 feet—the highest recorded at the time—as a result of the Category 1 storm that hit the area in August of that year. The above photograph, taken from the west bank of the river, looks over the Fairmount Water Works. The art museum is on the hill. Below, a crowd gathers on the pier by the waterworks to see the debris that had collected in the calm water below the dam.

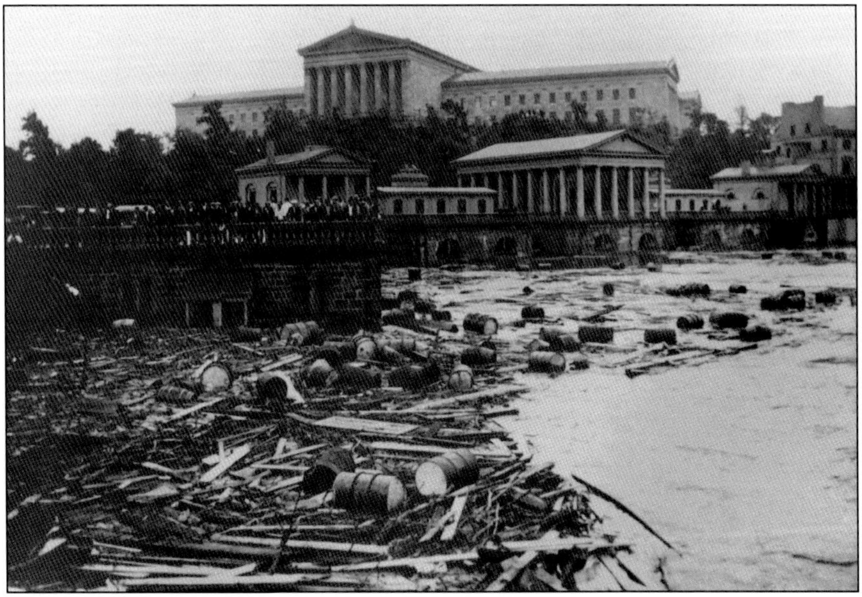

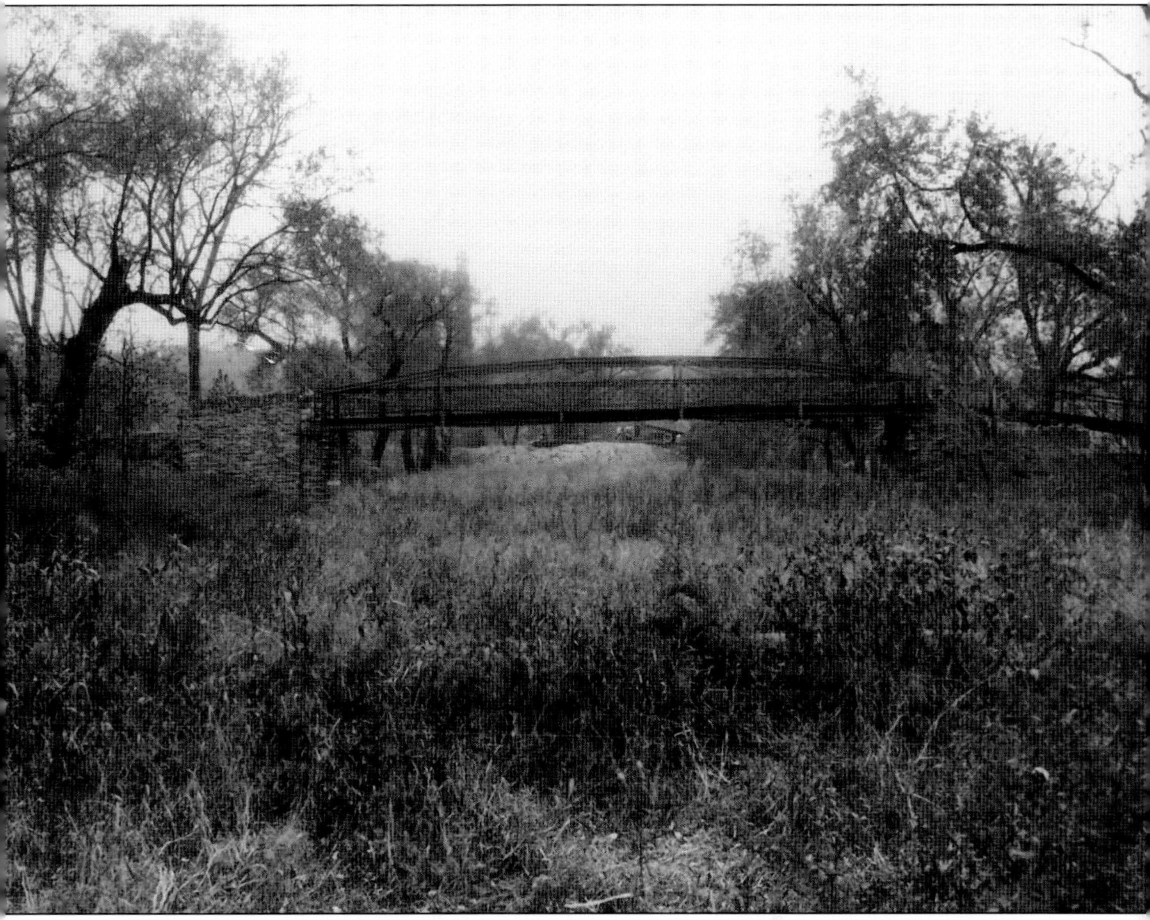

The primary purpose of the Schuylkill Canal was to carry anthracite coal from the northern coal region to Philadelphia; in fact, the Schuylkill Navigation Company's success was built on the downstream trade of this commodity. While dredging was a matter of routine maintenance on the canal, by the 1930s, so much coal silt had accumulated in the Schuylkill River that it was no longer navigable. Furthermore, the situation threatened the river's value as a water supply. Consequently, the Commonwealth of Pennsylvania undertook a desilting project to dredge silt from the river and pour it into canal beds and silt basins. This operation improved the river, but it ultimately destroyed the Schuylkill Canal; in the process, many locks and dams were buried by silt, dismantled, or neglected. This photograph looks north at an old canal bed believed to be the channel between Peter's Island and the west bank of the Schuylkill River.

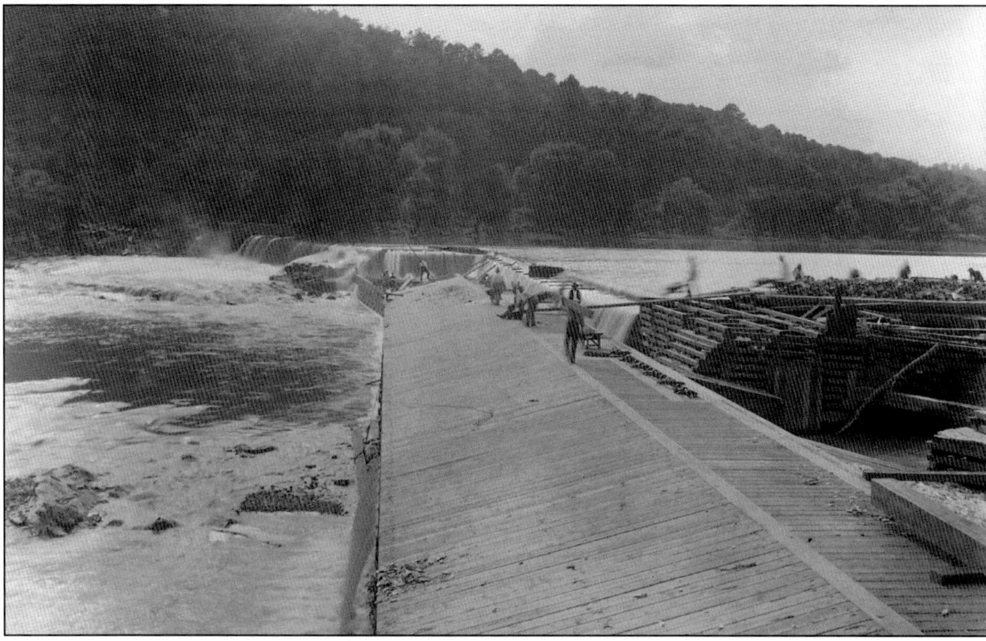

Originally built in 1818 by the Massachusetts contractor Ariel Cooley, the Flat Rock Dam (Dam 31) at Shawmont diverted water from the Schuylkill River into the Manayunk Canal to circumvent especially shallow, rocky areas that large boats could not pass through. The dam, named for a well-known natural rock formation in the river above Manayunk, was destroyed by a flood in 1839, requiring it to be repaired and rebuilt. These 1904 photographs show different stages in the building of a new dam below the old dam. Work on this project began on May 9 and was completed on November 25.

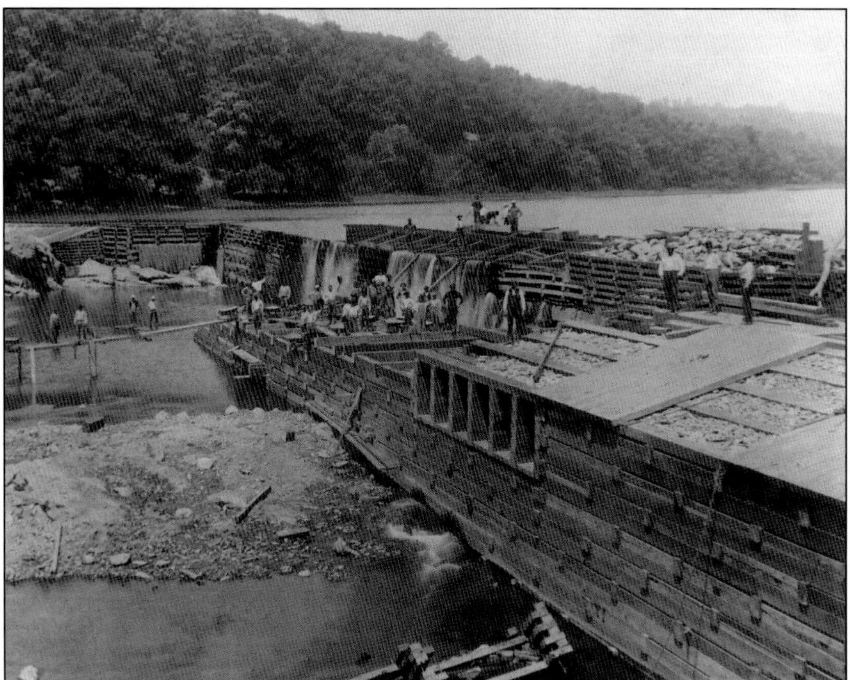

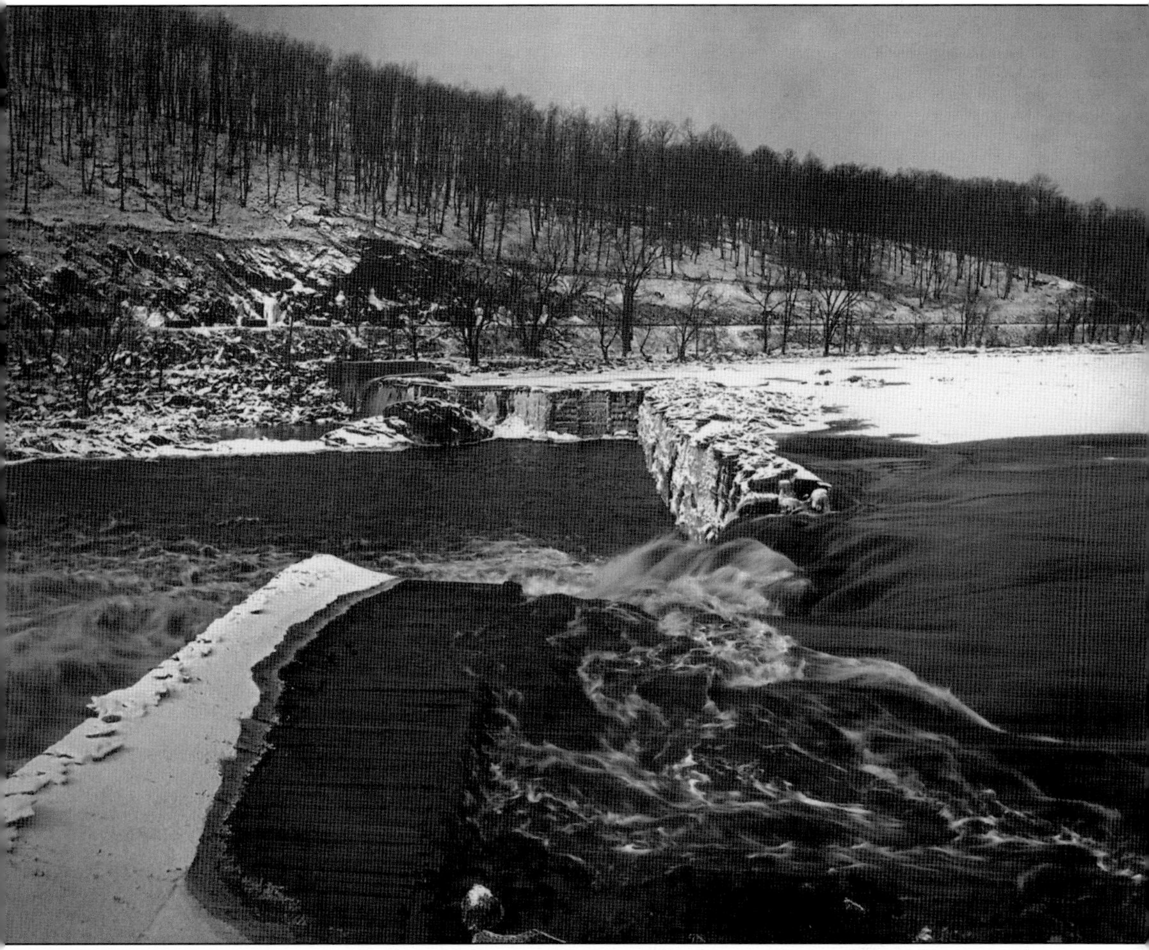

This serene winter photograph, dated February 27, 1904, offers an up-close view of a break in Flat Rock Dam near Shawmont. The mill town of Manayunk only came to be thanks to the construction of Flat Rock Dam, which provided the necessary industrial power source. It is no surprise that winter was a quiet time on the Schuylkill Navigation System. Melting snow occasionally resulted in flooding, which would sometimes affect various structures, such as breaks in dams and even damage to watercraft. In the background, railroad tracks can be seen. The Reading Company, chartered in 1871, became the holding company for the system of railroads, canals, and coal mines built by its predecessor, the Philadelphia & Reading Railroad Company, between 1833 and 1896. The Reading Company owned, leased, or held a controlling interest in rail lines throughout southeastern and central Pennsylvania, including the one shown here.

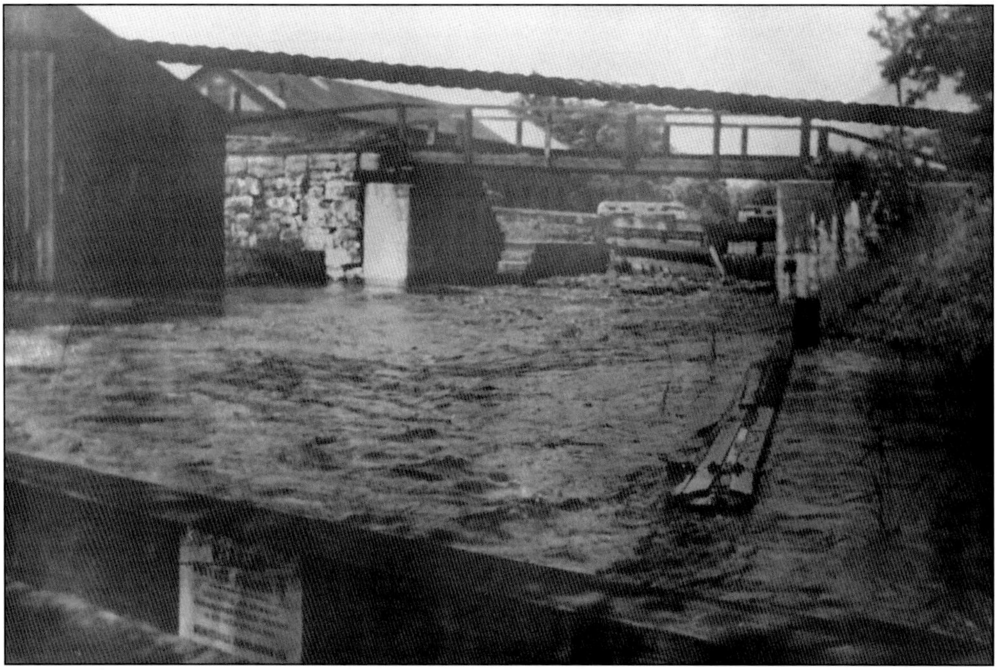

The land below lock 60 on the Schuylkill Canal is floodplain, and when the Schuylkill River floods, the canal acts as a large catch basin for the rising water to lessen the danger of flooding for the many properties that border the canal in Mont Clare and Port Providence. Unfortunately, residents here are no strangers to flood scenes, like this one in May 1942. These photographs, looking over lock 60 at Black Rock Dam (above) and of the actual ruptured lock gate (below), provide a glimpse of Mother Nature's power. The restored lock 60 is the only operating lock that remains on the Schuylkill River.

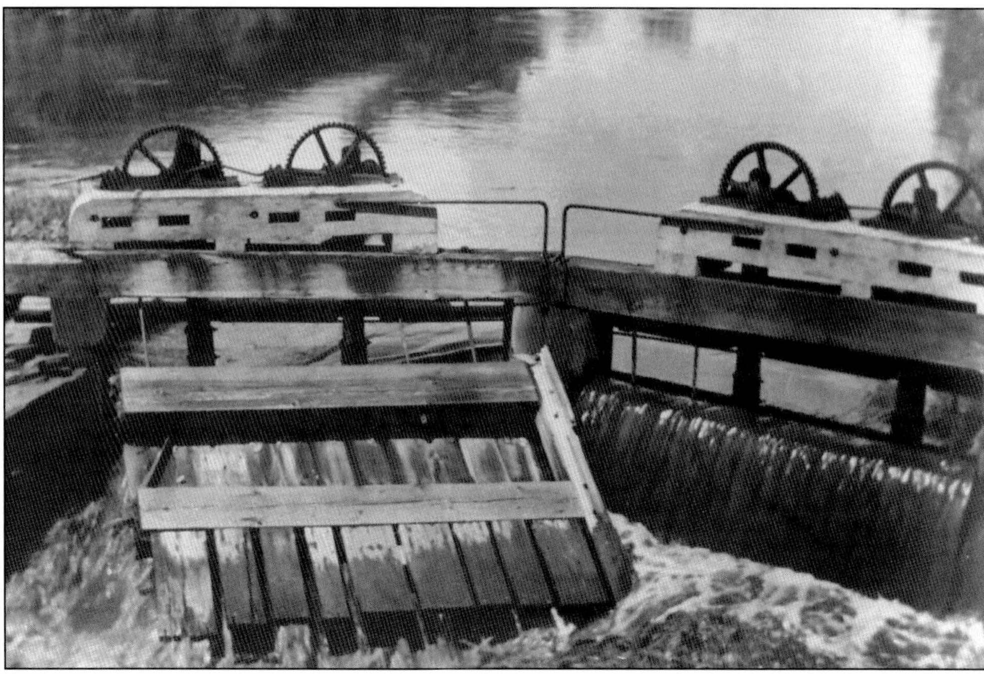

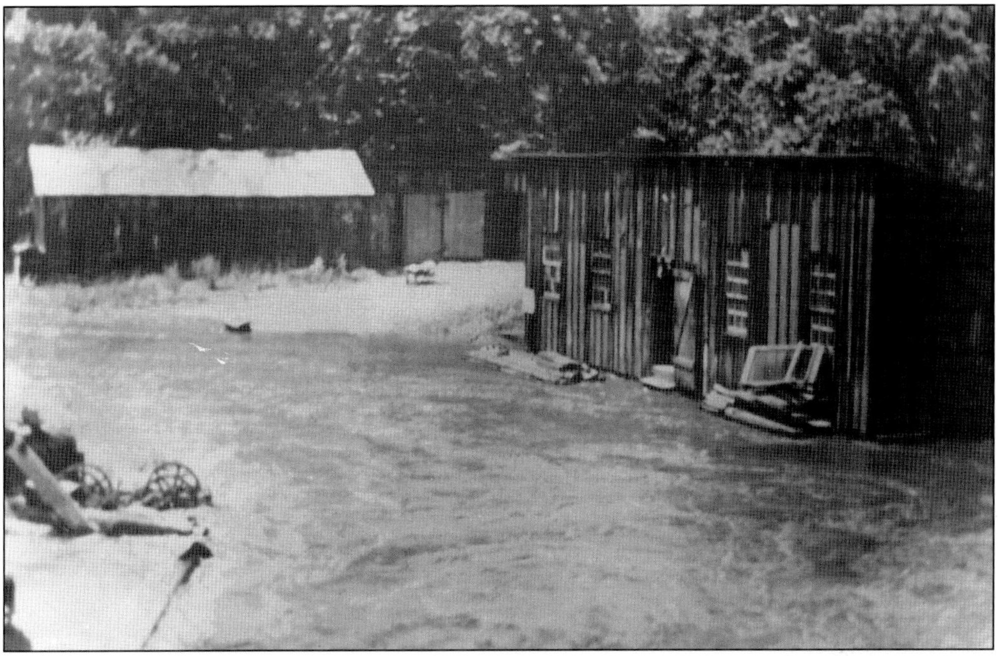

High-water conditions seen here at lock 60 near Black Rock Dam (Dam 26) during the flood of May 1942 brought water from the canal over the banks and to the doorsteps of the maintenance buildings and onto the towpath. Here, the lock (bottom left) is barely visible above the water.

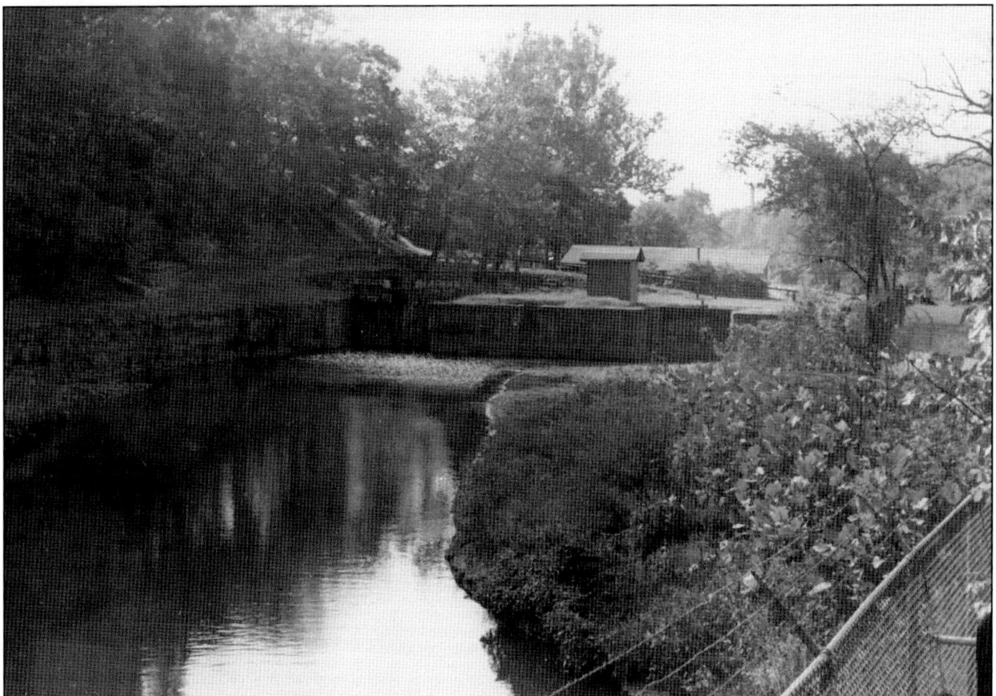

This photograph, taken from upstream on October 14, 1948, shows lock 60. The lock on the right was built in 1839 and later rebuilt into a canal feeder, or bypass sluice, so that in the event of a blockage, there would be a way to replenish the water supply.

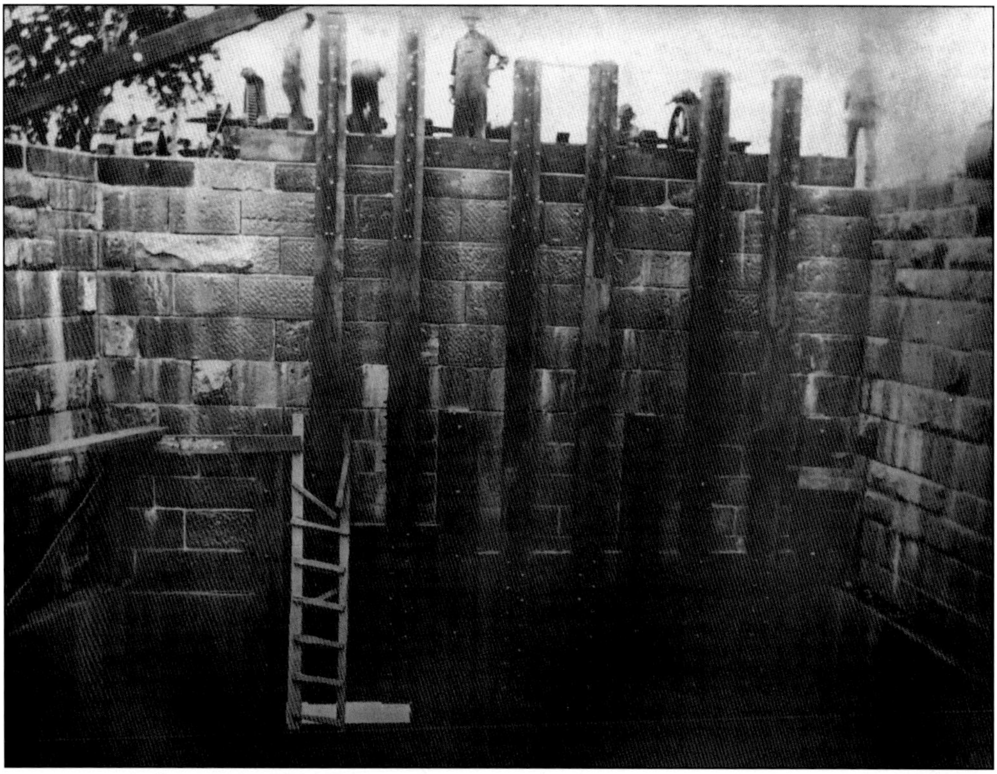

Men in coveralls work on the Vincent Dam (Dam 25 of the 32 total dams that were part of the complete Schuylkill Navigation System) under the direction of Michael Towers. He also had a part in the construction of the Vincent Canal. Shown above is the Schuylkill River elevation of the feeder gates. A canal-side view of the feeders (below) shows the cofferdam built around the gates to keep the water out. Cofferdams, also called coffers, were temporary enclosures built to allow the enclosed area to be pumped out so that major work, such as replacing a main dam, as in this case, could take place.

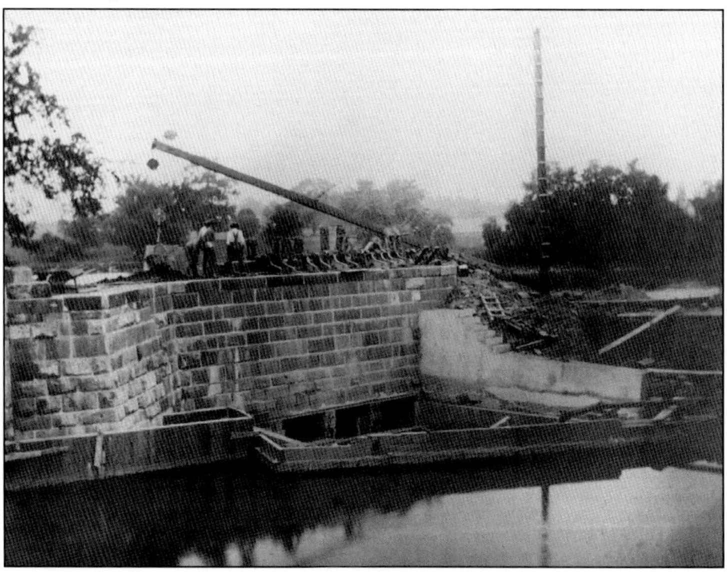

Workers take part in excavation efforts in the rebuilding of the feeders at Vincent Dam in Spring City in 1903. Dams were the most common feeders and could feed several locks below. All of the dams on the Schuylkill River were built of timber cribbing pinned with iron to the bedrock and filled with stone.

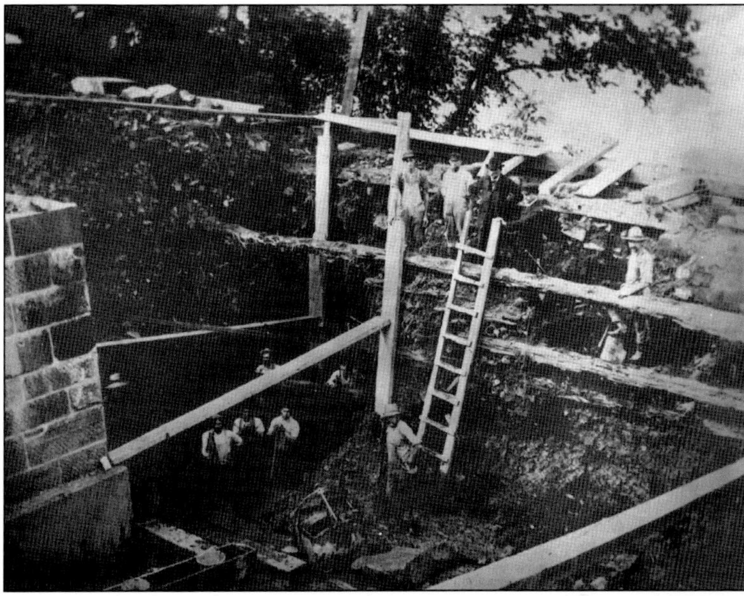

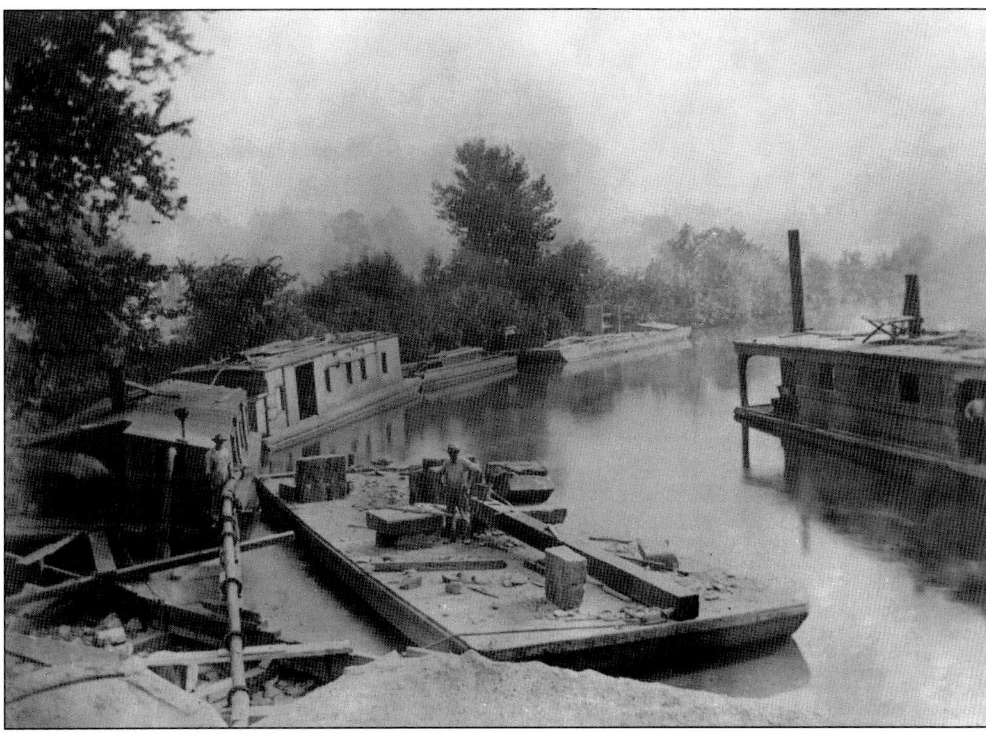

Various boats, including flat-bottomed scows and mechanic's barges, are seen on the Vincent Canal in 1903 during the rebuilding of the feeder gates at the Vincent Dam. The scow in this photograph appears to be actively in use as part of the work in progress. Boatmen had living quarters in the stern of the larger boats, just under the tiller.

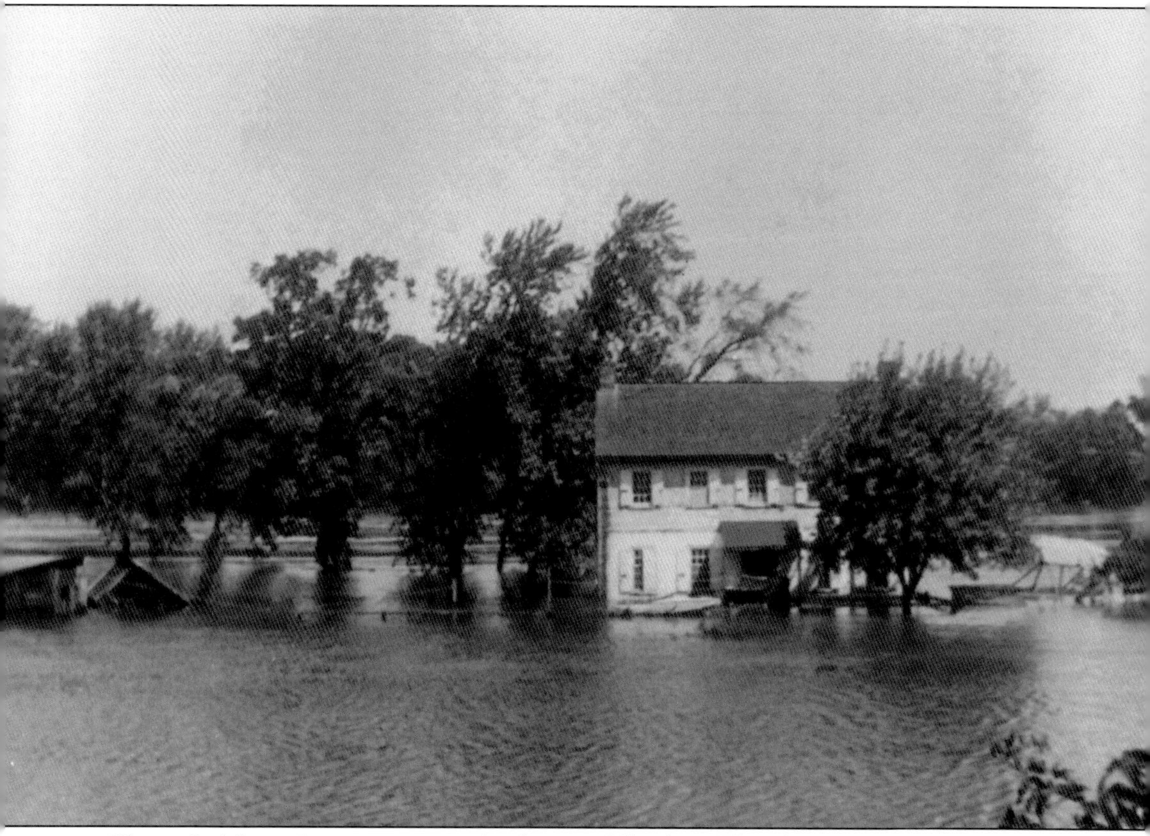

Obviously, life on the water carries the danger of flooding. That danger is even more imminent when the location is situated between two bodies of water, as in the case of this lock tender's house just above Spring City in Parker Ford, seen here in 1933 during high water. The small bridge crossed over the Girard Canal outlet lock (lock 57, or Schwartz's Lock) at its upper end. The lock is under water in this scene. The Girard Canal stretch of the Schuylkill Canal began at Dam 24—also called Lewis's Dam and later Big Reading Dam—and ran for 22 miles from Reading to Parker Ford. While the canal is most remembered for its transportation of anthracite coal, other types of freight, such as lumber, stone, marble, flour, grain, and other farm products, were also hauled along the waterway.

Four

That Was Then

After 1850, silt from the coal washeries operating upstream began to clog the channels, making navigation difficult. Profits also began to lag because of increased competition from the Reading Railroad. The section of the canal above Schuylkill Haven (lock 12) was abandoned by 1872 due to the silt problem, yet coal was shipped by canal from Schuylkill Haven until 1887, when the Reading Railroad acquired its all-rail route to New York. Coal silt made its way farther downstream with every high-water period until the channels were too choked to support commercial activity. In 1888, to the surprise of many, the Reading Railroad announced that the canal would be closed above Port Clinton. It was at this time that coal could finally be shipped by rail to the major markets. The writing was on the wall. Animal-powered water vessels were becoming outmoded by steam railroads. By 1932, all nonrecreational boat traffic on the Schuylkill Canal officially ceased. While this may have marked the end of an era, much good resulted. The canal created many business opportunities as well as jobs, and it can be credited for putting numerous little towns on the map, so to speak. In fact, the canal was not only important for these towns, but it also holds historical significance for the state as a whole.

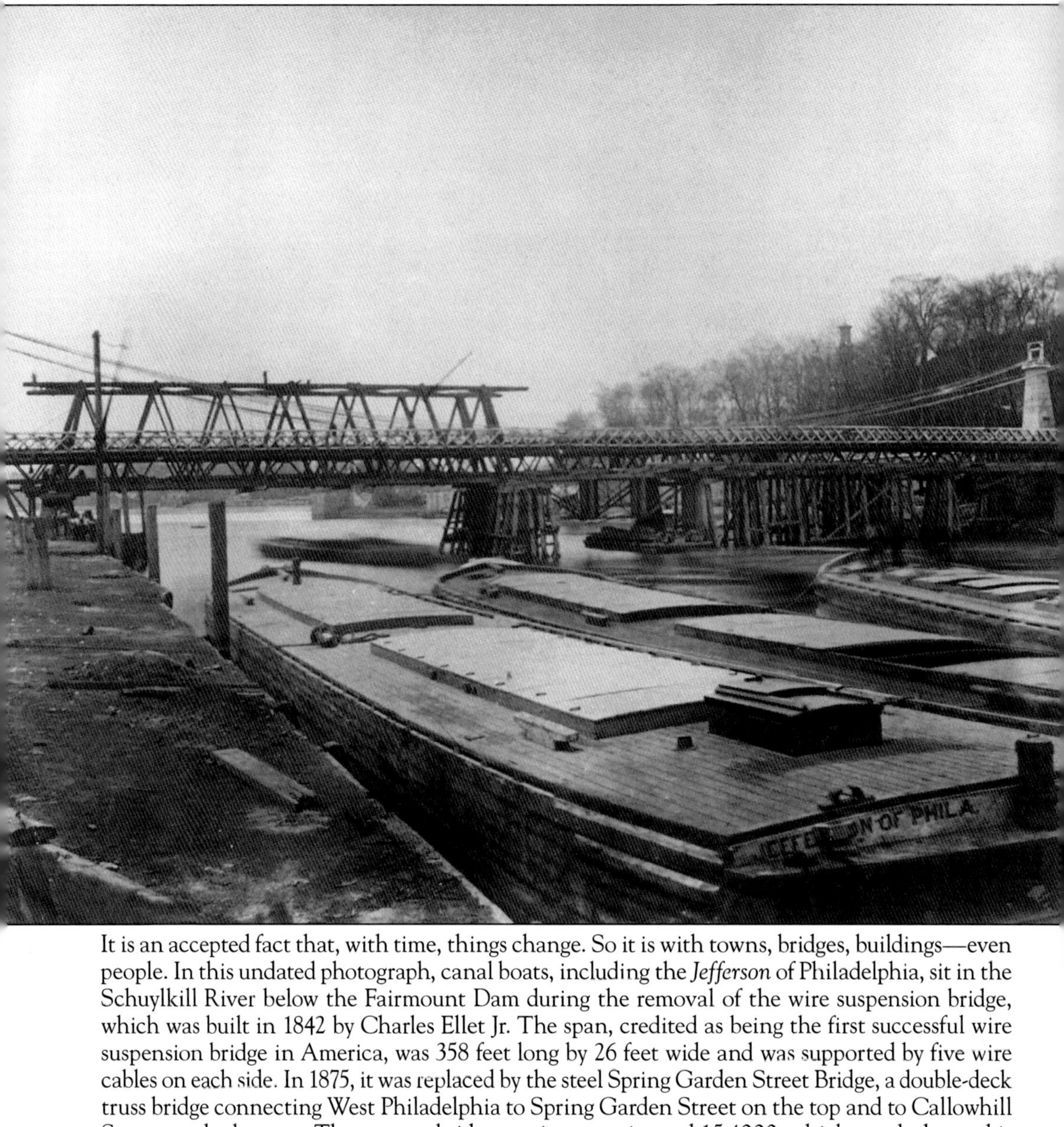

It is an accepted fact that, with time, things change. So it is with towns, bridges, buildings—even people. In this undated photograph, canal boats, including the *Jefferson* of Philadelphia, sit in the Schuylkill River below the Fairmount Dam during the removal of the wire suspension bridge, which was built in 1842 by Charles Ellet Jr. The span, credited as being the first successful wire suspension bridge in America, was 358 feet long by 26 feet wide and was supported by five wire cables on each side. In 1875, it was replaced by the steel Spring Garden Street Bridge, a double-deck truss bridge connecting West Philadelphia to Spring Garden Street on the top and to Callowhill Street on the bottom. The current bridge carries an estimated 15,4000 vehicles each day and is presently undergoing a multimillion-dollar makeover.

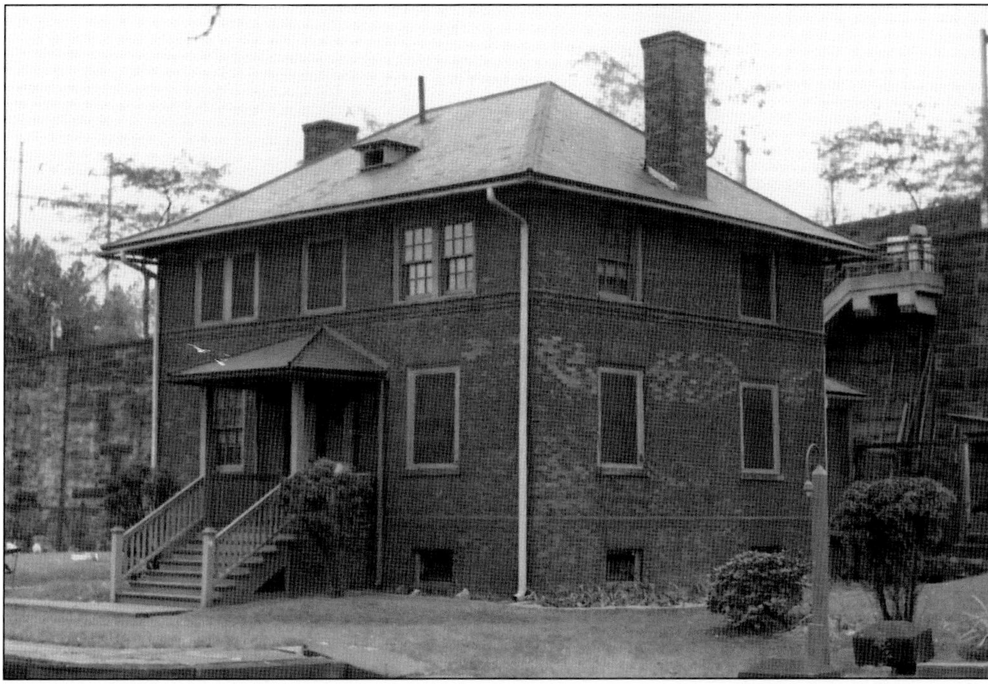

The Schuylkill Navigation Company began operating in 1825 and was quite successful for many years, thanks to the demand for anthracite coal, which the company's navigation system transported. In fact, 1859 was the most successful year for the company—even though competition for the highly profitable coal trade by the Philadelphia & Reading Railroad had begun to chip away at its financial stability from the moment the railroad was up and running in 1842. Toward the end of 1915, a mere 30 boats were estimated to still be in service. It is hard to believe that these photographs of the lock 72 lock tender's house (above) and of locks 71 and 72 at Fairmount Dam (below) were taken so long after, in October 1948.

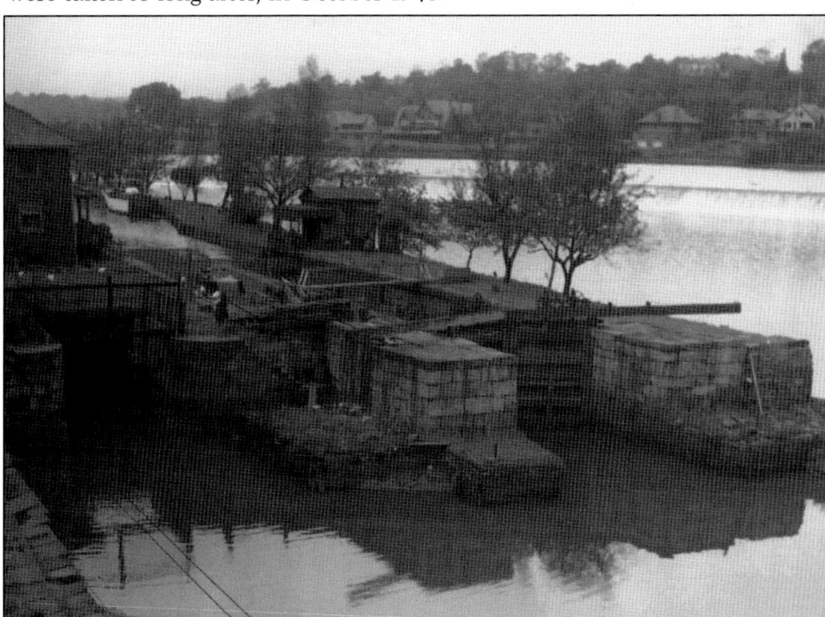

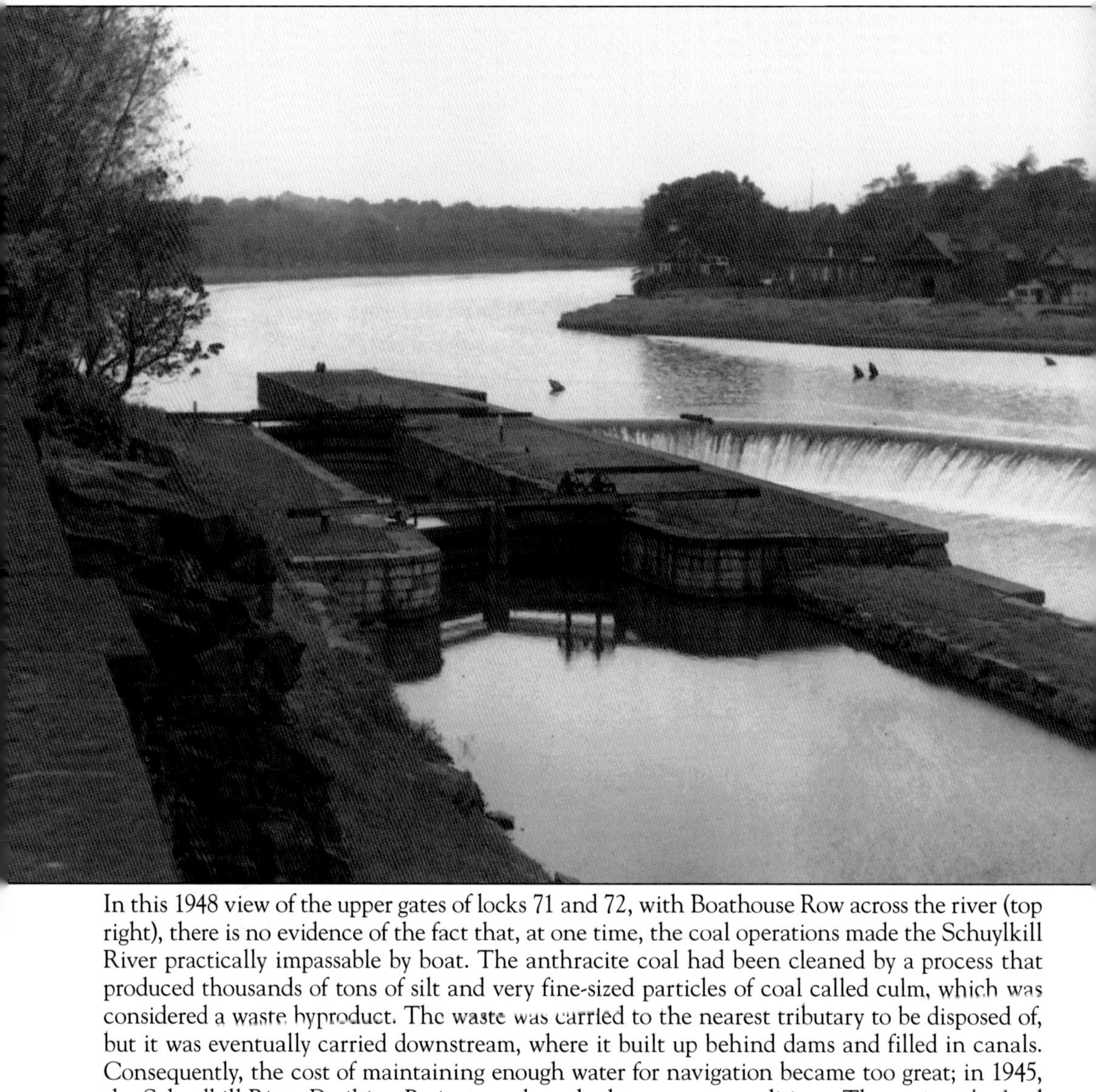

In this 1948 view of the upper gates of locks 71 and 72, with Boathouse Row across the river (top right), there is no evidence of the fact that, at one time, the coal operations made the Schuylkill River practically impassable by boat. The anthracite coal had been cleaned by a process that produced thousands of tons of silt and very fine-sized particles of coal called culm, which was considered a waste byproduct. The waste was carried to the nearest tributary to be disposed of, but it was eventually carried downstream, where it built up behind dams and filled in canals. Consequently, the cost of maintaining enough water for navigation became too great; in 1945, the Schuylkill River Desilting Project was launched to correct conditions. The project dredged silt from the river and poured it into canal beds and silt basins.

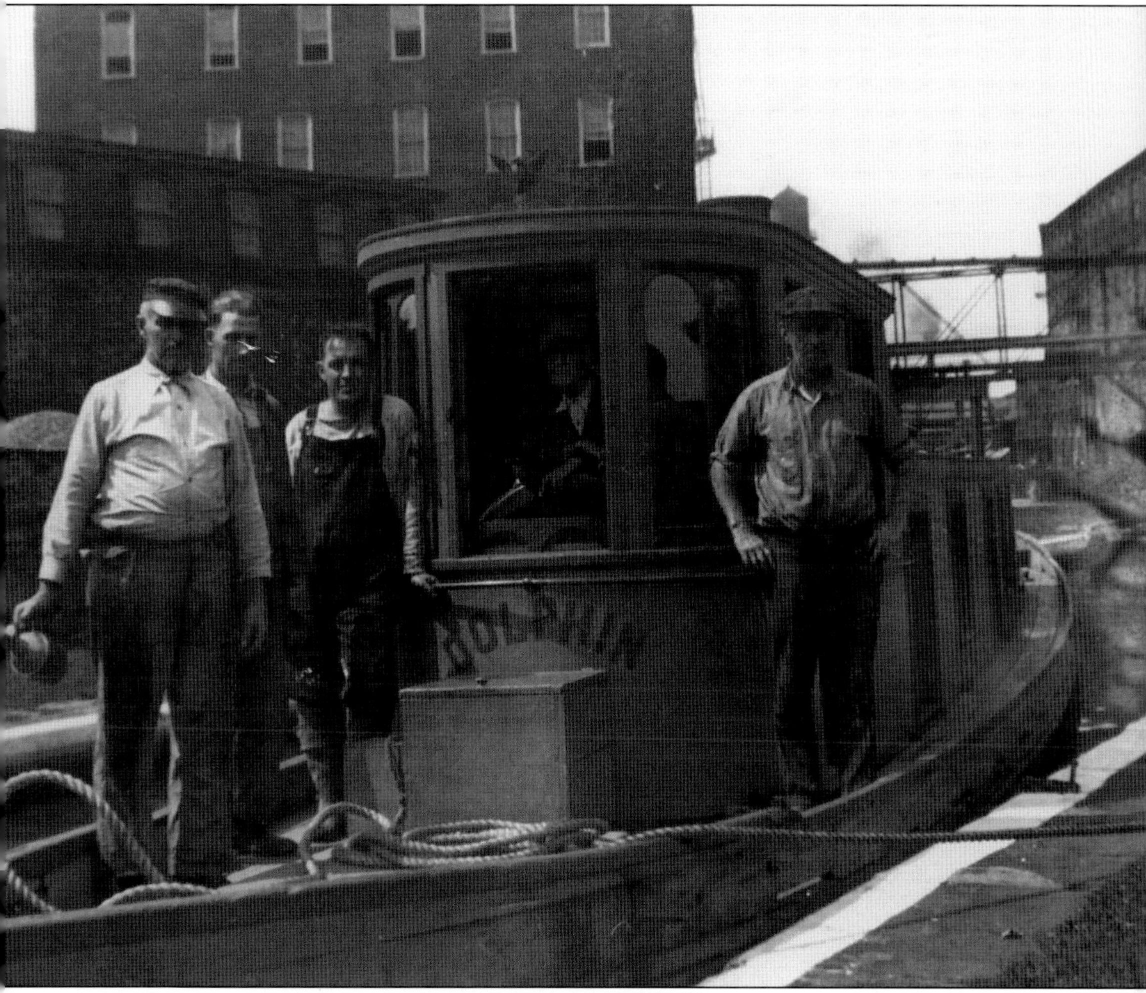

The *Dolphin* was a tugboat built in 1858 at Union Boiler Works, a company headed by F.J. Obert in Reading. The boat was used on the Schuylkill Canal to tow dredges, mud scows, and canal boats. In the 20th century, lock 60 on the Oakes Canal in Mont Clare served as the homeport for the boat and its crew. Pictured here on the *Dolphin's* last dredging trip in 1937 are, from left to right, Vincent Moyer (engineer), Floyd Crowl (spud tender), Jim Hinkel (scow tender), Rubin Waters (pilot), and Billy Bean (deckhand). The boat is in the upper chamber of the Manayunk Canal. Today, the pilothouse of the *Dolphin* is on display at the C. Howard Hiester Canal Center in Berks County.

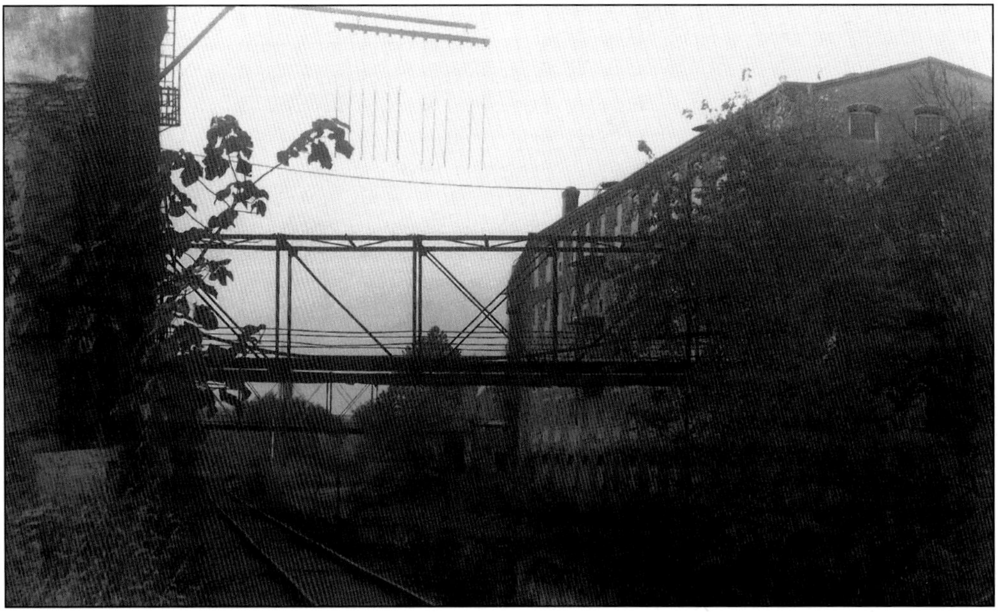

Above, the old S. Schofield Woolen Mill buildings can be seen on both sides of the Manayunk Canal. The bridge at center was used by workers to access the mill, while the bridge in the background crossed the canal to the Green Lane Bridge. The below photograph was taken from a point just above the buildings. The story of the Schofield brothers' business endeavors is quite a tale, with involvement in producing blankets, yarn, and more. At the height of business, the mill's complex spanned from Lock Street to Rector Street, occupied both sides of the canal, and completely encompassed Venice Island between the river and the canal.

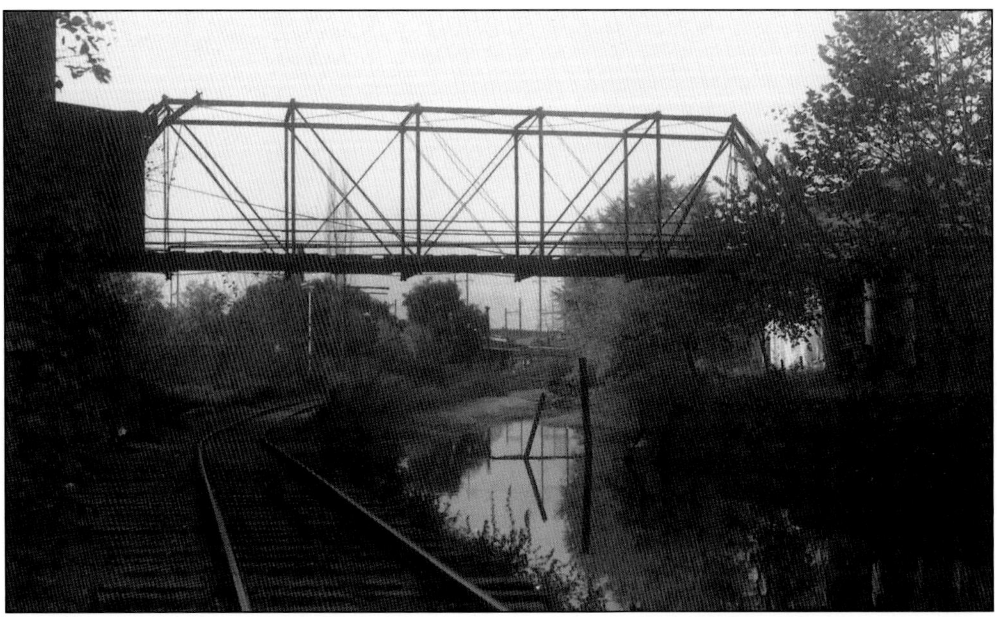

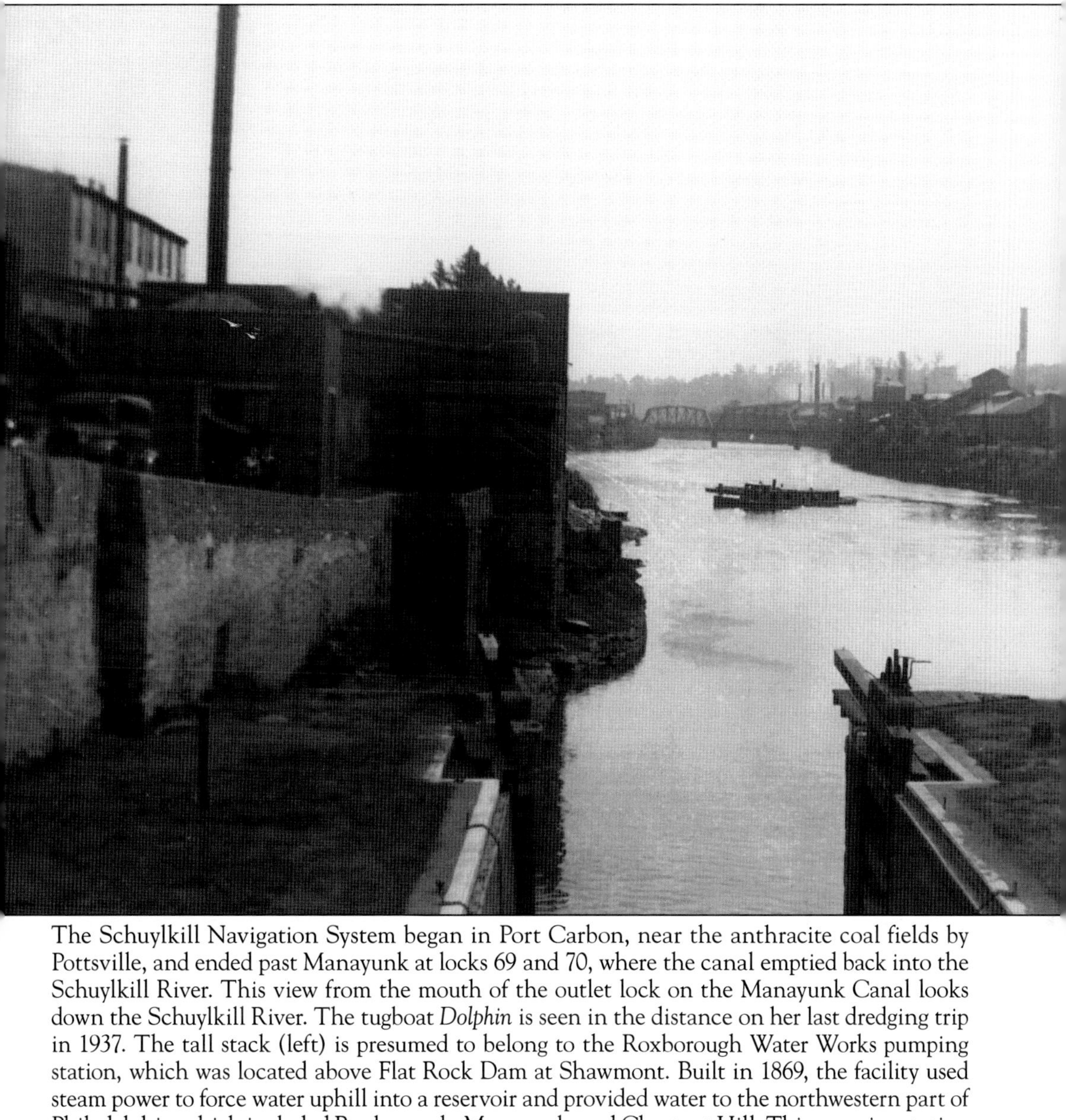

The Schuylkill Navigation System began in Port Carbon, near the anthracite coal fields by Pottsville, and ended past Manayunk at locks 69 and 70, where the canal emptied back into the Schuylkill River. This view from the mouth of the outlet lock on the Manayunk Canal looks down the Schuylkill River. The tugboat *Dolphin* is seen in the distance on her last dredging trip in 1937. The tall stack (left) is presumed to belong to the Roxborough Water Works pumping station, which was located above Flat Rock Dam at Shawmont. Built in 1869, the facility used steam power to force water uphill into a reservoir and provided water to the northwestern part of Philadelphia, which included Roxborough, Manayunk, and Chestnut Hill. This pumping station was expanded in the 1890s to increase the capacity of the Roxborough Works and reach a larger part of the city.

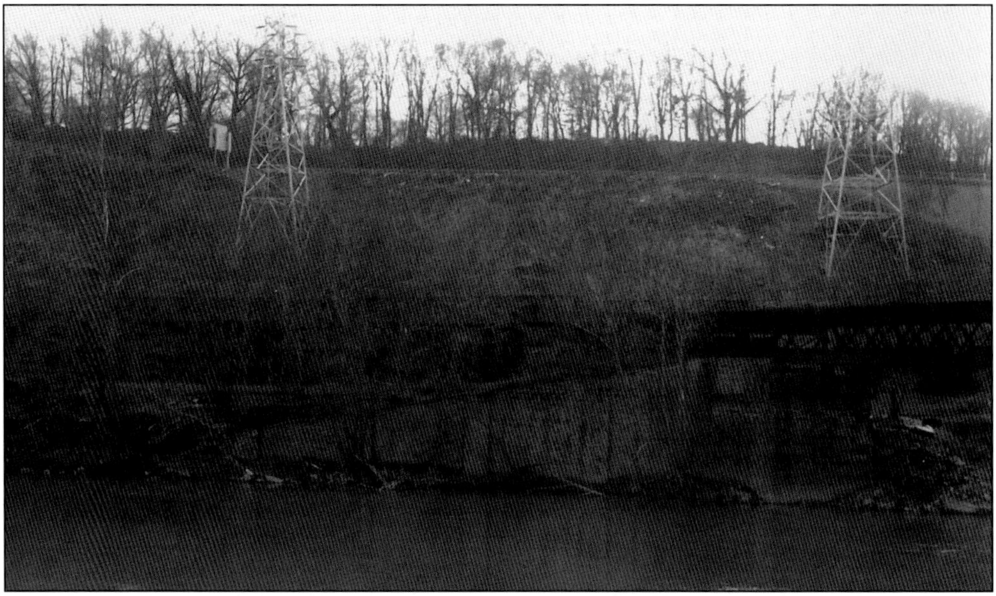

These photographs of the Venice Island Branch Bridge over the Schuylkill River were taken on March 6, 1976. The western shore abutment is shown above. The bridge was originally built as a towpath bridge by the Schuylkill Navigation Company, but it was rebuilt in 1889 by the old Reading Company to carry the Venice Island Branch railroad as well as the towpath over the river. Note the length of the incline of the towpath; mules once used this bridge to cross the river. The Schuylkill Navigation Company even had a mule farm of its own, located on the Berks and Chester County line.

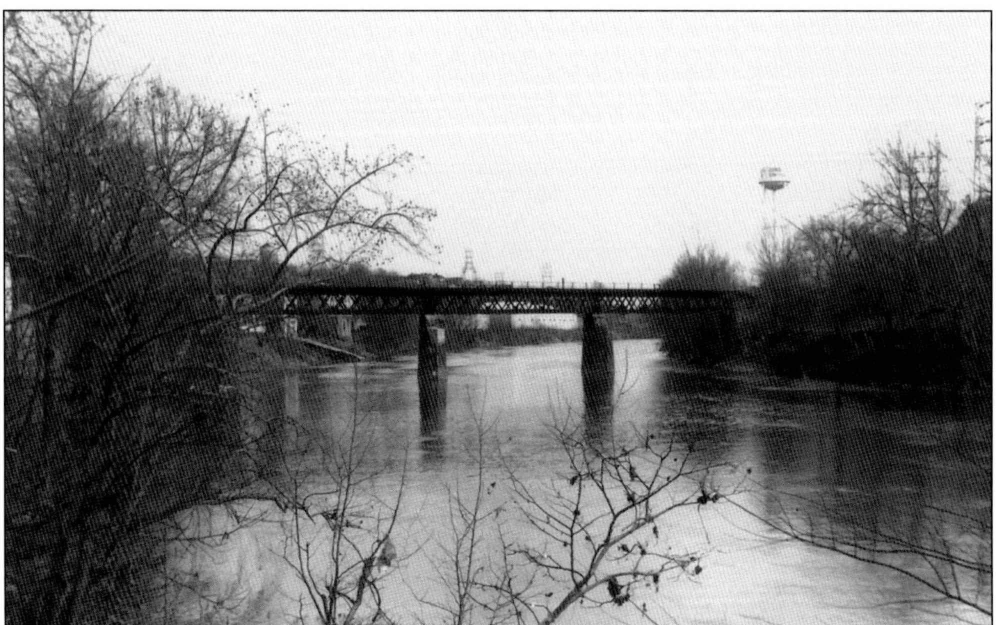

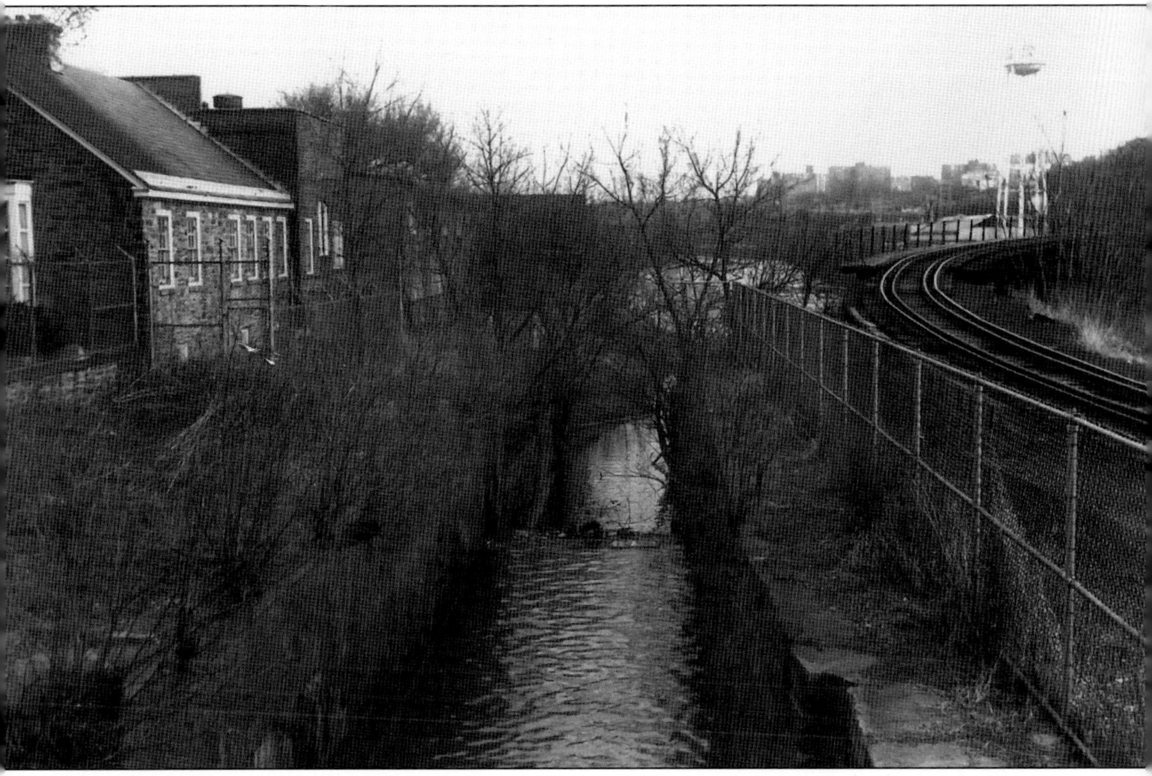

The Manayunk Canal, completed in 1818, was first used for travel in 1822. The canal's initial lock system comprised a single channel at the upper lock and multiple channels at the lower lock. On the Schuylkill Navigation System, locks were typically between 75 and 80 feet long and about 17 feet wide. This 1976 photograph shows the neglected Manayunk Canal at its outlet locks, fenced off for safety reasons as well as to keep out vandals. The railroad tracks (right) are still in use today. The Philadelphia & Reading Railroad opened in 1842 and immediately competed with the canal. When the canal was leased by the Reading Railroad in 1870, commercial use virtually ceased. In 1889, the railroad opened the Venice Island spur. Today, this section of the Schuylkill Canal is one of two that been renewed.

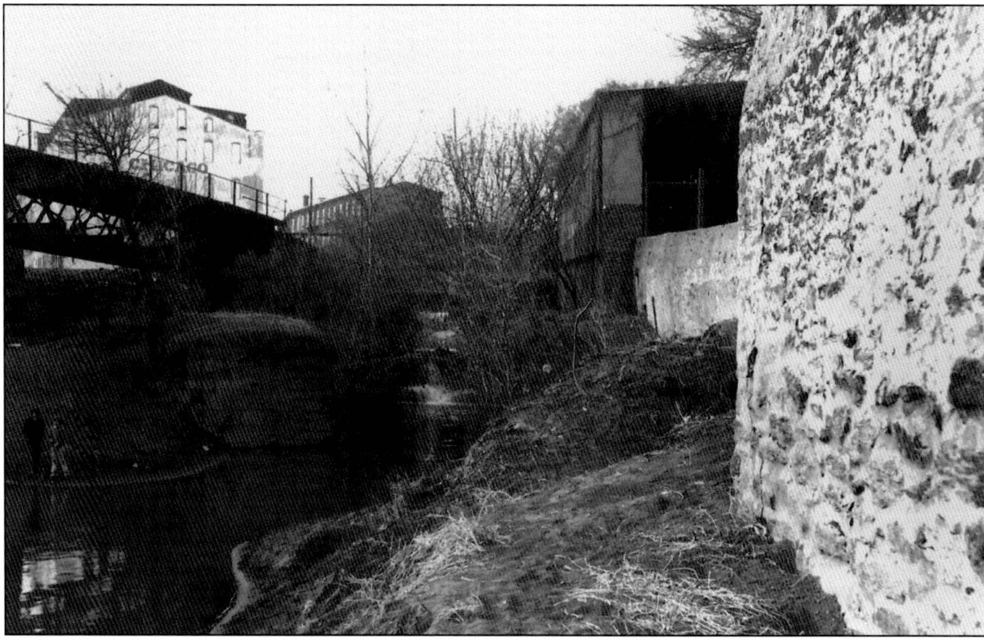

The above photograph, taken in 1976, provides a different perspective, looking upstream into the outlet locks on the Manayunk Canal. The white building beyond the bridge (upper left) is seen front and center in the below photograph from 1974. This is the old S. Schofield Woolen Mill building, which was torn down in the summer of 1977. This site is now home to RichardsApex, Inc., a family-owned company that supplies high-performance metal-working fluids. The bridge to the right of the mill in the below photograph appears in other photographs, taken from the other side of the building and across the canal.

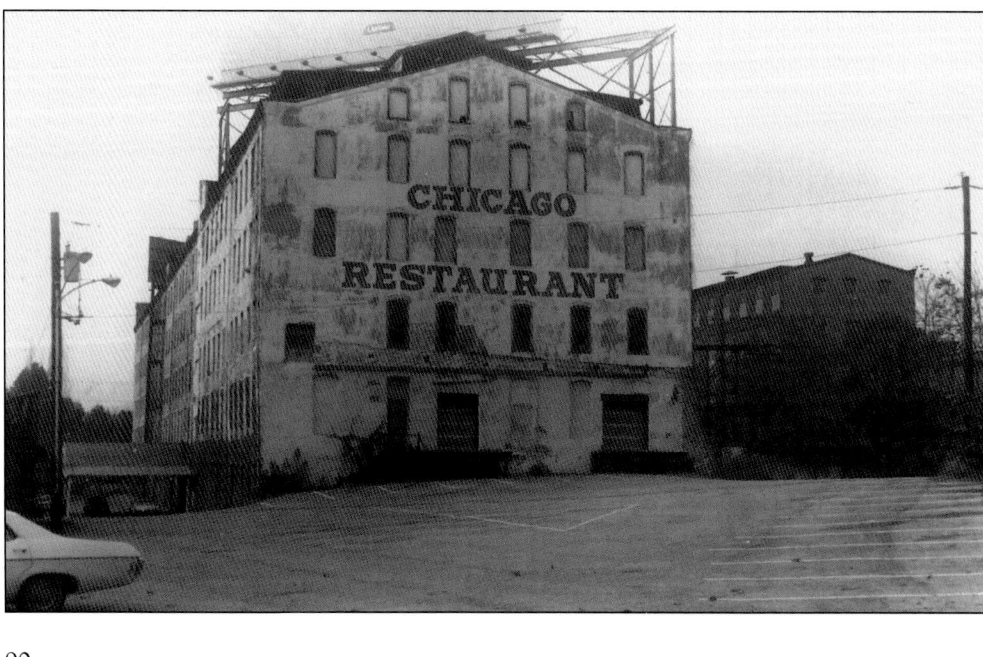

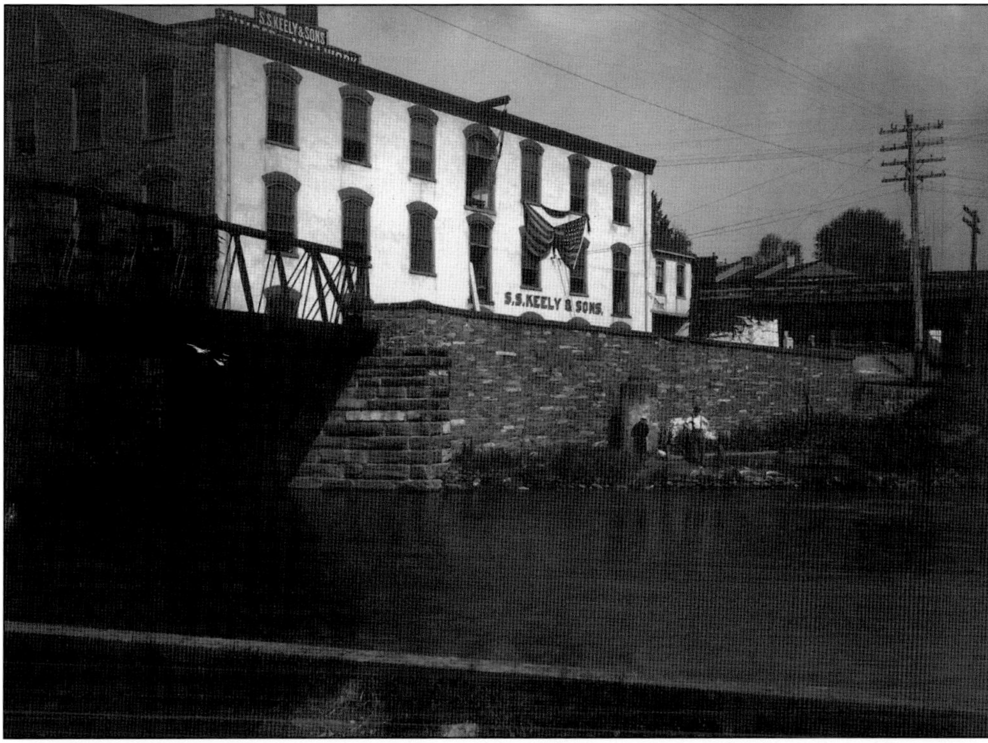

These photographs show the Leverington Avenue Bridge over the Manayunk Canal, with the former S.S. Keely & Sons Lumber and Millwork building in the background. Though 113 years have passed, the scene remains relatively unchanged. The bridge clearly has been rebuilt at some point over the years, and the towpath has been expanded and paved to improve its recreational use by walkers, runners, and bikers. Fairmount Park, in partnership with the Philadelphia Water Department, is proposing additional improvements to the Manayunk Canal, including minor restoration work on the upper locks and sluice house, bank stabilization work, and removal of sediment to increase water flow into and through the canal. (Below, courtesy of the author.)

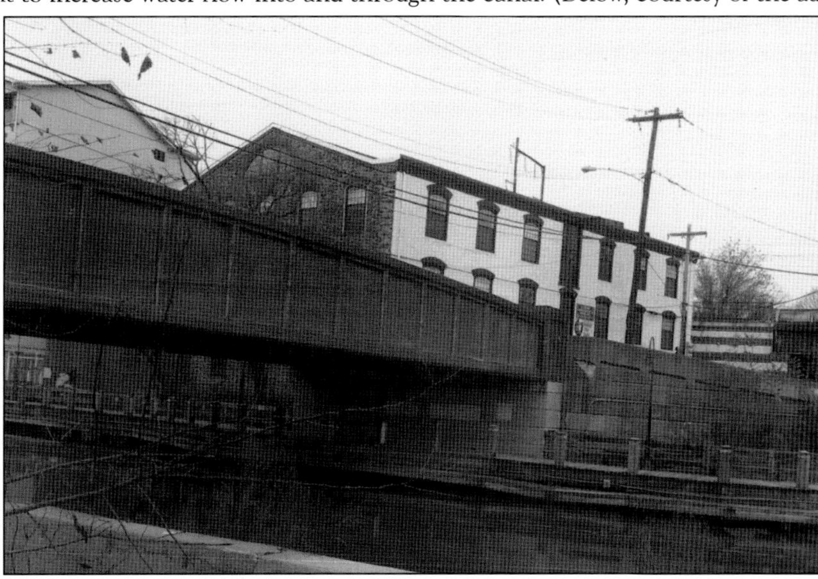

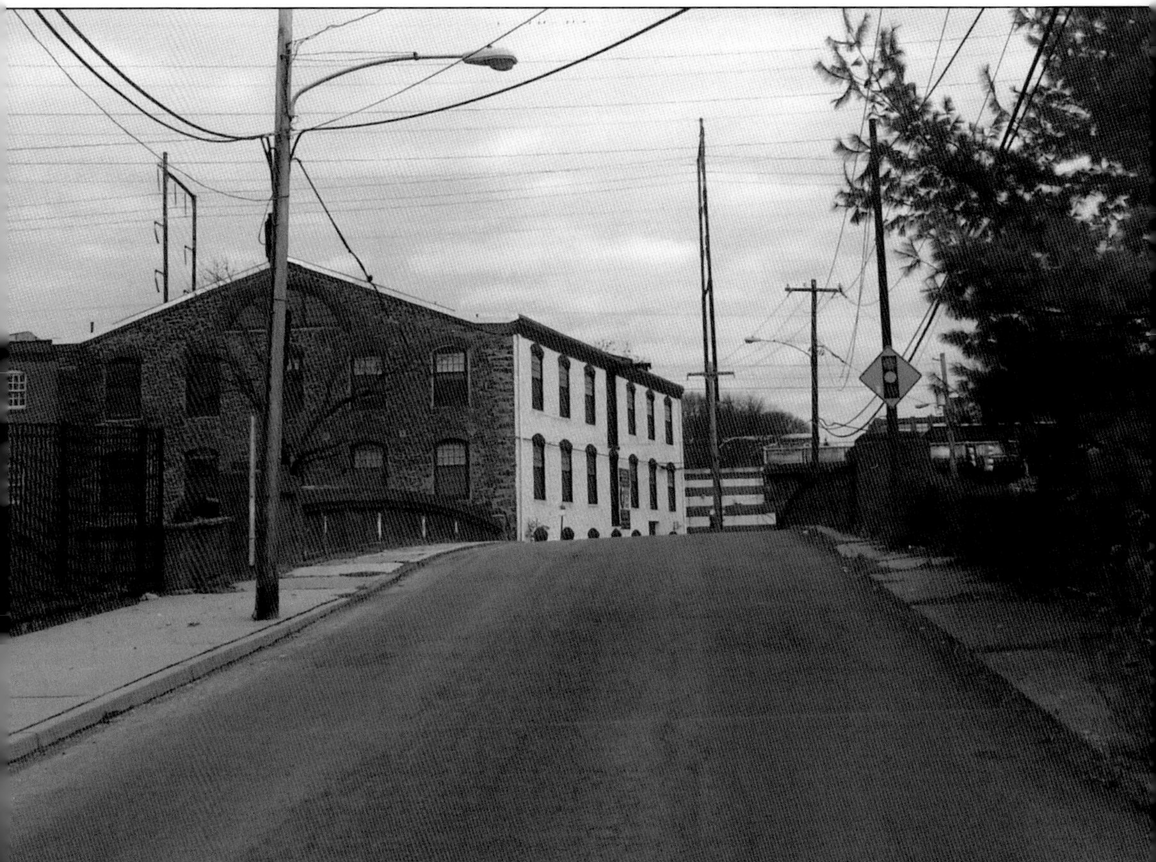

The original name was Flat Rock, after a rock formation in the river. Many believe that the modern name, Manayunk, comes from a Lenape word meaning "a place to drink," referring to the Schuylkill River as a source of water. This 2014 photograph was taken on the Leverington Avenue Bridge, showing the former S.S. Keely & Sons Lumber and Millwork building (left), which now houses condominiums. In the canal era, the bigger mill buildings were located on Venice Island between the river and the canal, though many operated on both sides of the canal, which workers accessed by bridge. Interestingly, offices, hotels, banks, and residential buildings usually ended up on the north side of Main Street. Little development—or redevelopment, for that matter—took place here after the early 1900s. Today, the Manayunk Main Street Historic District is listed in the National Register of Historic Places. (Courtesy of the author.)

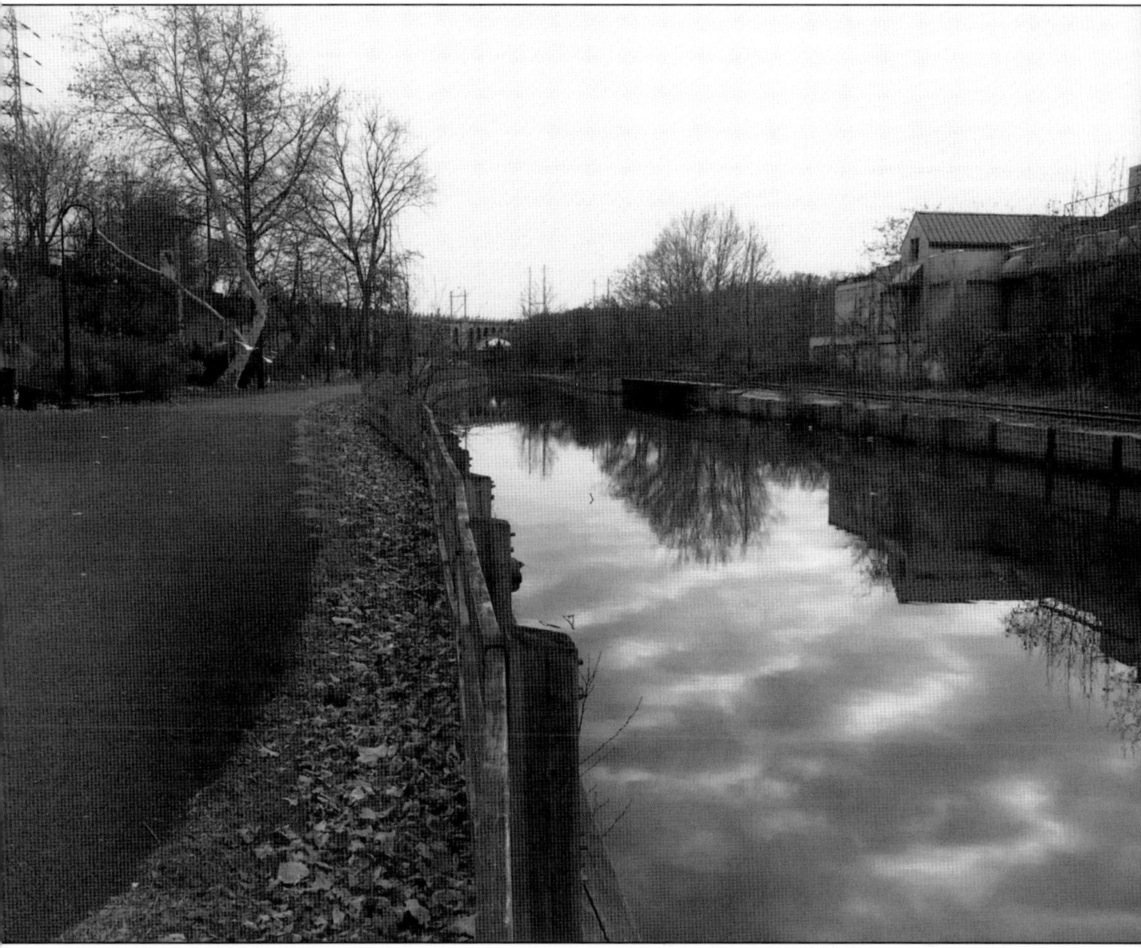

This is a 204 photograph showing the view down the Manayunk Canal, which itself is in the Philadelphia Register of Historic Places. The paved towpath (left) is located behind Main Street, and railroad tracks run on the opposite side of the canal. Beyond the tracks at right is a building that belonged to the now-closed Carmella's Restaurant between Leverington Avenue and Green Lane on Venice Island. There are development proposal plans for a 4.5-acre parcel on that land. In the distance (center) is the historic Manayunk Bridge, which opened in 1918 and is now an inactive railroad crossing, closed for 28 years. A new project is under way to connect the Cynwyd Heritage bicycle and pedestrian trail in Lower Merion Township to Manayunk across the Schuylkill River on top of this old structure, which is known for its amazing views. (Courtesy of the author.)

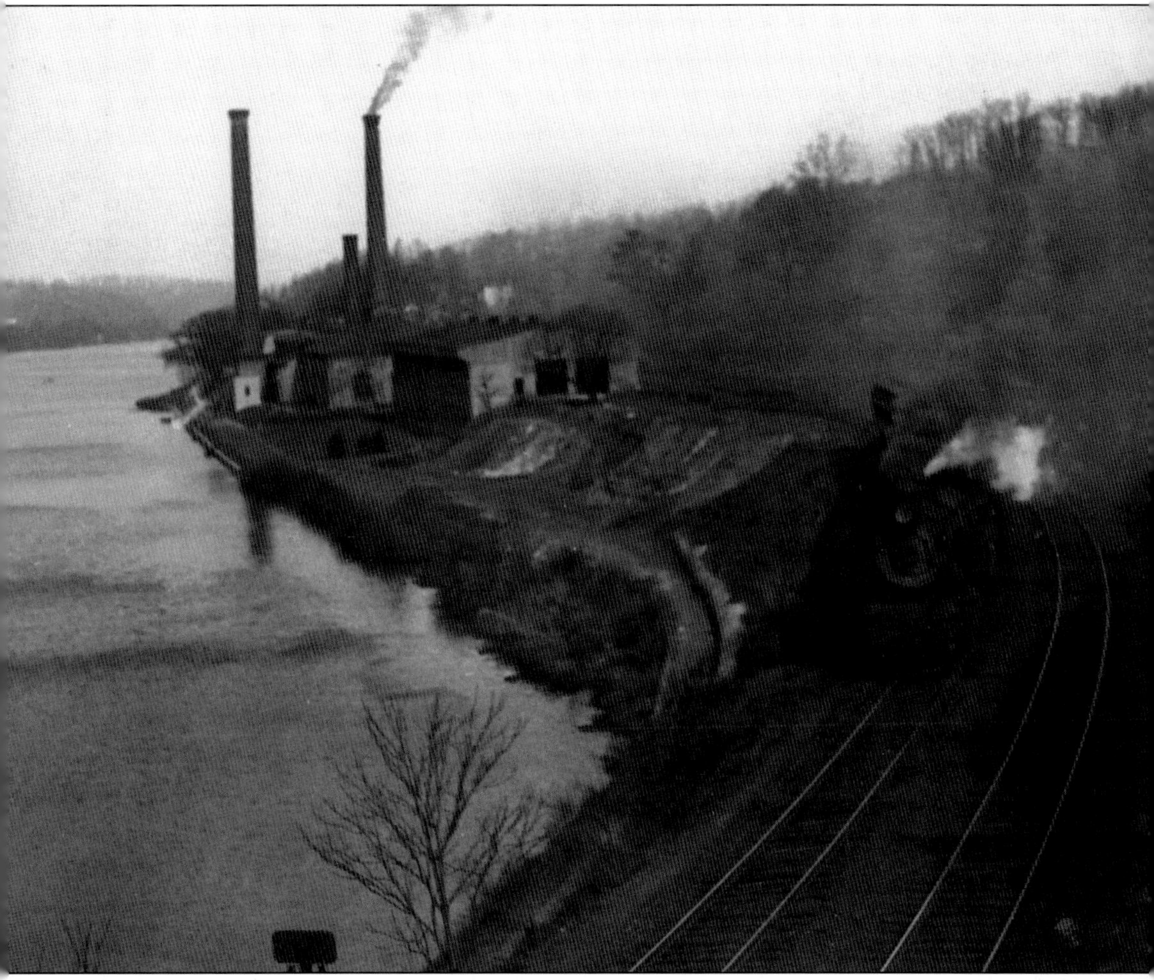

The railroad is credited for the downfall of the Schuylkill Canal, and it is no wonder. The Philadelphia & Reading Railroad opened in 1842, providing transportation between Port Carbon and Philadelphia; in only two years, it carried more coal than the canal. In answer to this new competition, the canal was widened to accommodate larger boats, and tolls were lowered. Unfortunately, these efforts were in vain. The Reading Railroad leased the canal in 1870, and finally, in 1949, the bankrupted Schuylkill Navigation Company deeded all of its properties to the Commonwealth of Pennsylvania. This undated photograph was taken from upstream on the Schuylkill River from a point just above Flat Rock Dam. The towpath cut out along the bank of the river for canal traffic is seen below the passing steam engine. The Knickerbocker Ice Company building is at center; the three stacks of the Roxborough Water Works stand behind it.

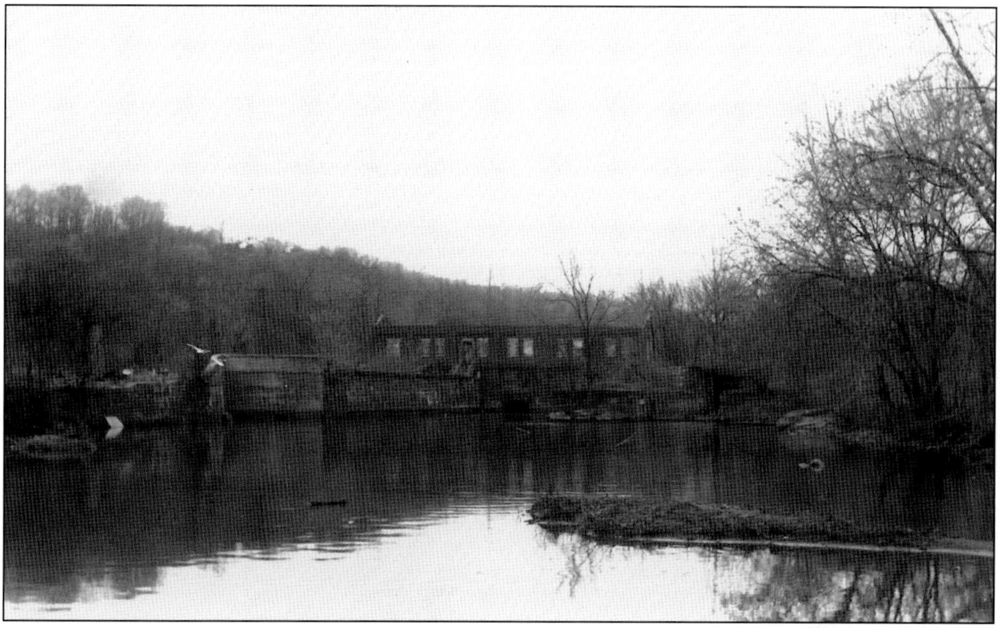

The above photograph, taken in 1976, looks downstream at the now-defunct Shawmont sluice house (center), sometimes referred to as a feeder house, and the old lock 68 (right) at Flat Rock Dam. A closer look at the feeder section (below) shows a date stone from 1883 that bears the initials of the Philadelphia & Reading Railroad Company. The water level in the canal was of major importance to the operation of the mills along its banks. While the canal was in operation, water from the river was channeled into a sluiceway and then either let through or held back by the sluice gates.

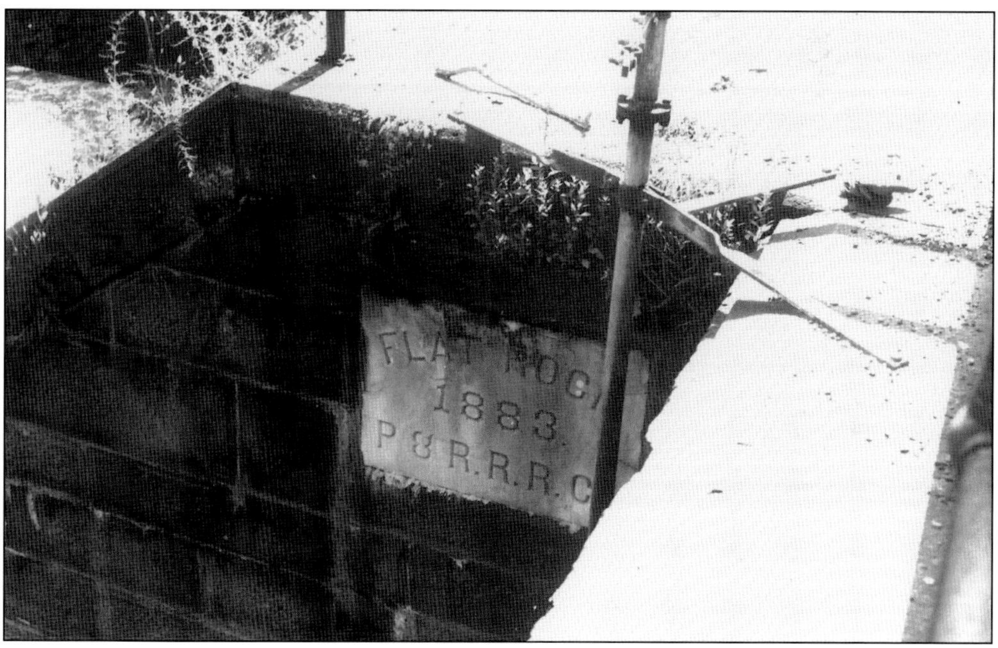

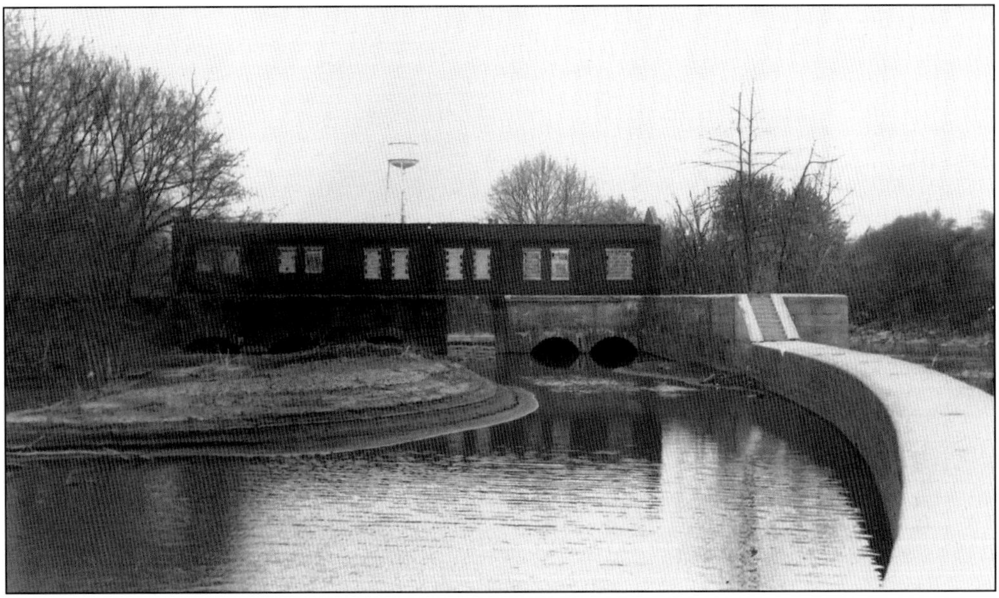

The feeder house at the head of the Manayunk Canal is seen above from upstream. The remains of the interior of the feeder house are shown below in September 1976. Waterpower from the dams was a power source for local mills, and the Schuylkill Navigation Company received a profit from this operation. The machinery shown below was once used to operate the sluice gates to regulate the water level and keep the mills running. Without adequate water in the river, the mills would experience a reduction in power, which was less than ideal.

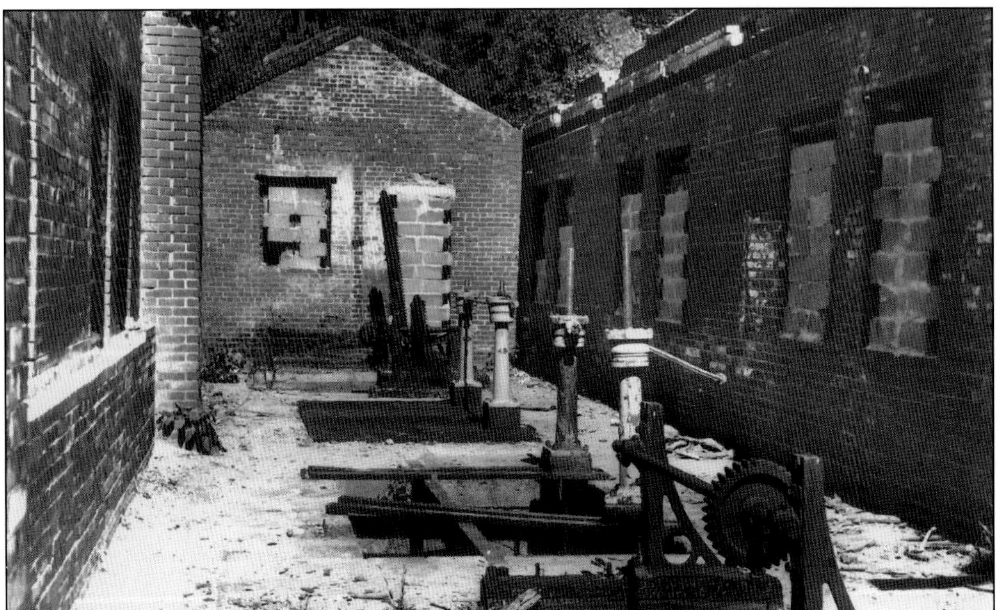

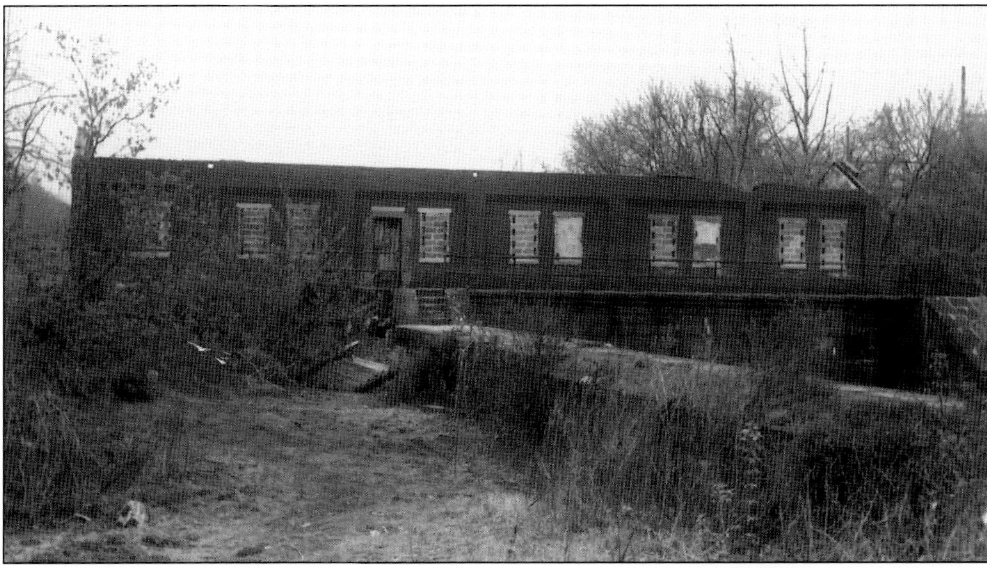

Now in ruins, the Shawmont sluice house is a reminder of another way of life long ago. The facility, shown above in 1976, looks only slightly different than it did in 1948 (below). The facility was named after local inventor Thomas Shaw, who devised several permanent improvements for the railroad. Nearby Shawmont Station was also named for Shaw. Fairmount Park and the Philadelphia Water Department have proposed improvements to this area, including minor restoration on the upper locks and sluice house, bank stabilization, and the removal of sediment to increase water flow into and through the canal.

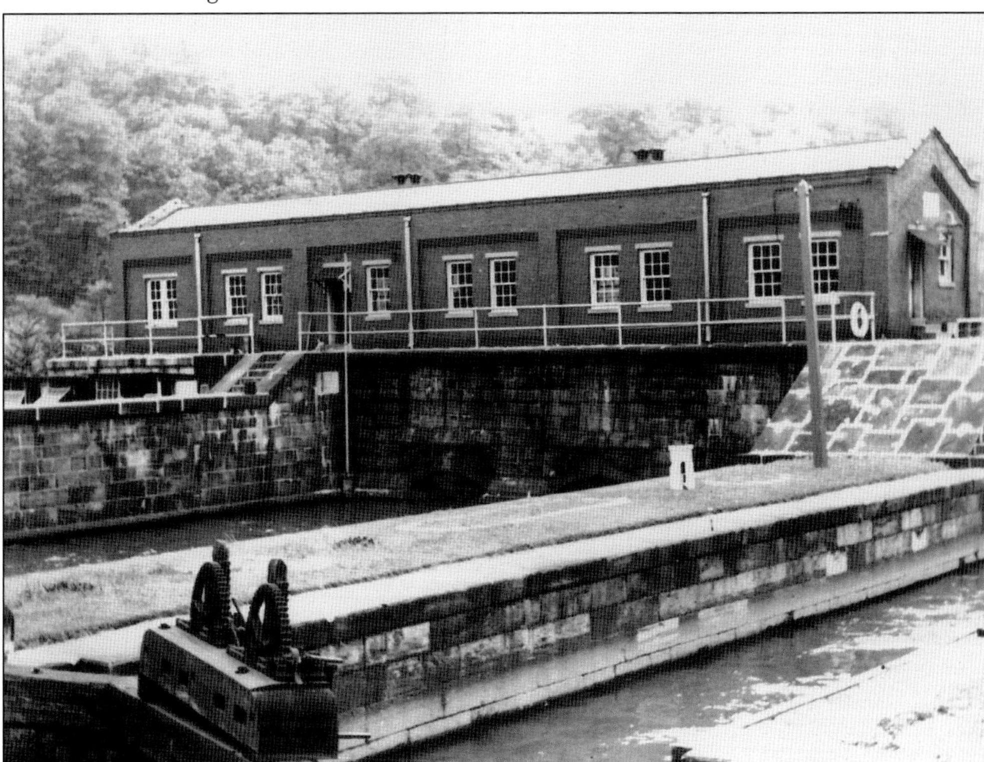

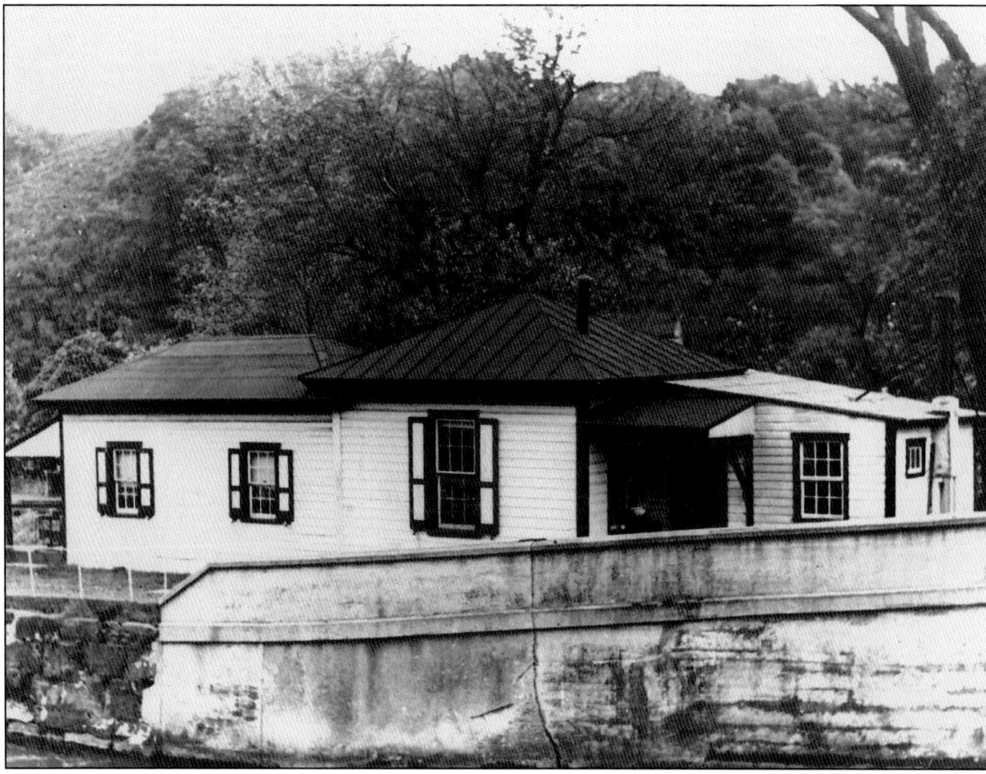

Those who worked along the waters in the canal era were spared the headache of today's workweek commute. Most of those who worked on boats also lived on them, and those who worked on land commonly lived nearby, as in the case of the tenders of the feeder or sluice houses and the locks. The feeder tender house (above) at Flat Rock Dam was built in 1919. Its proximity to the feeders enabled the tender, also called the watchman, to quickly adjust the feeders when needed. The stone lock tender's house (below) at lock 68 was built in 1846 and was a mere 530 square feet in size.

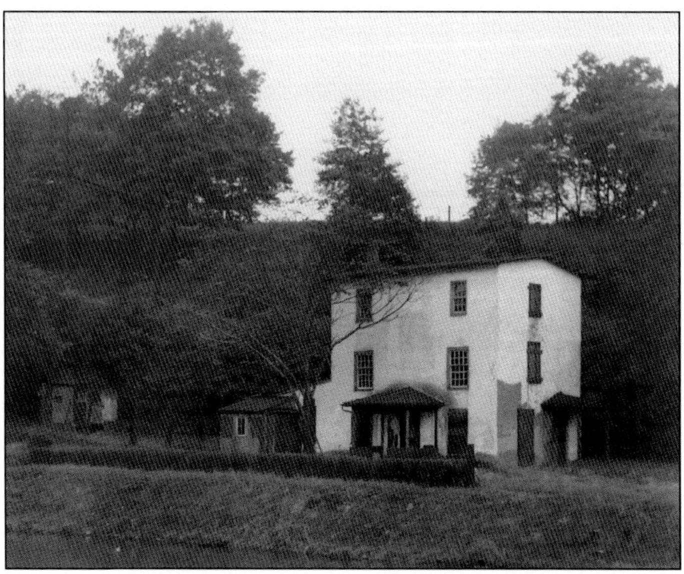

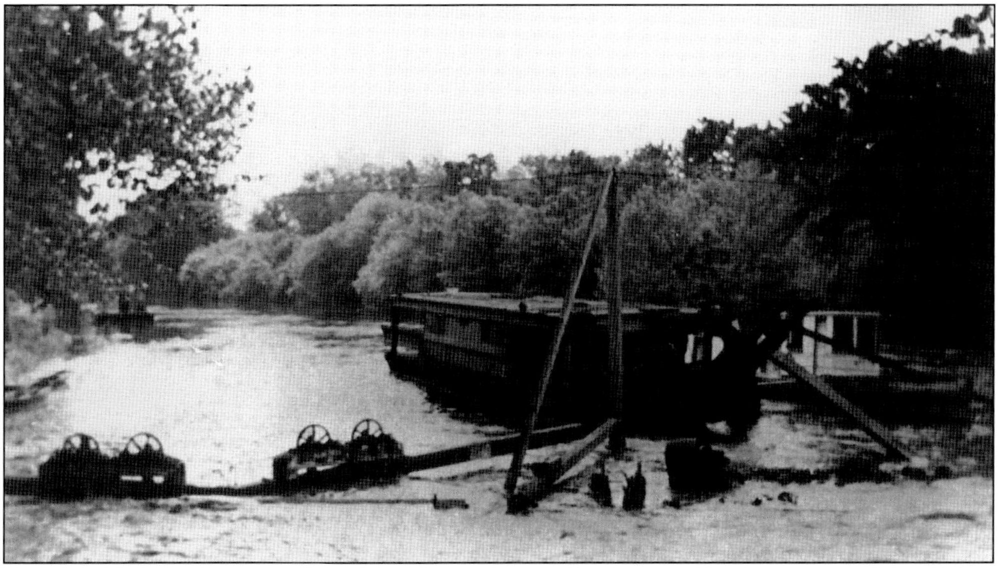

Moving back up the Schuylkill Navigation from the Manayunk Canal through the Conshohocken and Norristown Canals, the next section is the Oakes Canal, shown on this page. Above, the tugboat *Dolphin* and the Schuylkill Navigation Company's dredge No. 2, which it towed, are in storage at the lower gate at lock 60 during high water. The below photograph, taken around 1940, shows the end of an era. Dredge No. 2 is seen here just before she was destroyed. The last coal to have been delivered here at Black Rock was in 1919.

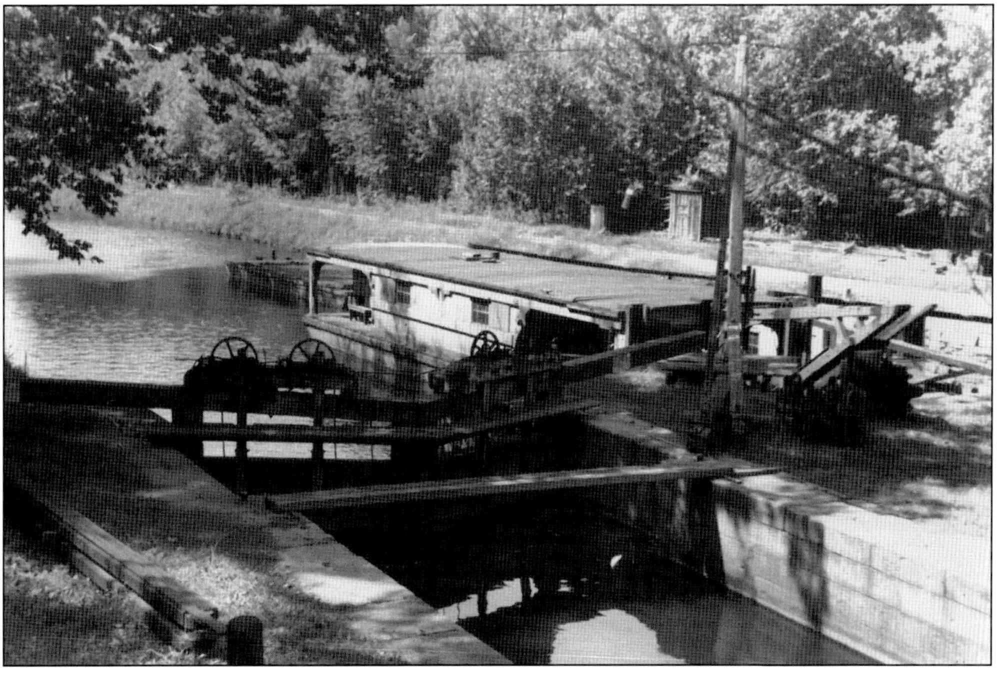

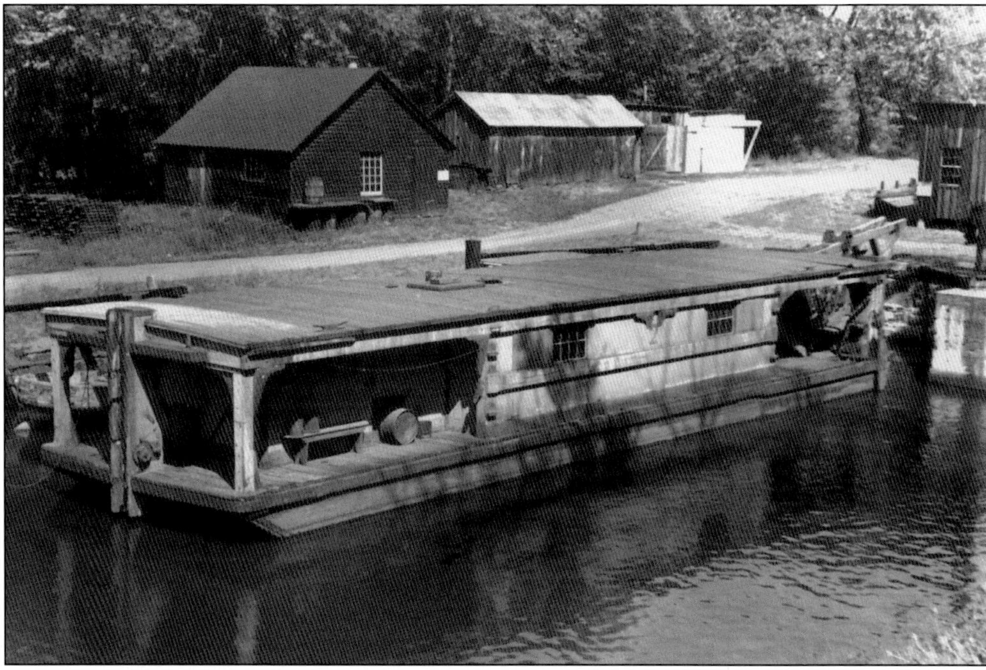

Dredging was a full-time, nonstop process between March and November to remove silt and other sediment from the canal. These materials were loaded onto a scow and taken to a desilting basin. If not dredged regularly, the waterway would become impassable. Here, dredge No. 2 at lock 60 is seen prior to being broken up in 1940.

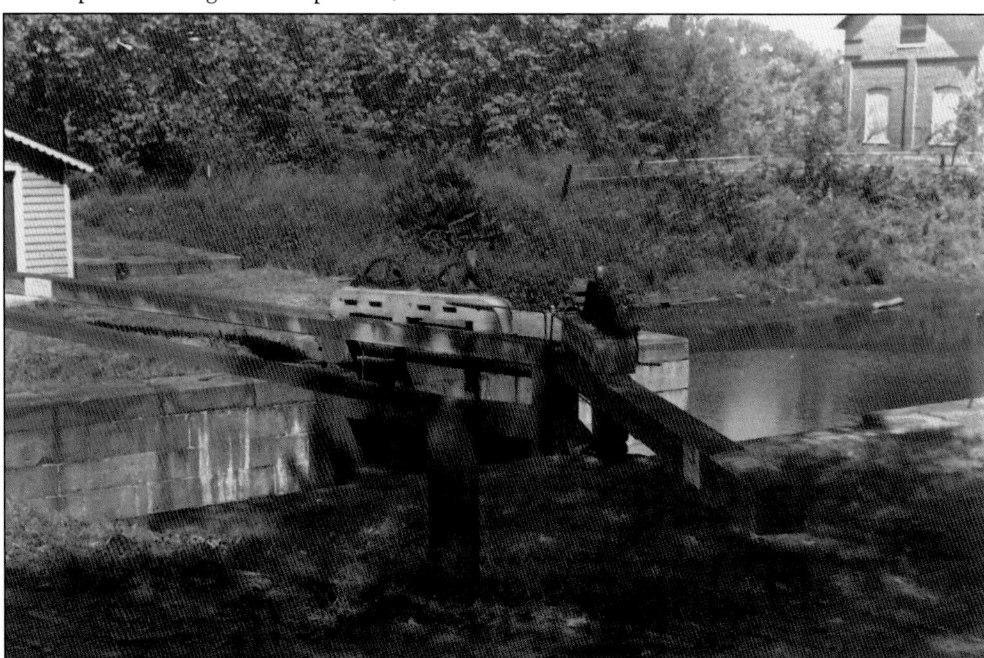

This is the upper gate of lock 60, originally built in 1839 as a twin lock. When the canal was widened in 1846, the larger lock was replaced with an even longer lock to accommodate bigger boats; the smaller lock was used as a bypass flume to convey water around the new lock.

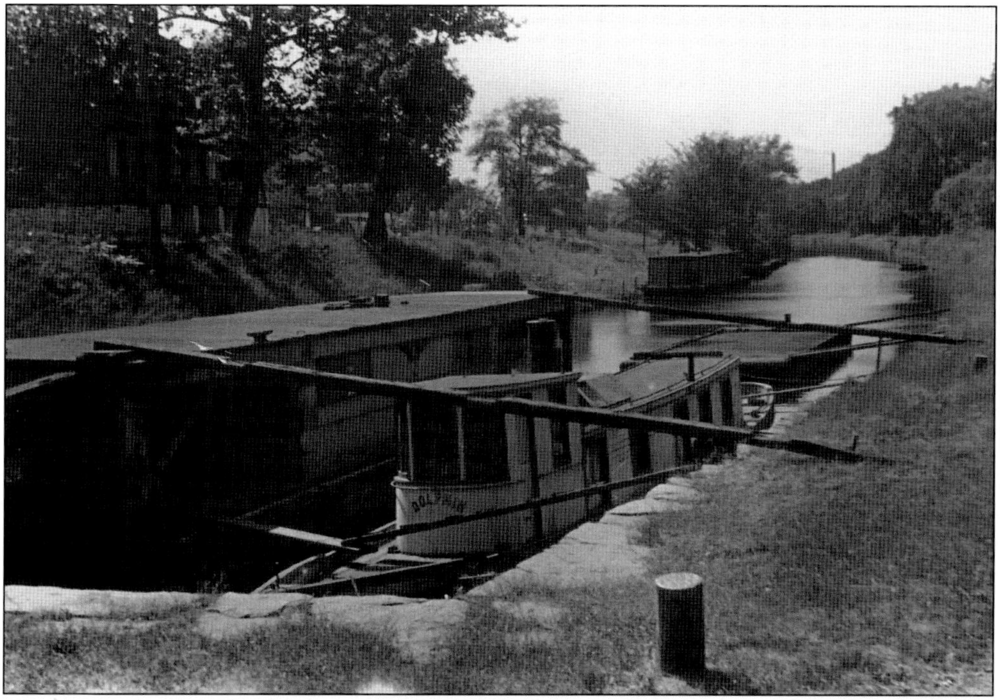

The above photograph provides a view down the Oakes Canal from lock 60, with the *Dolphin*, dredge No. 2, a lumber scow, and the mechanic's barge next to and behind the tugboat. The *Dolphin*, owned by the Schuylkill Navigation Company, was used on its navigation system to tow these types of watercraft. To keep these boats watertight, they were often caulked with a durable, rope-like fiber called oakum. In the 20th century, lock 60 in Mont Clare served as the homeport for the boat and her crew. These photographs were taken in 1940, just before the boats were dismantled, as they had served out their need.

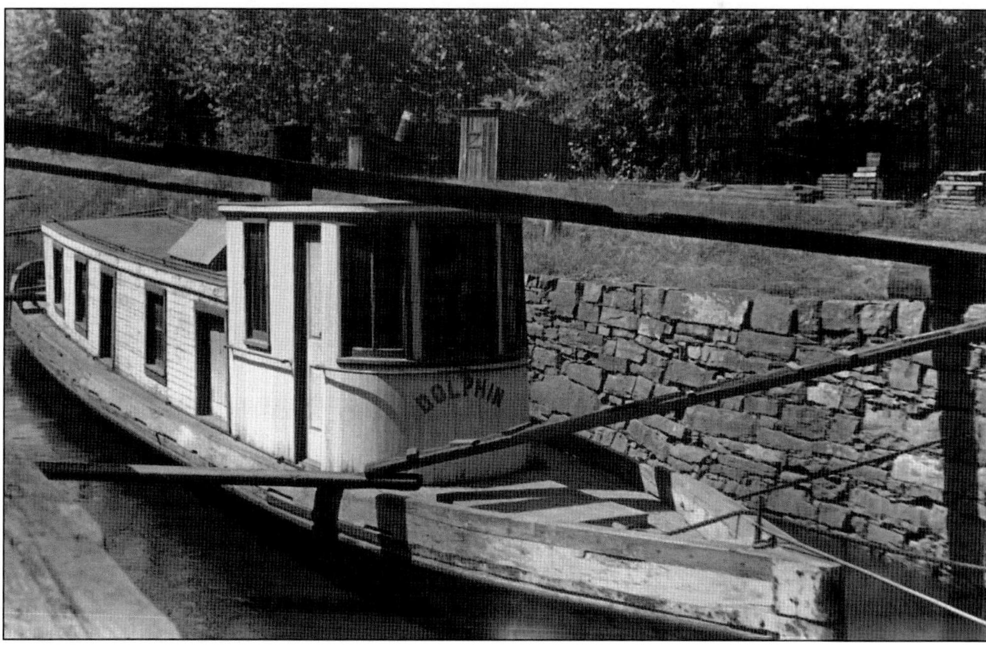

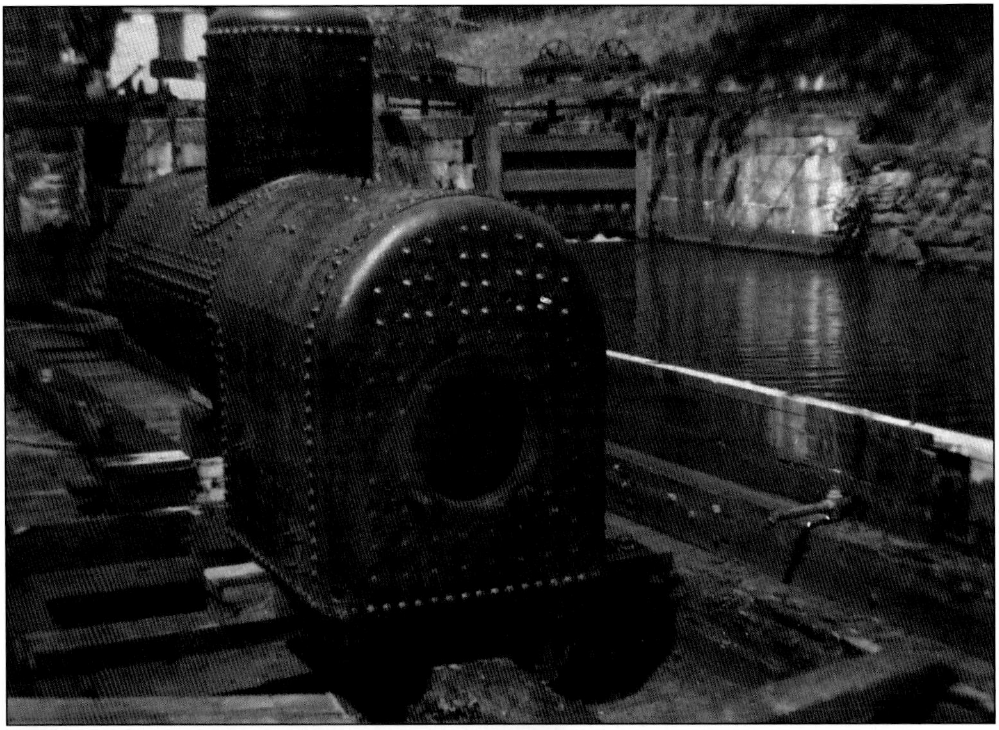

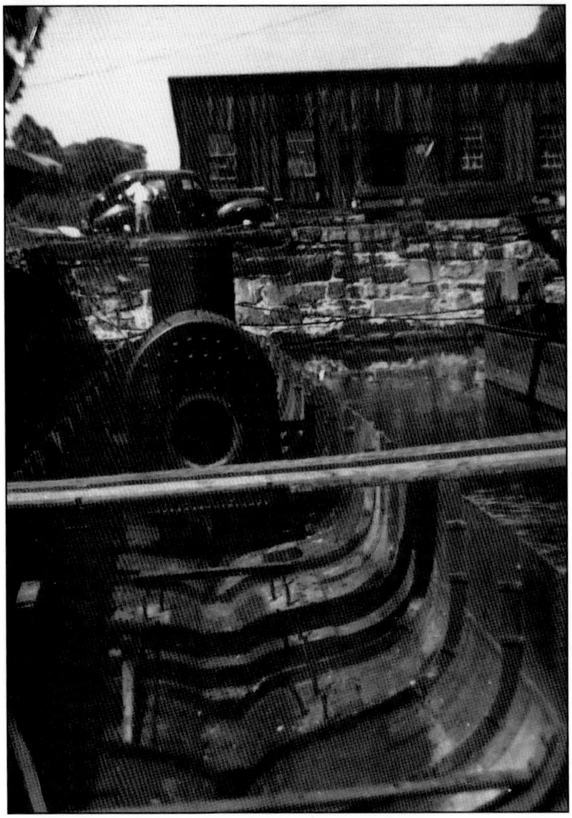

Shown above are the boiler of the *Dolphin* as well as dredge No. 2. The below photograph shows the cut-down hull and boiler of the retired tugboat from its stern side. A man named C. Howard Hiester, whose family owned the Hiester Boatyard, gathered relics from the Schuylkill Canal and eventually acquired the largest private collection of 19th-century canal memorabilia in America. In 1976, he donated his collection of approximately 1,400 artifacts to the Berks County Parks and Recreation Department. In 1986, the C. Howard Hiester Canal Center, named in his honor, was opened. There, one can see the *Dolphin's* pilothouse.

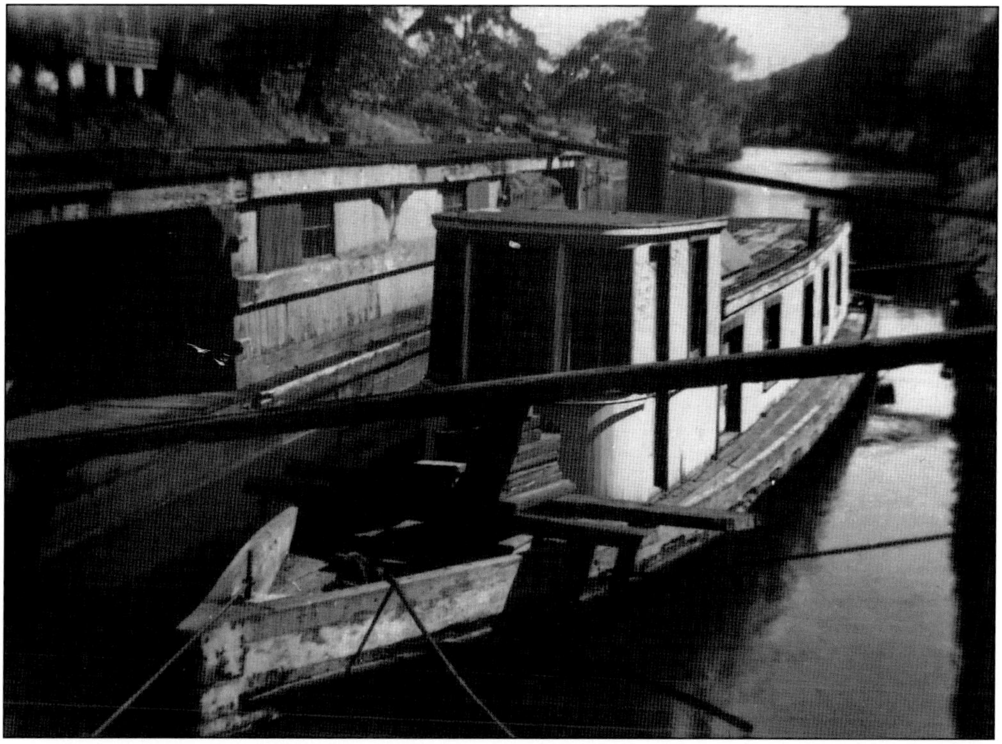

Ironically, the very reason for the dredge boat's creation (to dredge the canals and remove silt and sediment) was also a big reason for the failure of the waterway on which it operated. By 1872, the dredges that maintained the canal had a hard time keeping the channel free of buildup. The above photograph shows a bow view of the *Dolphin's* cut-down hull and boiler during dismantling operations, with dredge No. 2 seen on the left. The below photograph shows yet another view at lock 60 on the Oakes Canal during the process. This section of the Schuylkill Canal had been dug by hand in 1820.

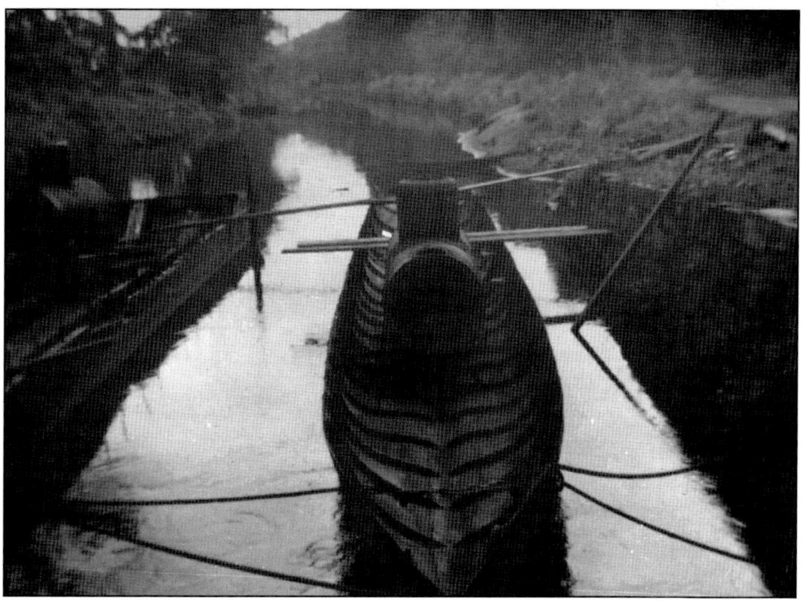

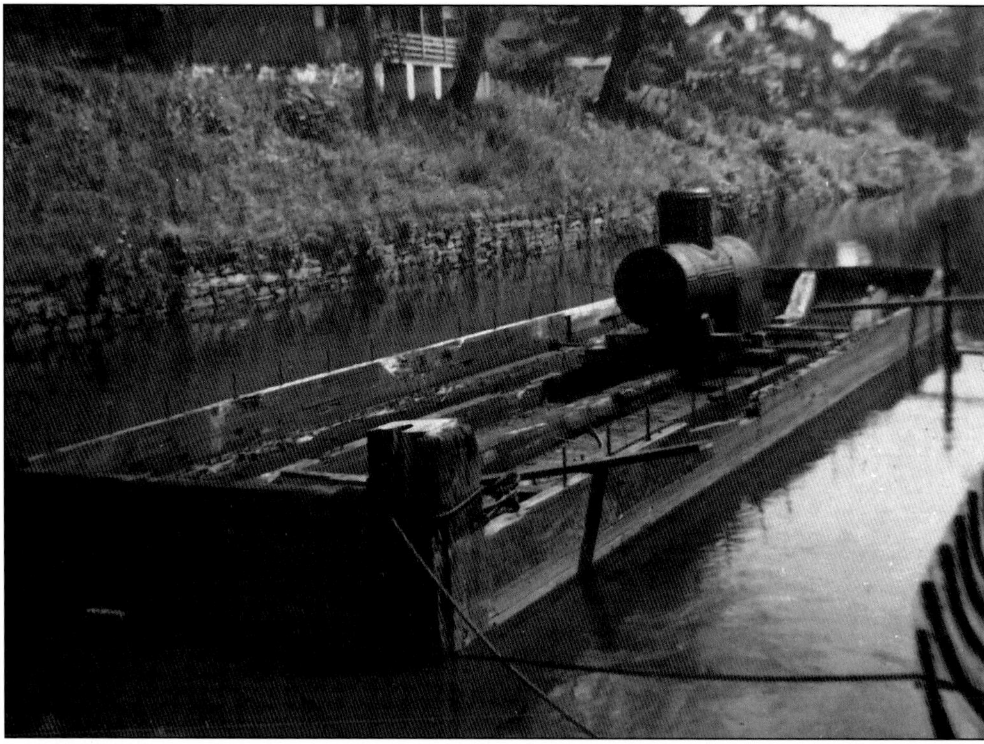

The Phoenix Iron Company was almost exclusively doing its shipping to Philadelphia via the Phoenixville Branch Canal link to the Oakes Canal by 1828. It was a major producer of cannon for the Union army during the Civil War. Over the years, use of the canal to transport commodities dwindled; pleasure boats last used the canal in the 1940s. These 1940 photographs offer different angles of dredge No. 2 (above, center and below, right) and the *Dolphin* (below, left) at lock 60 before being taken apart. The building behind the boats in the below photograph was the carpenter's shop. It no longer exists.

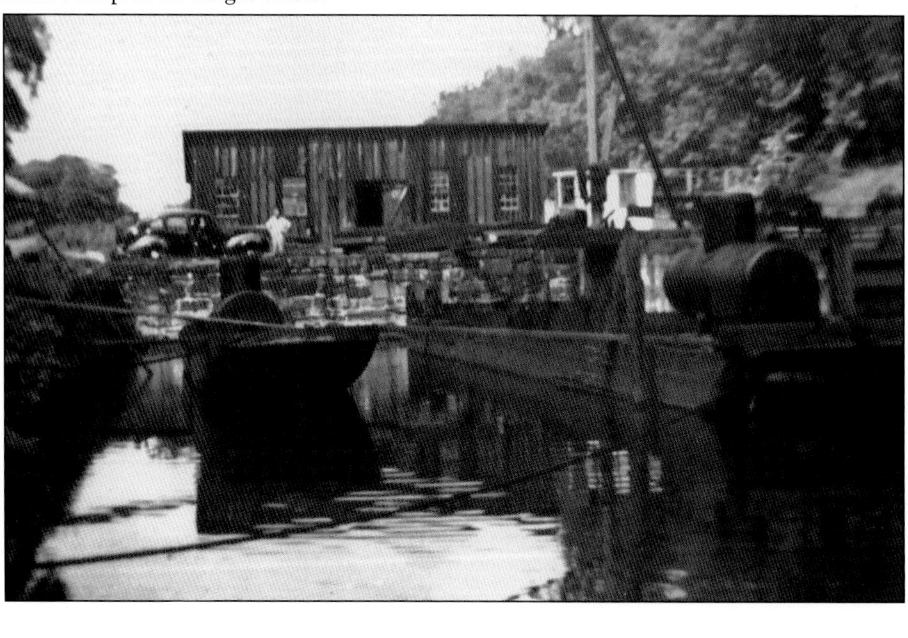

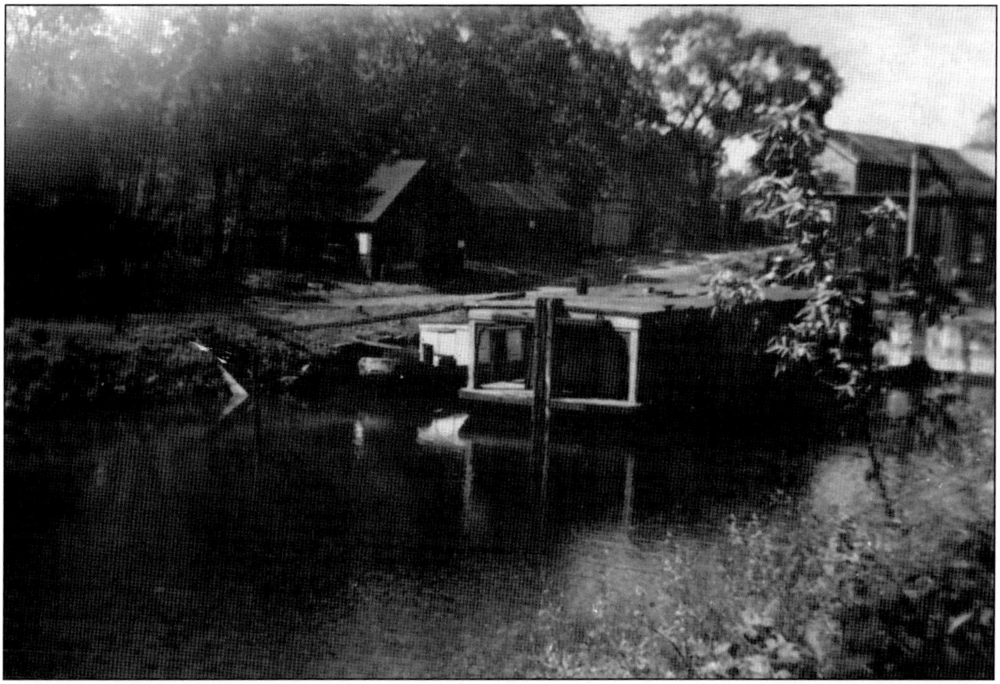

Thomas Oakes, an engineer and millwright, was born on August 13, 1777. Not only was he highly involved in the design of the Fairmount Water Works in Philadelphia, but he was also the principal engineer of the Schuylkill Navigation Company. The section of the navigation system between Phoenixville and Mont Clare was named after him. Incidentally, Mont Clare is where the infamous outlaw Harry "the Sundance Kid" Longabaugh was born in 1867. Oakes died in 1823 from an illness (suspected to be malaria) that affected many canal workers at the time. These photographs show the *Dolphin* and dredge No. 2 below lock 60.

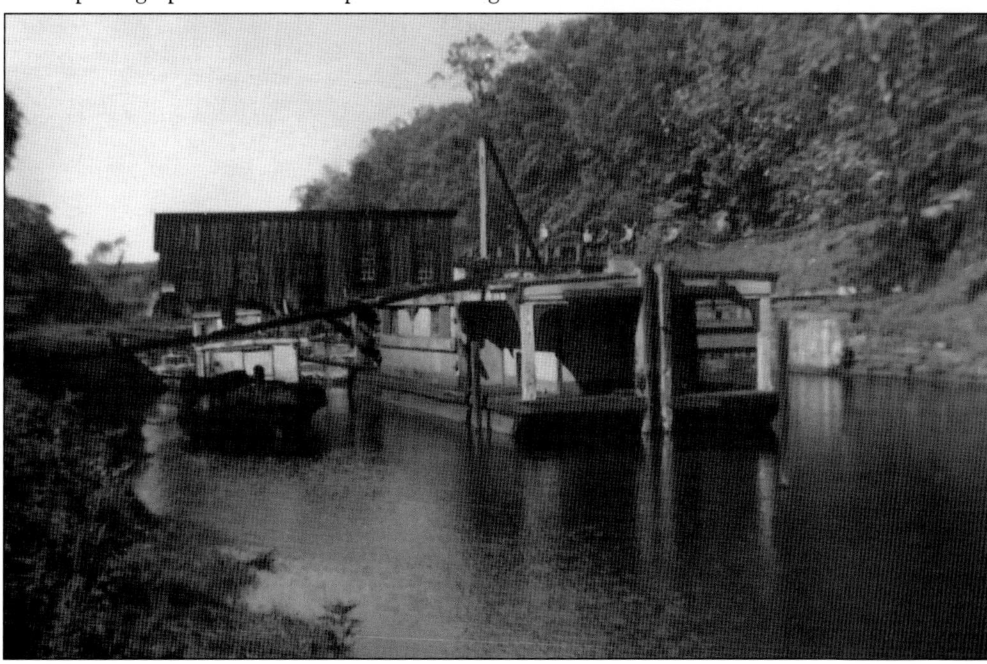

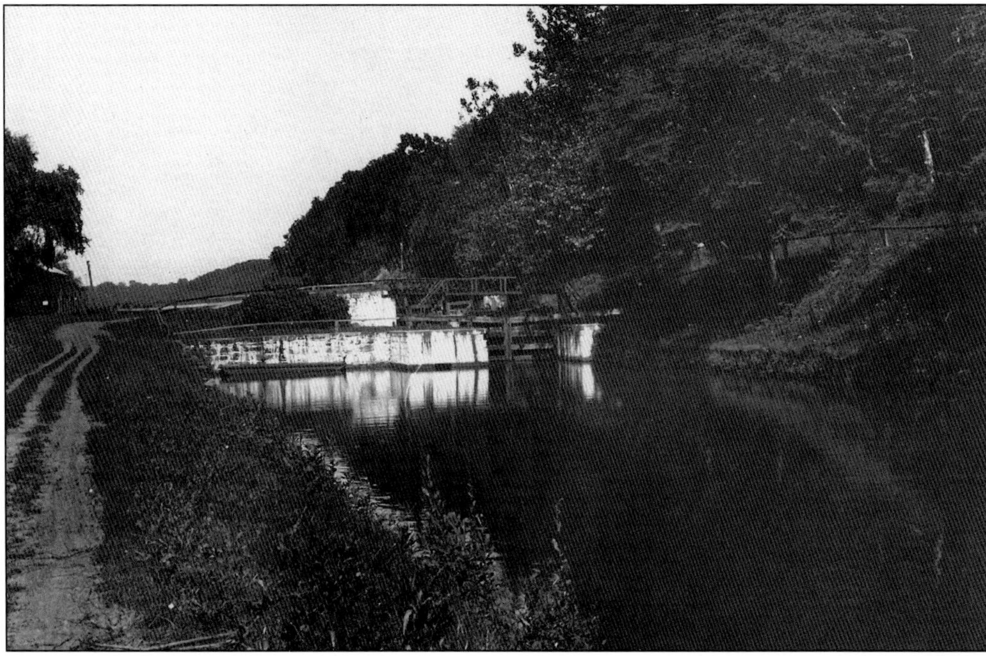

The channel of the Oakes Canal is shown above in 1919. Boats would head down this canal after passing through lock 60. The towpath is visible at left. Today, this path is paved and used daily by vehicles as well as bikers, walkers, and runners. The lock tender's house is just out of view on the right. The below photograph, taken from upstream, shows the part of the 1839 twin lock that was converted into a feeder. Various maintenance buildings stand above the feeder, including the lock tender's shanty (left).

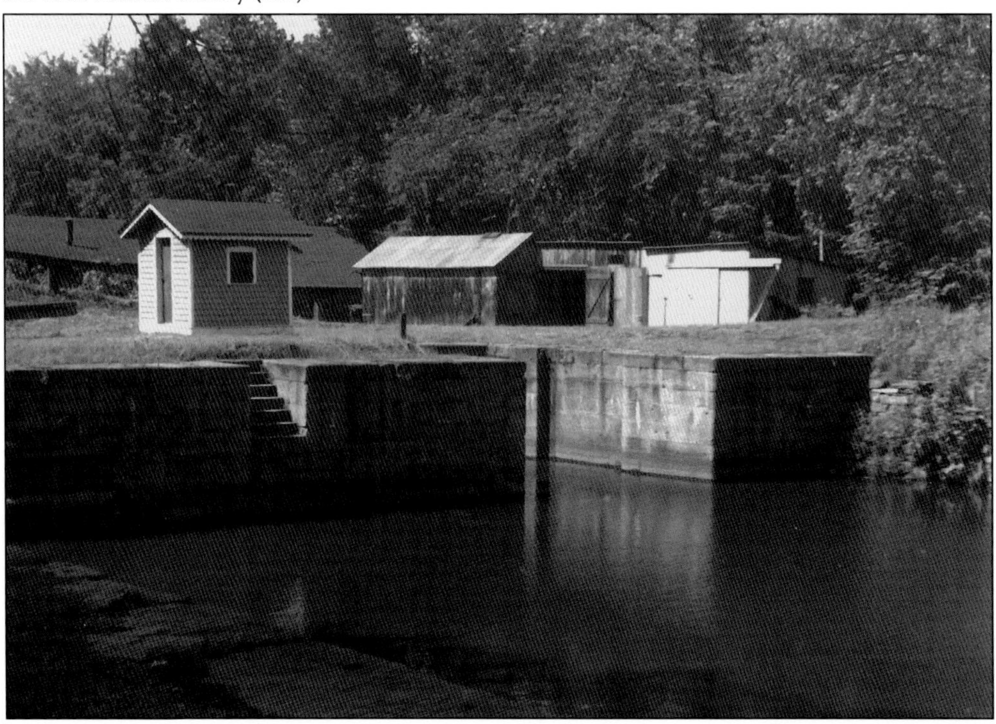

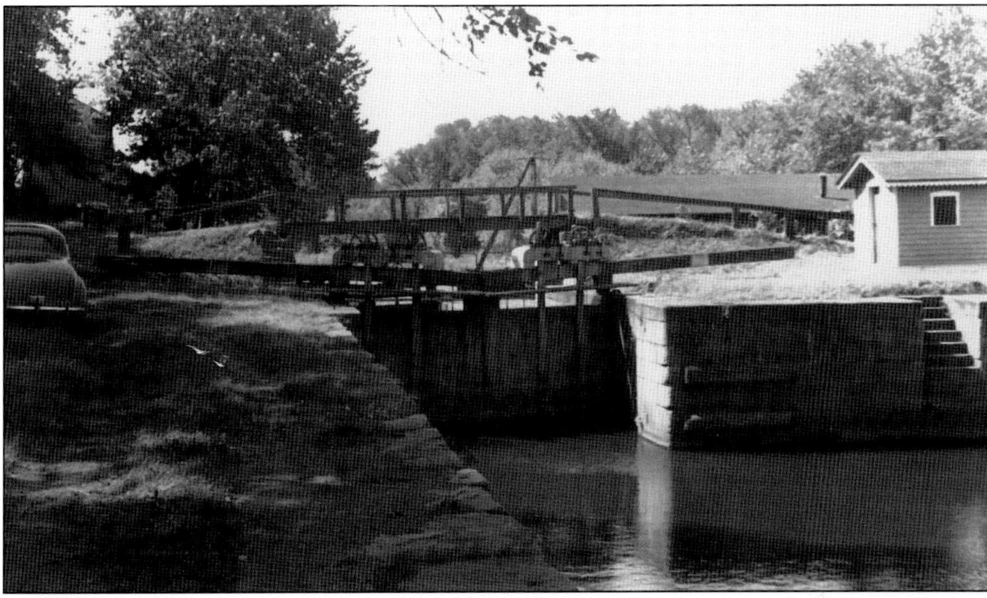

A forebay is the portion of a lock immediately upstream of the upstream lock gates. This 1940 photograph provides a clear view of the upper gate at lock 60, the guard lock of the Oakes Canal portion of the Schuylkill Navigation. Both the lock tender's house (left) and shanty (right) are in view.

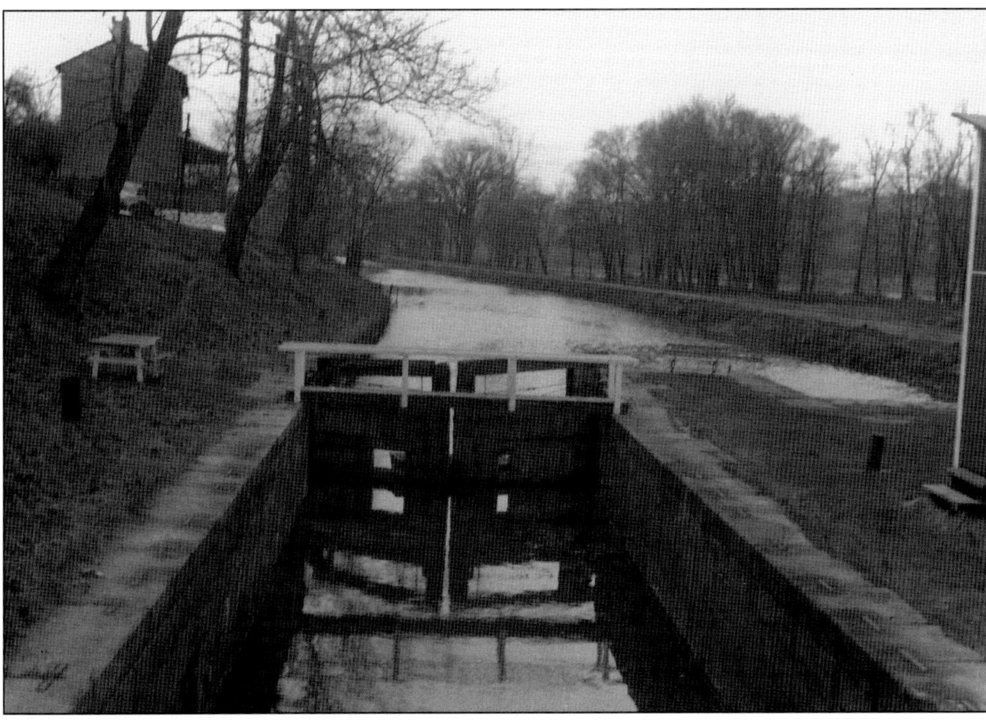

This is the view one would have after passing through the upper lock gates shown in the photograph above. Straight ahead are the lower lock gates; before them is a small truss bridge that allowed people to cross from one side of the canal to the other. This bridge has been replaced by a larger, wider bridge to accommodate vehicles.

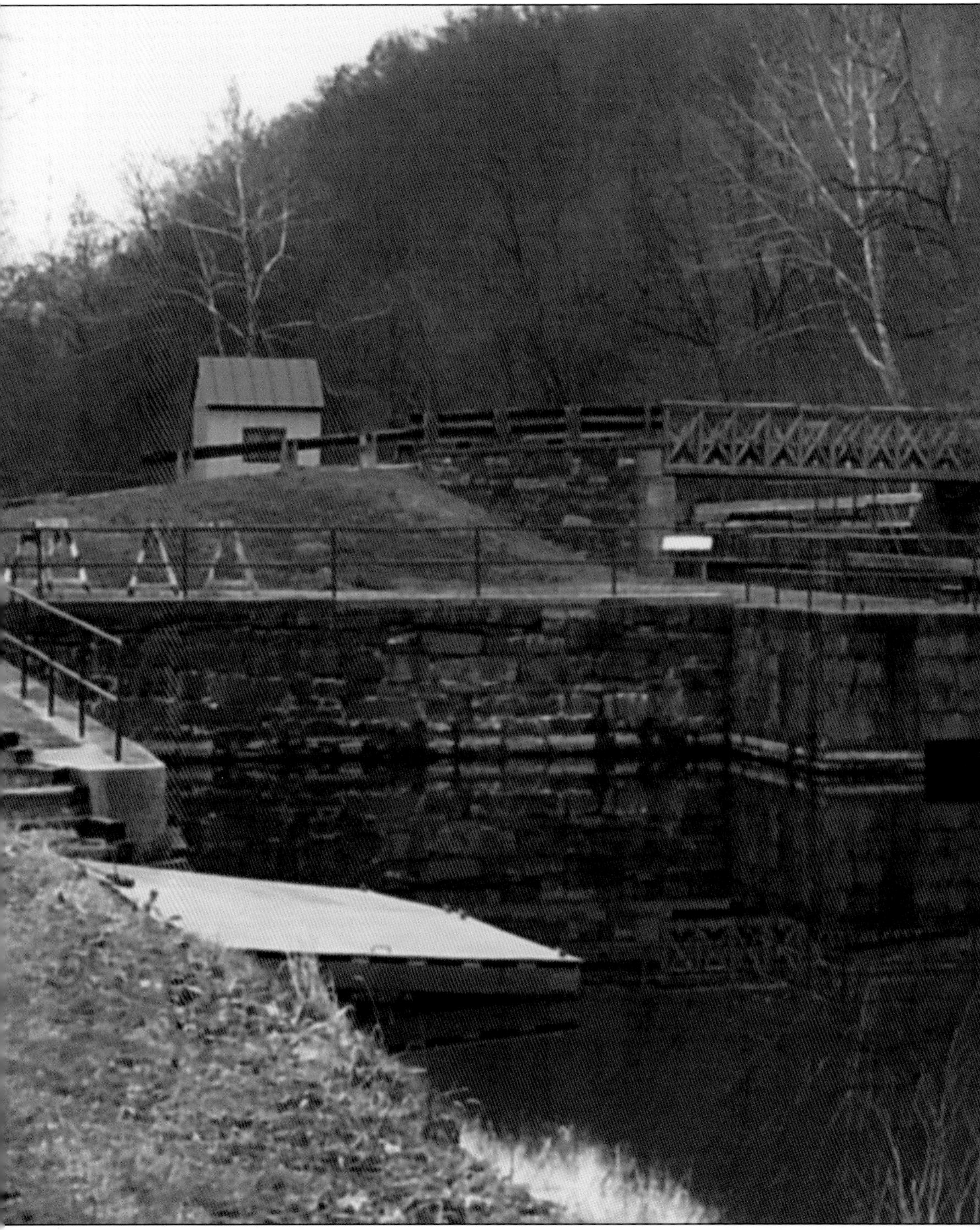

This current photograph features a floating dock (left), which boaters use to exit the Oakes Canal, as well as lock 60 (right). Mule drivers of the canal era led their mules across the small truss bridge (seen over the lock) to stay on the towpath. The little white building was the lock tender's shanty. Thanks to funds from several grants, the Schuylkill Canal Association was able to restore lock

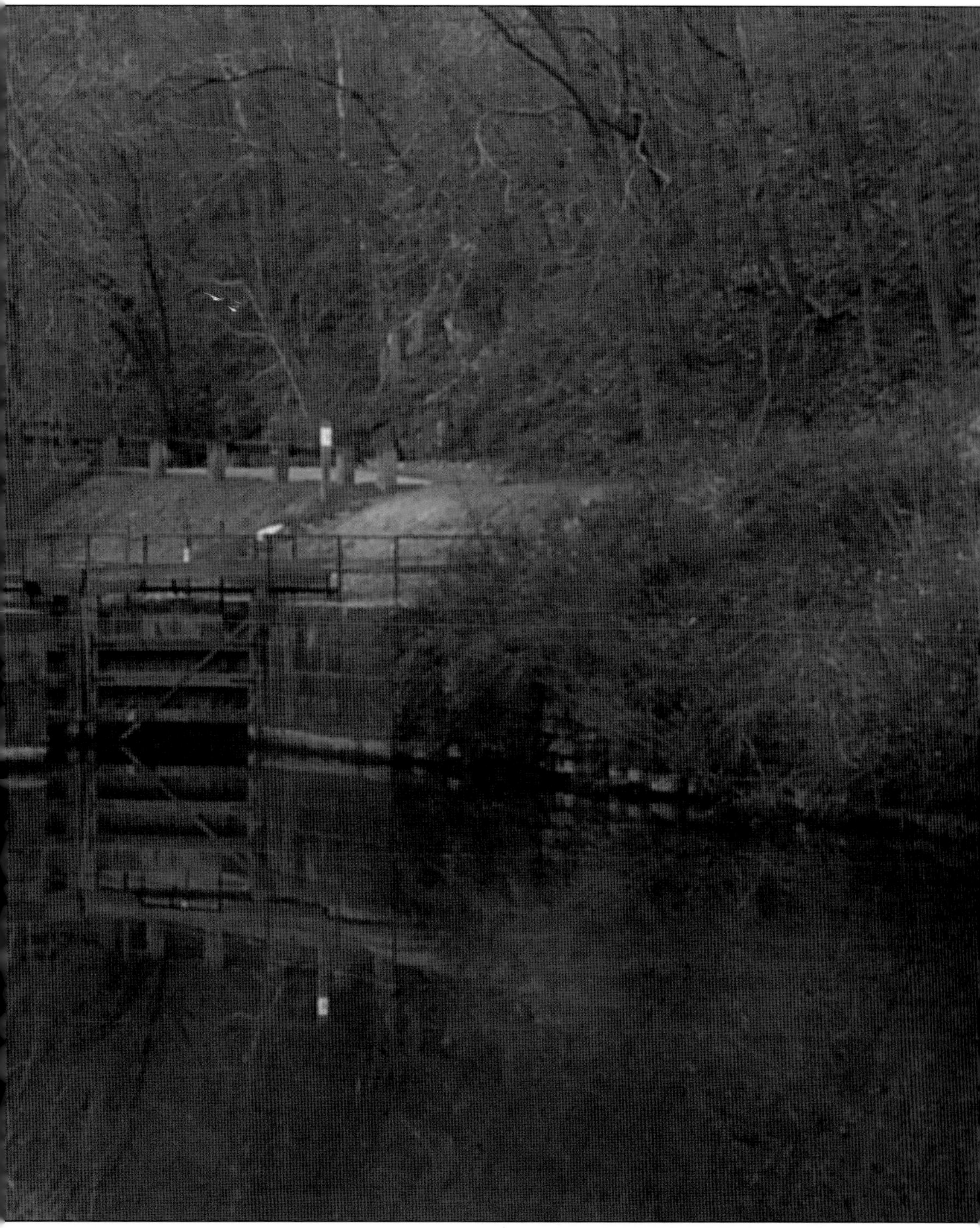

60, its gates, and the truss bridge, which was made to look like the 1820 original yet handle the weight of today's vehicles. These restoration projects were wrapped up in February 2005. This photograph shows the typical, lowered wintertime water level. (Courtesy of the author.)

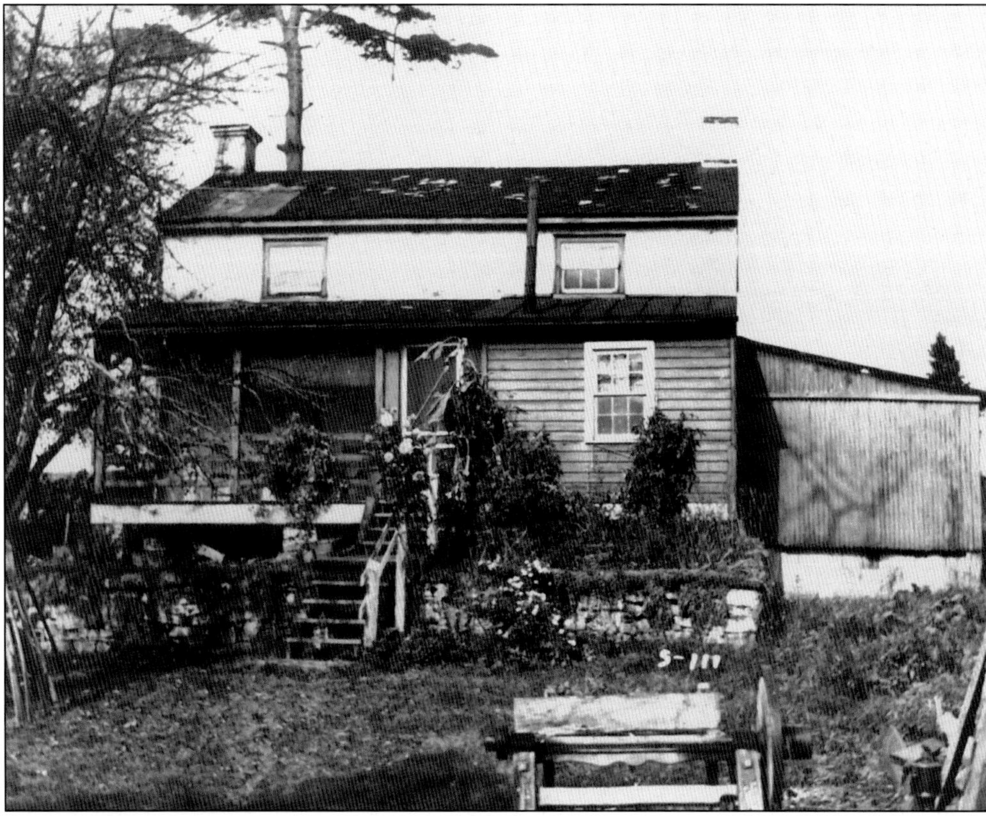

Emmanuel Schaeffer was reportedly the last lock tender to live in the dwelling at lock 60 in Mont Clare. He and his widowed sister eventually moved out in the early 1970s, after which the house was boarded up. By this time, the building was in a deteriorated state, much like the unidentified house above, and had a bad leak in the roof. The lock 60 tender's house is shown below in its restored form on March 2, 1975. Today, an old player piano that belonged to the Schaeffer family sits in the living room.

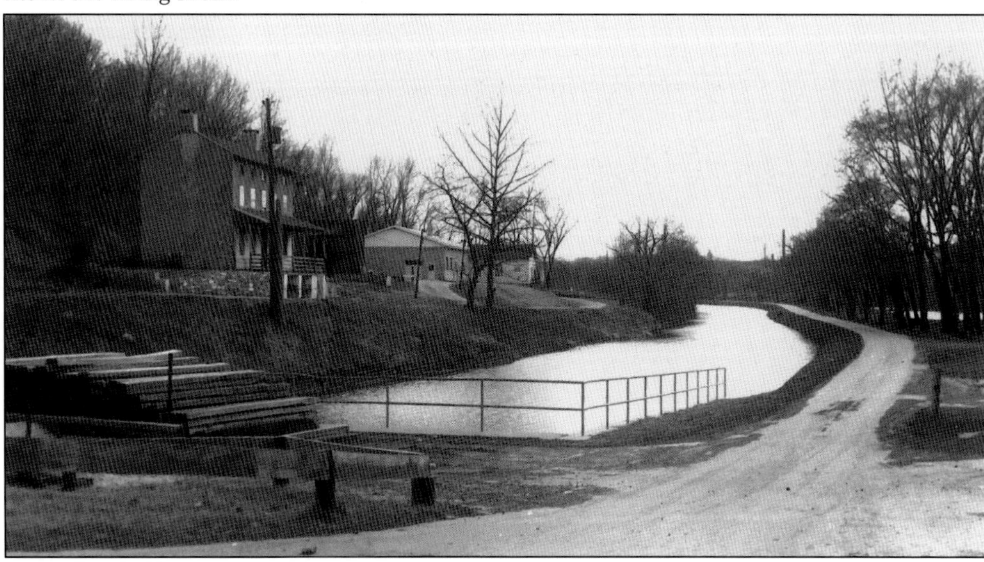

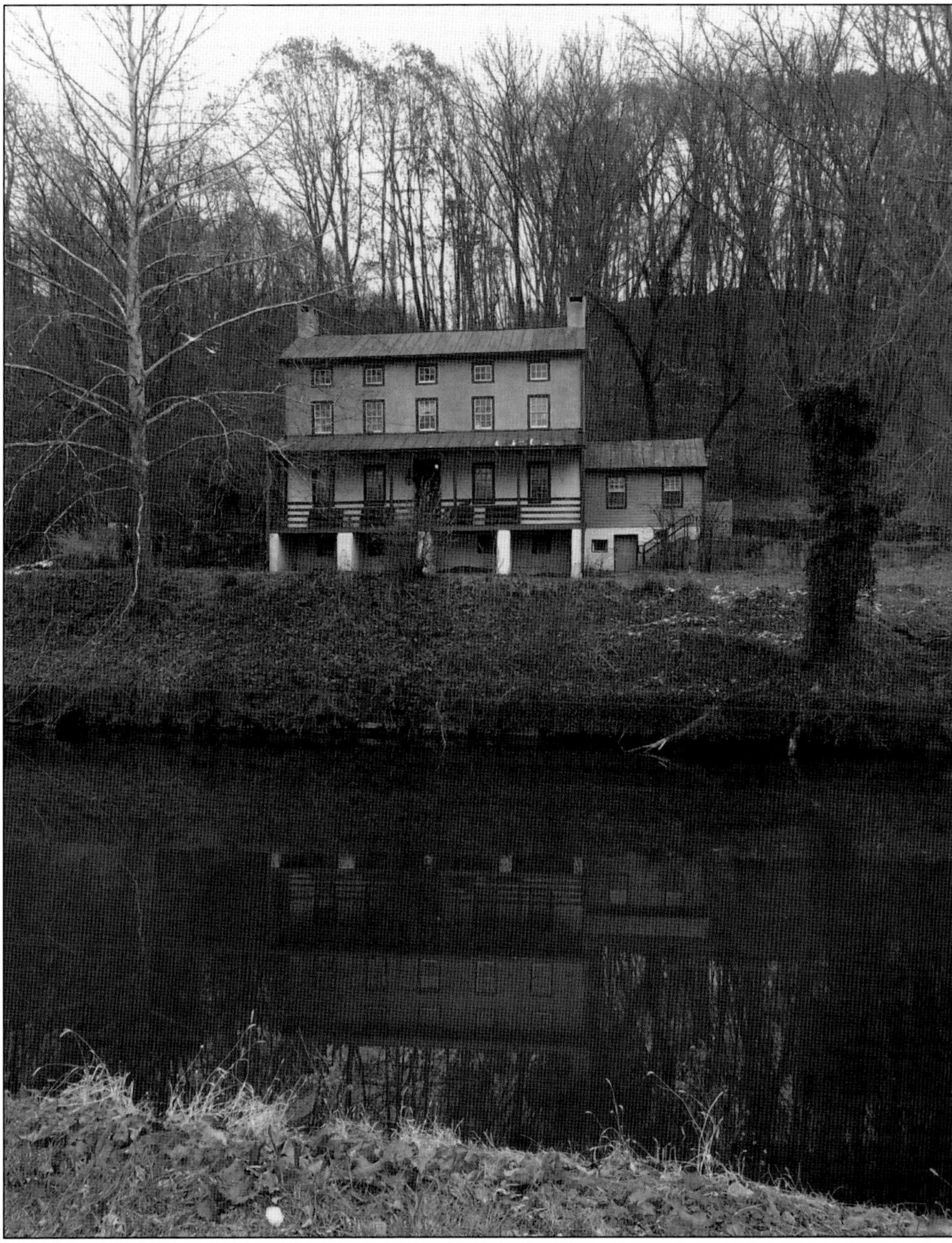

This 2014 photograph shows the lock tender's house at lock 60 as it currently stands. Built during the Schuylkill Canal's first expansion period in 1836, it was home to the lock tender and his family and overlooks the lock as well as the head of the Oakes Canal. The house was inhabited until the 1970s, after which it was abandoned and badly vandalized. In 1983, Upper Providence Township and the Schuylkill Canal Association (SCA) began restoration efforts. The house consists of three stories, with the SCA's administrative office located on the second floor. On the first floor, two rooms hold exhibits, historic photographs and documents, a library, maps, pamphlets, and souvenirs for sale. The house now serves as the association's visitor center and is open to the general public on the third Sunday of each month. (Courtesy of the author.)

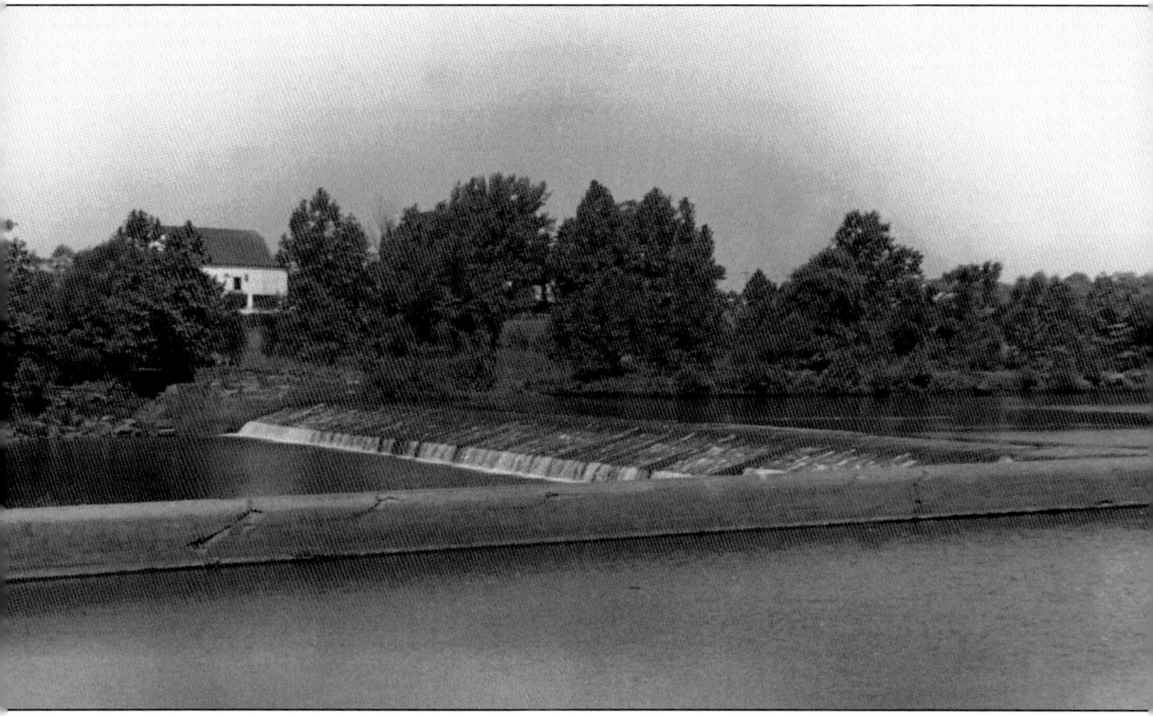

Black Rock Dam, pictured in the background in 1940, is a low head dam on the Schuylkill River between Phoenixville and Mont Clare that feeds the Oakes Canal (foreground). It was built by the Schuylkill Navigation Company in the early 19th century as a stone-filled, timber crib dam to create a slackwater pool for the navigation system. Of the original timber crib dams, only Black Rock and Norristown remain. In 1828, a lock was added to the Chester County side of the dam as part of the Chester County, or Phoenix(ville) Branch Canal, but this canal was damaged in 1869 due to flooding. Today, the power company Exelon owns the dam; in 2009, it built a fish ladder on the Chester County side of the dam to allow American shad, a native fish that migrates from the Schuylkill River to the Atlantic Ocean and back, and other migratory fish to travel freely upstream on the river.

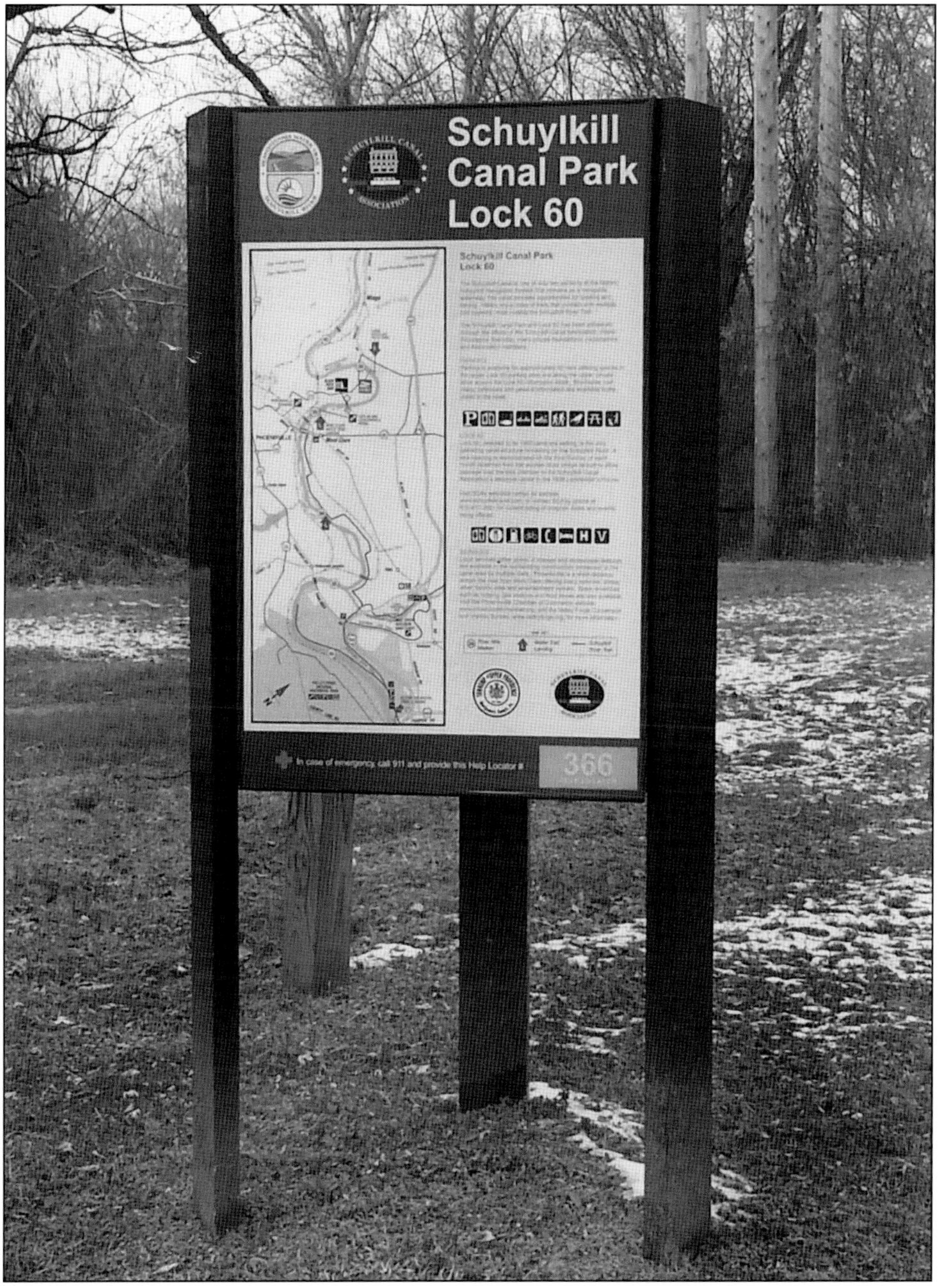

The canal at lock 60 is one of only two stretches of the Schuylkill Navigation System that still hold water today, and the lock itself is the only operating one on the river. The land surrounding the Oakes Canal section of the navigation system and lock 60 is now used recreationally and is formally called Schuylkill Canal Park, as indicated on this sign. The park is at the center of the Schuylkill Navigation Canal, Oakes Reach Section in the National Register of Historic Places. The area attracts both locals and those from neighboring communities. Individuals visit the park to fish, hike, bike, paddle, picnic, and more. The site is also the location of the Schuylkill Canal Association's annual fundraiser, known as Canal Day, which takes place on the last Sunday in June and draws an estimated 3,000 people. (Courtesy of the author.)

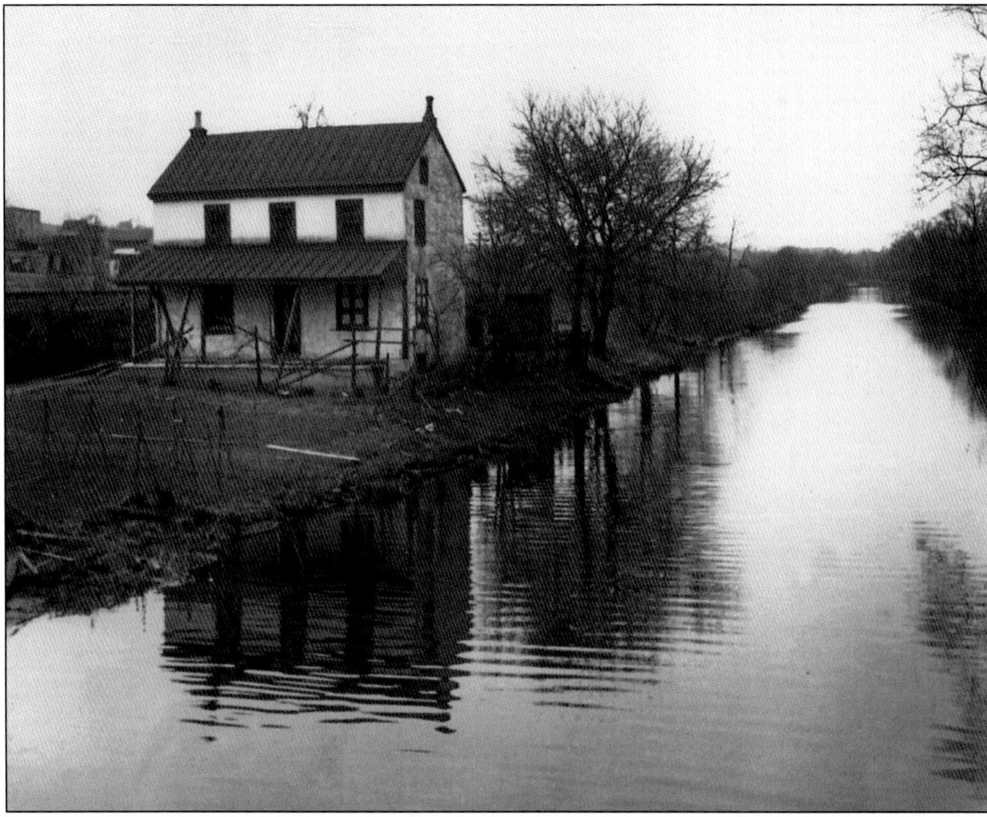

Moving up the Schuylkill Navigation System from Mont Clare, a canal boat would pass through the locks on the Vincent Canal. The lock tender's house (pictured here in 1959), located near what is believed to be Wissamer's Lock (lock 59), below Spring City, stands as a reminder of a time long gone. (Photograph by Harold W. Amster.)

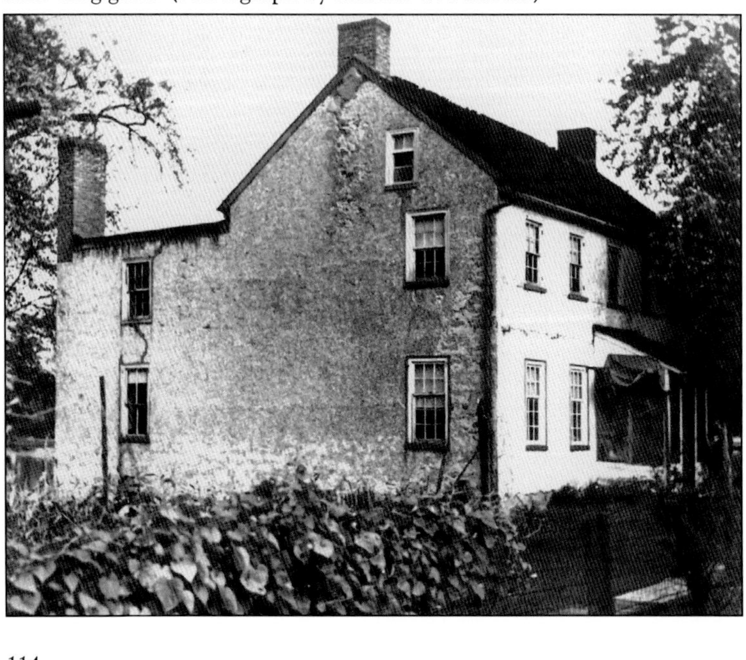

From the Vincent Canal, watercraft would enter outlet lock 57 (Schwartz's Lock), built by Alexander Lawrence, on the Girard Canal. This photograph, dated October 14, 1948, shows the lock tender's house at this lock in Parker Ford, East Vincent Township. The 430-square-foot house, built in 1836, was torn down around 1968.

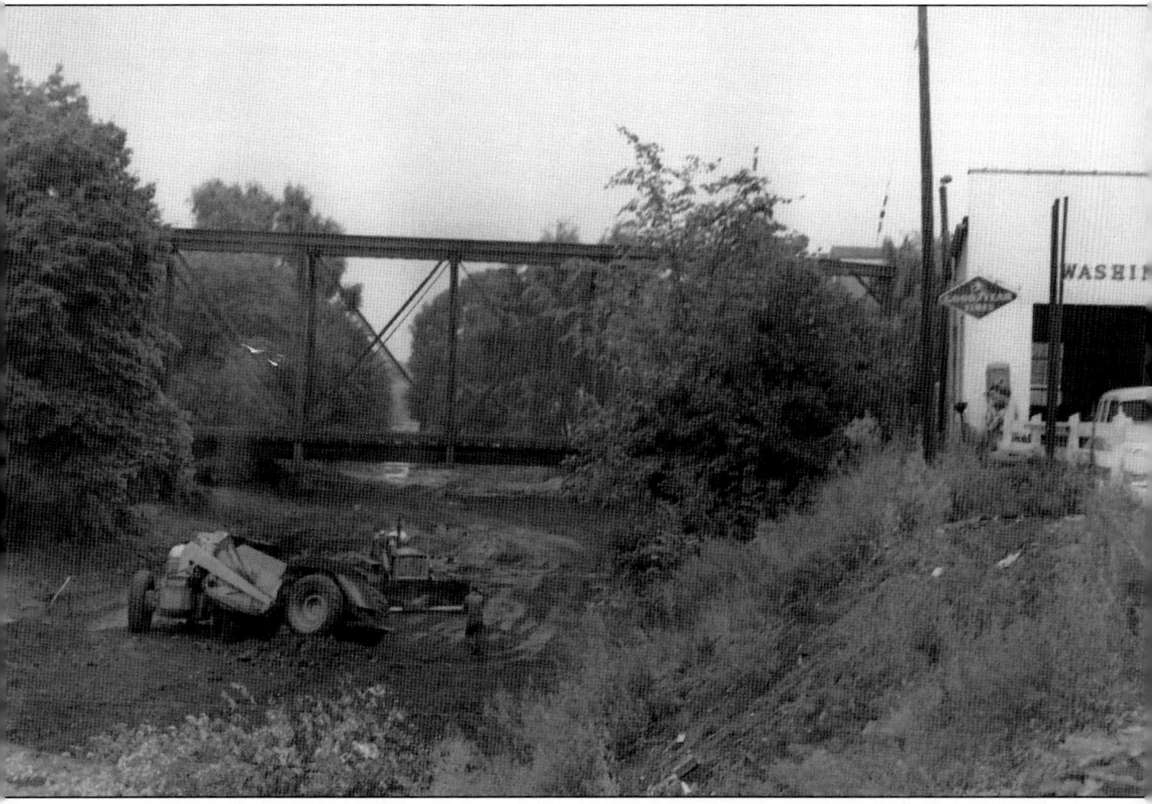

The completion of the Schuylkill Navigation System did wonders for many towns along its banks. Spring City was no exception. Houses were built along Main Street next to the Vincent Canal; in the 1840s, both the Spring City Stove Company and the American Wood Paper Company set up shop with the intentions of using the canal to bring in raw materials needed by their operations and then to send out their finished products. This view down the Vincent Canal from the bridge between Spring City and Royersford was taken in September 1950, when the borough of Spring City was filling in the canal bed. In the background, a bridge used by the Philadelphia & Reading Railroad stretches over the old canal. Today, the canal may no longer run between these towns, but there is no doubt they got to be where they are today because of it. (Photograph by Wilbert Amster.)

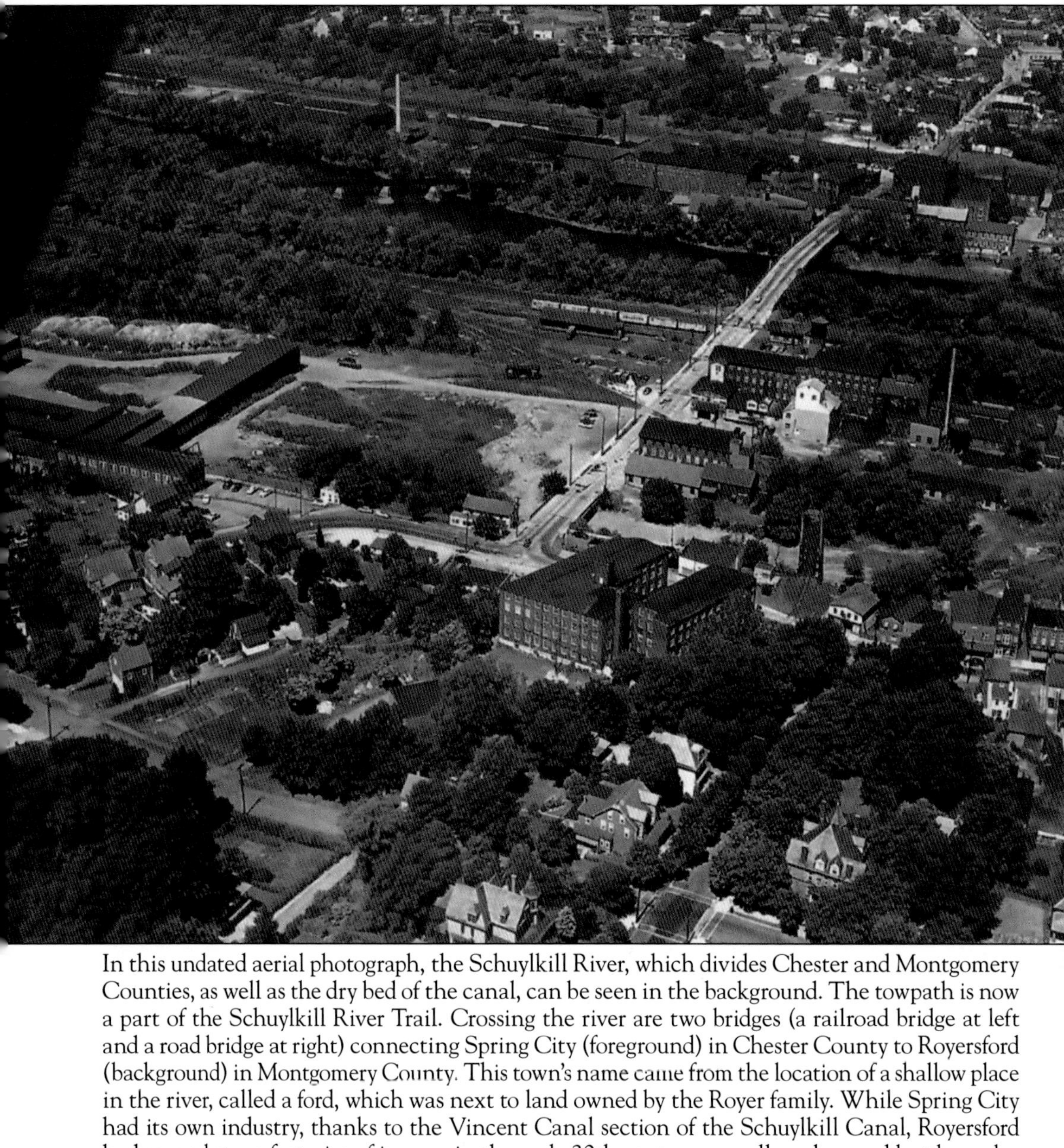

In this undated aerial photograph, the Schuylkill River, which divides Chester and Montgomery Counties, as well as the dry bed of the canal, can be seen in the background. The towpath is now a part of the Schuylkill River Trail. Crossing the river are two bridges (a railroad bridge at left and a road bridge at right) connecting Spring City (foreground) in Chester County to Royersford (background) in Montgomery County. This town's name came from the location of a shallow place in the river, called a ford, which was next to land owned by the Royer family. While Spring City had its own industry, thanks to the Vincent Canal section of the Schuylkill Canal, Royersford had several stove factories of its own in the early 20th century, as well as glass and bottle works, silk mills, and other manufacturing plants. (Photograph by Harold W. Amster.)

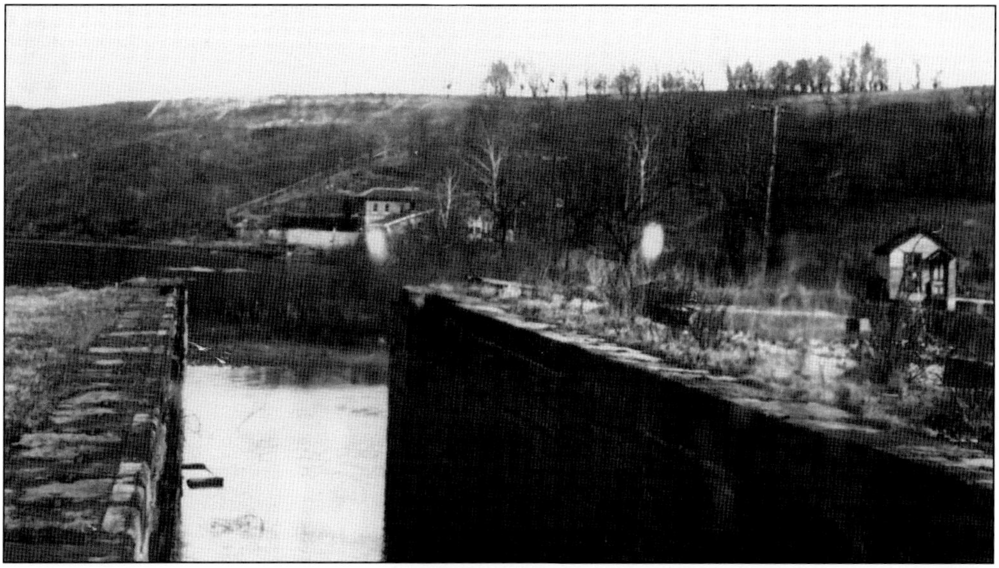

It is believed that this undated photograph is looking through lock 59, or Wissamer's Lock, down the Schuylkill River at Cromby. The lock tender's shanty stands unassumingly on the right. In April 2011, the paved segment from Spring City to Cromby of the Schuylkill River Trail opened, including a new trailhead near the old Cromby Power Plant.

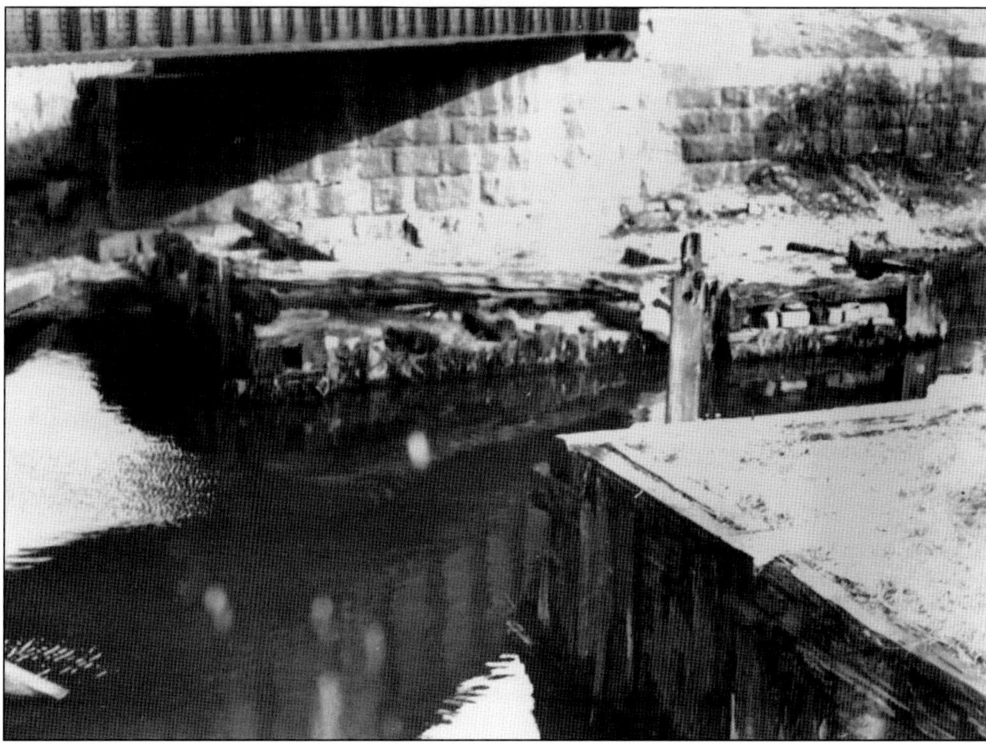

Here lie the remains of the stop gate below Towers' Lock (lock 58), where the Pennsylvania Railroad Bridge crosses the Vincent Canal in Spring City. This site also happens to be located behind the infamous Pennhurst State School and Hospital. Today, only 28 miles of the original 108-mile canal system still exist.

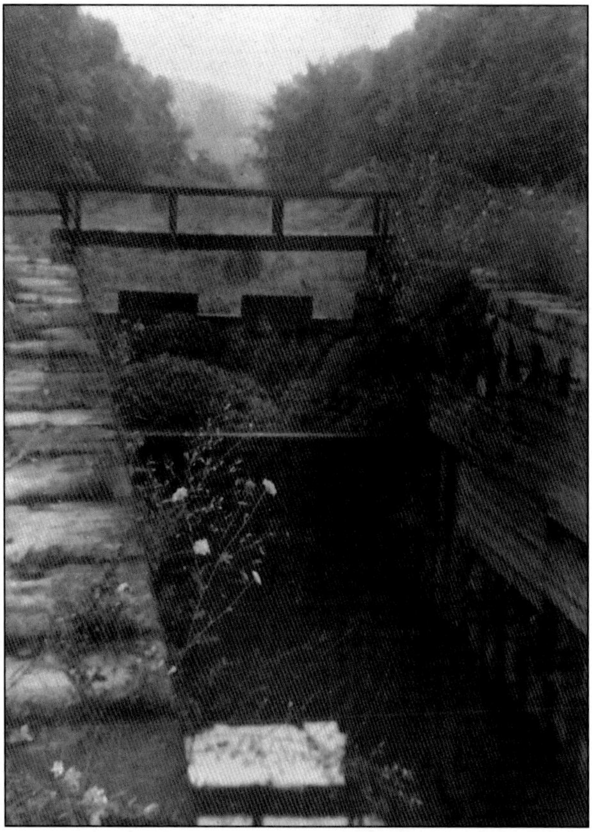

The photograph at left looks up the Vincent Canal through the lock at Cromby. A small truss bridge still stands above the gate. Aside from the overgrown vegetation, the scene is reminiscent of a time of unwatering, when the water was emptied from the canal to inspect it or simply perform routine maintenance and repairs to its structure. However, the photograph was taken before the lock was filled in. In 1948, the lock 59 stone lock tender's house (below) was still well maintained and in overall good shape.

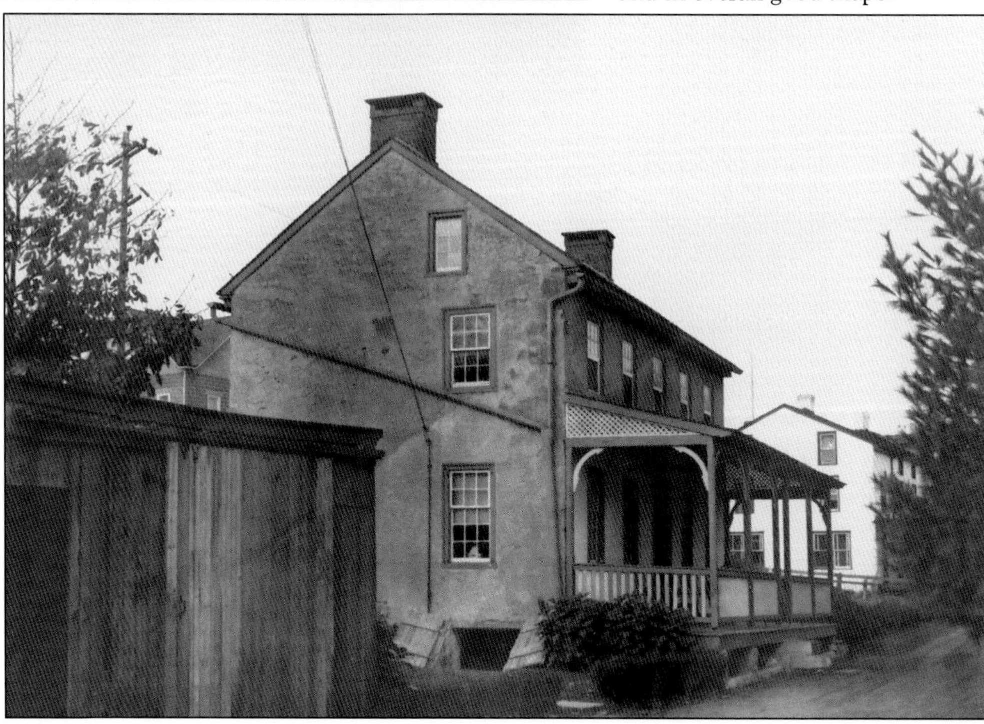

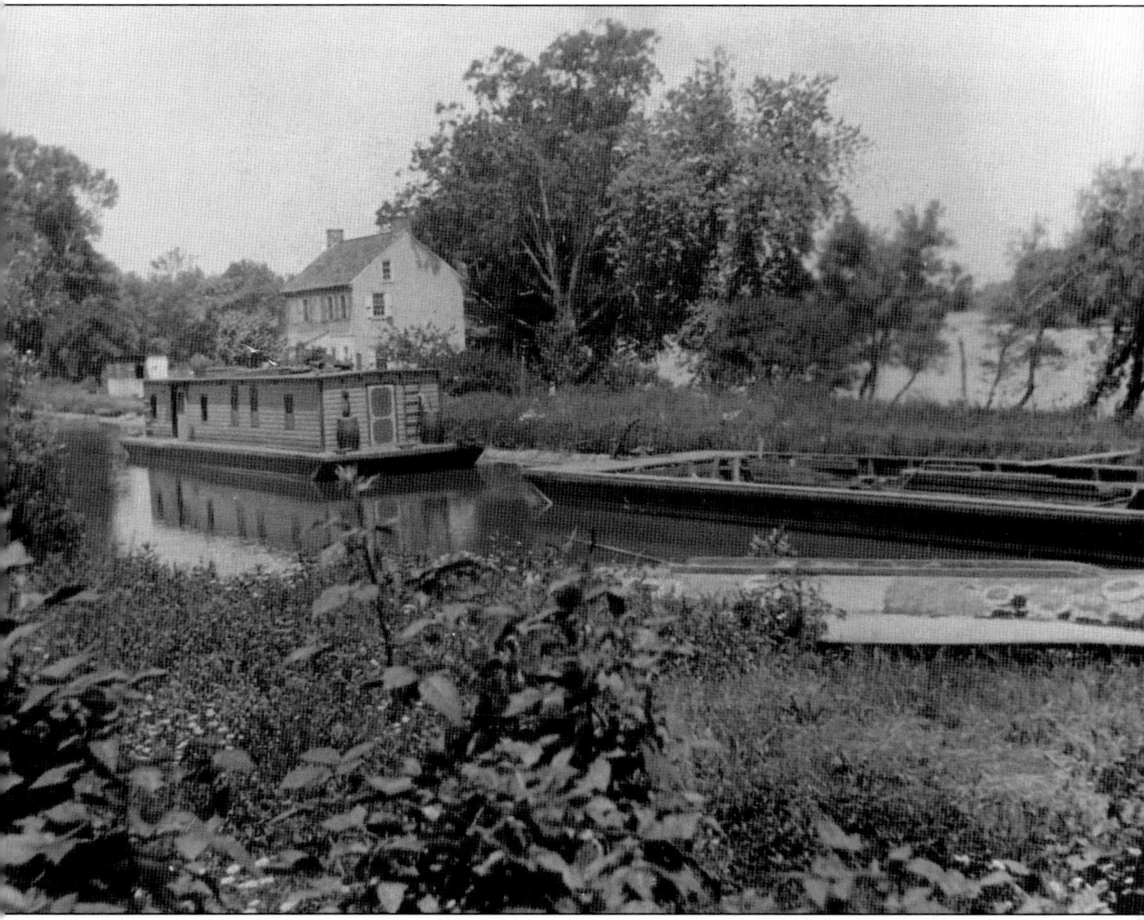

In 1926, a mechanic's barge and lumber scow are seen near Schwartz's outlet lock of the 22-mile Girard Canal, named after the wealthy Stephen Girard, a French-born philanthropist and banker who is credited with saving the US government from financial ruin at the time of the War of 1812. These boats, reportedly the last of their kind, are seen on the water here by Mrs. Ben Reitnour, who lived in the house next to the filter plant that supplied water for Spring-Ford (the area consisting of the sister towns of Spring City and Royersford). Ben Reitnour himself also worked at the plant, which was partly constructed of stone and built into the side of Crab Hill, next to the Pennsylvania Railroad line and Schwartz's Lock. Across the canal, behind the barge, stands the lock tender's house; behind the house is the Schuylkill River.

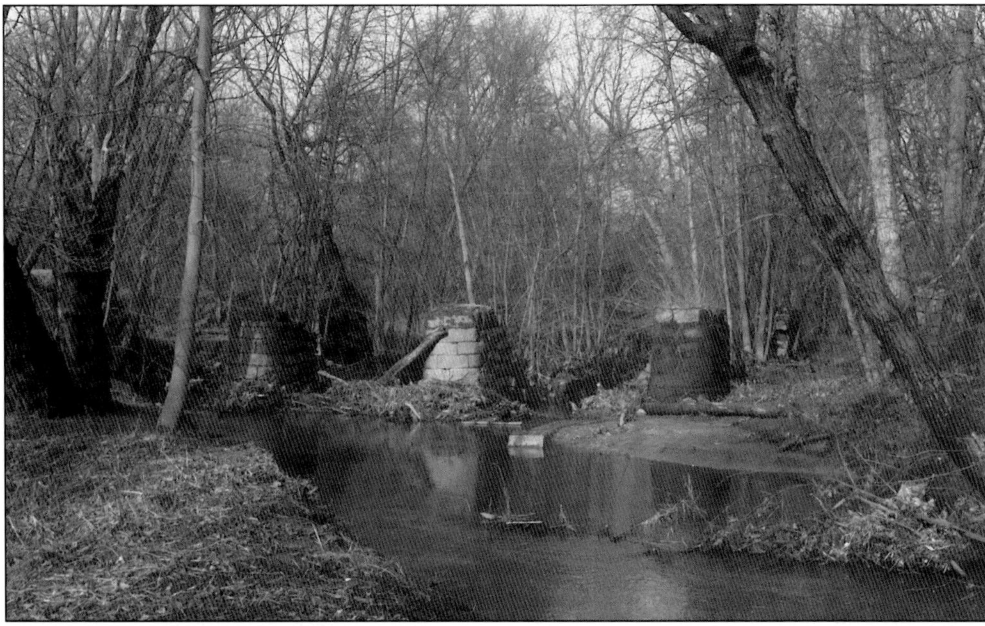

The Pigeon Creek aqueduct was a four-span wooden bridge with stone abutments and piers at the intersection of Route 724 and Linfield Road, just below lock 56 in Parker Ford. It is thought that the structure was built around 1846, though it was entirely rebuilt in 1866, with the piers extended on the south (berm) side. This aqueduct was unique, in that it was made of wood despite being located on a fairly large creek. It also differed from other aqueducts on the Girard Canal because it was constructed of reddish-brown stone, not gray fieldstone. These photographs show the remains of the piers of the Pigeon Creek aqueduct. Below, the bridge is seen from the berm side.

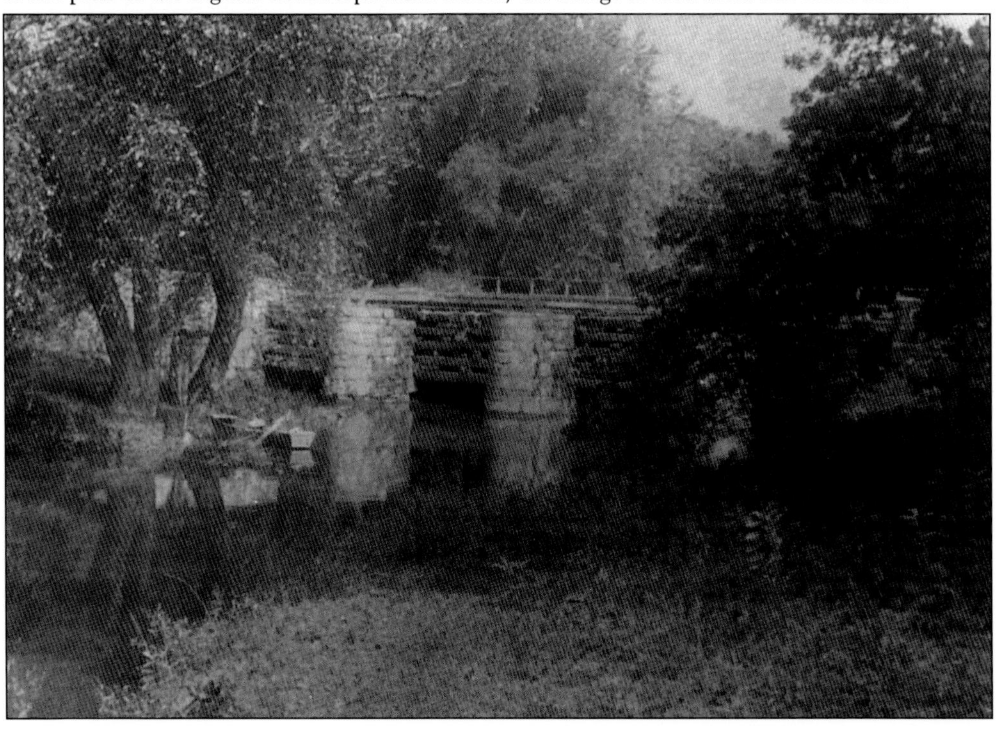

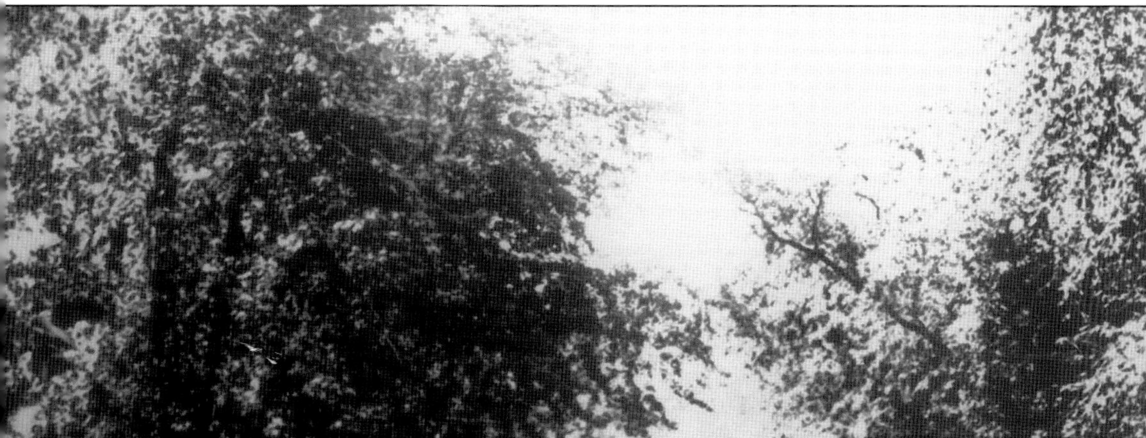

The Girard Canal extended the length of the Schuylkill River for 22 miles, beginning at Pigeon Creek. This 1959 photograph provides a partially obscured view of the Pigeon Creek aqueduct at Parker Ford. A mile upstream was lock 57, built by Alexander Lawrence. Remains of the Girard Canal, its aqueduct, and lock 57 are still visible. At another spot on Pigeon Creek stretches the 35-foot-long, two-lane Baptist Church Road Bridge, built in 1916 by John Parker Corcoran and set among active farms in northern Chester County. Pigeon Creek is now considered a watershed, known for its high-quality water. It, along with French Creek, Pickering Creek, and Valley Creek, complete the Schuylkill River tributary drainage and are all hydrologically linked. The municipalities that make up these watersheds are a part of the Green Valley Association's Sustainable Watershed Management Program. (Photograph by W.B. Coleman.)

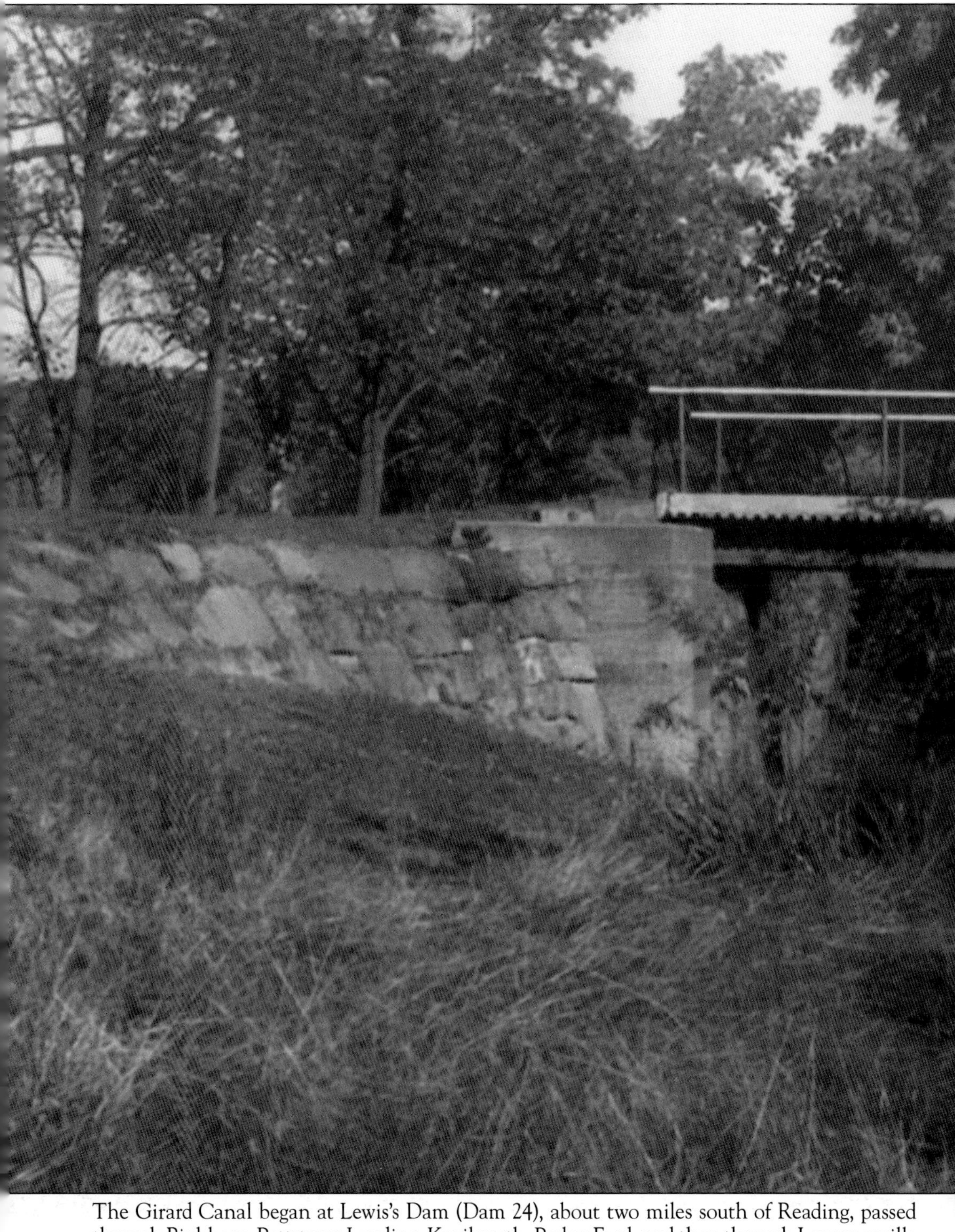

The Girard Canal began at Lewis's Dam (Dam 24), about two miles south of Reading, passed through Birdsboro, Pottstown Landing, Kenilworth, Parker Ford, and then through Lawrenceville before reentering the Schuylkill River at the Girard Outlet close to Spring City. Just off this part of the canal at Parker Ford stands the Henry Parker house, built in 1801, and its 5.5 acres

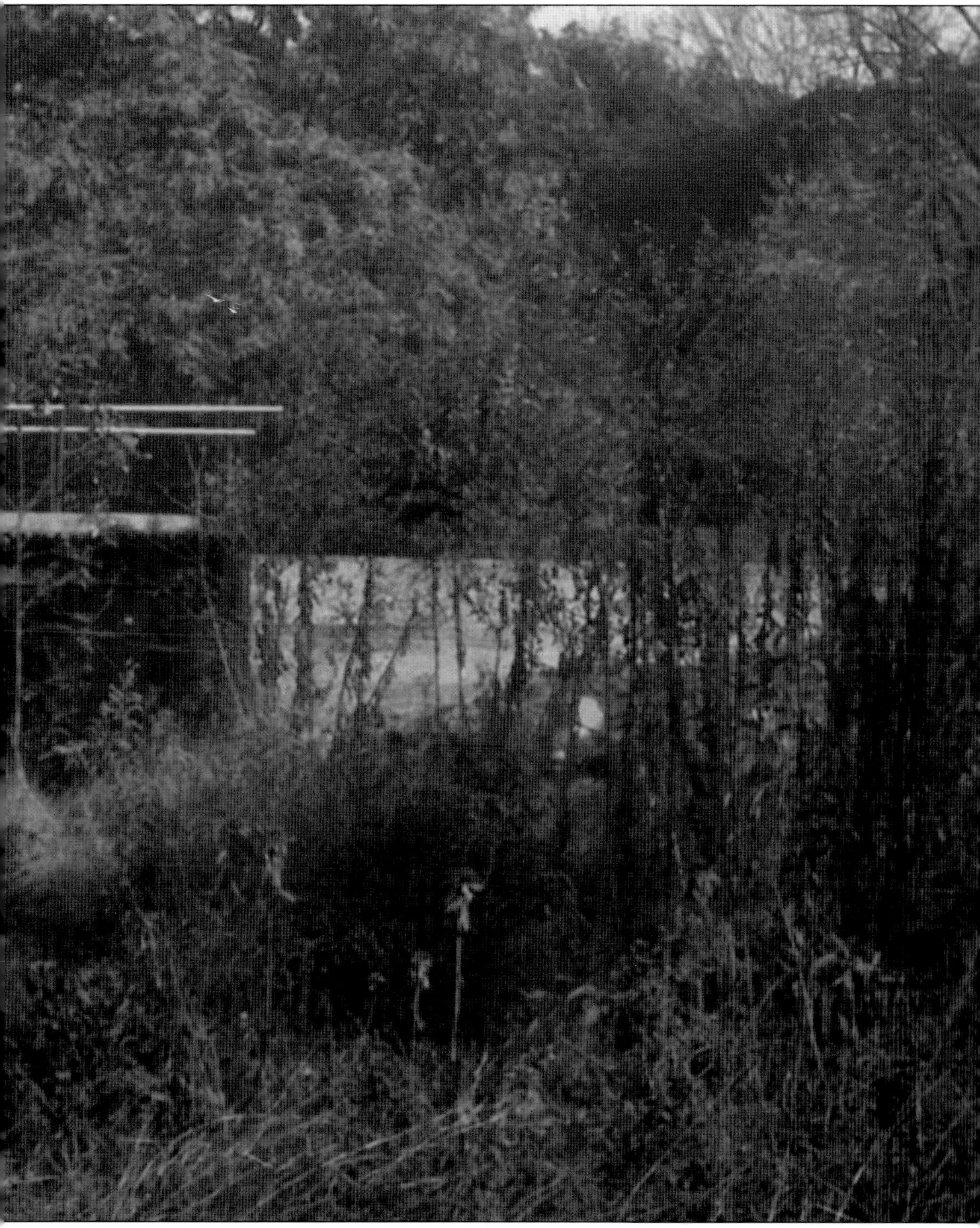

of property. Henry Parker's father, Edward, built the Parker Ford Tavern across from the house in 1766 and operated it until 1787. This 1973 photograph shows the dried-up bed of the Girard Canal, with a truss bridge still intact above it.

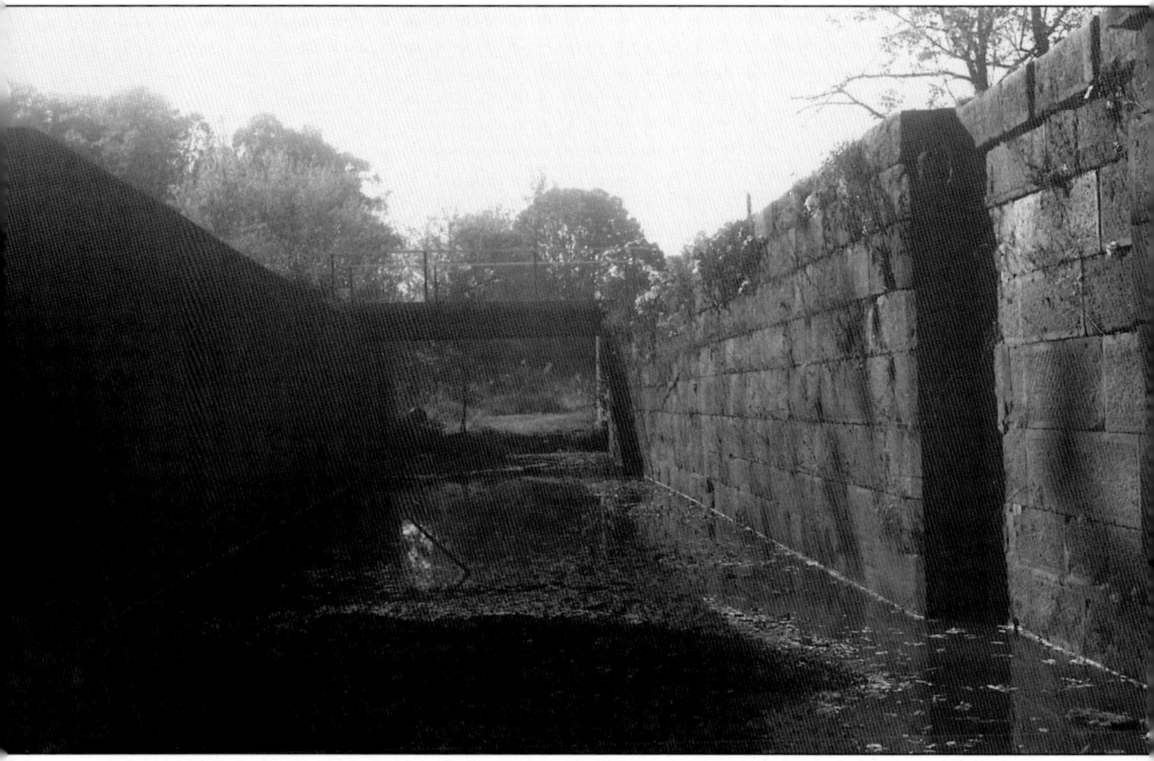

The very first lock chambers on the Schuylkill Navigation were built using rough stone and mortar. These were then lined with wood when it was evident that the construction was not adequate. In 1833, the Schuylkill Navigation Company starting using cut stone and hydraulic cement or dry masonry lined with wood planking in the construction of these structures. This 1973 photograph looks up the Girard Canal from within the lock between the upstream and downstream gates at where the previous photograph was taken. Most of the locks on this section of the Schuylkill Canal were doubled during the 1830s. In 1846, when most of the Schuylkill Navigation was enlarged, so, too, was the Girard Canal. The work consisted of widening and deepening the channel, as well as replacing the locks and constructing bridges and aqueducts. Trails allowing visitors to view these canal artifacts have been proposed.

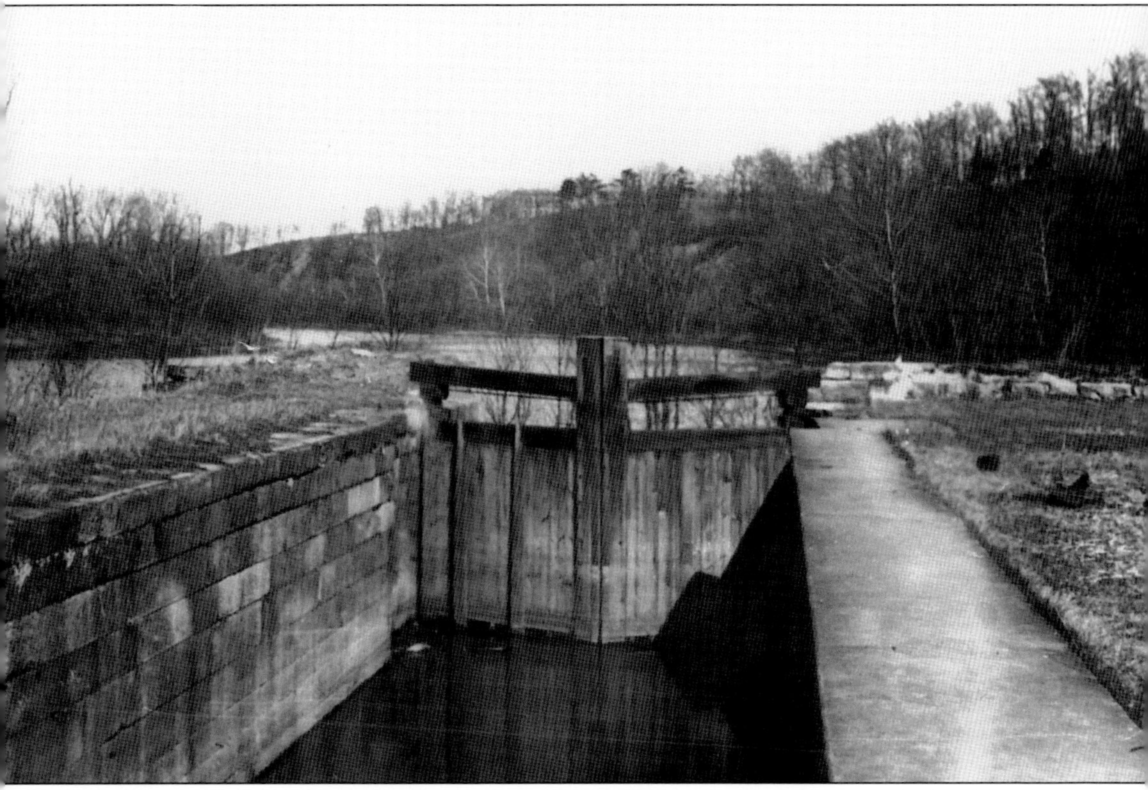

This photograph shows the lower gate of lock 57, the Girard Outlet, which was built with cut stone and masonry. Beyond the gate is the Schuylkill River. The original lock, built in 1820, was doubled in 1835. Although not seen here, there is a date stone in the north (left) wall bearing the date 1835. Both walls of the lock chamber had been constructed with stone, but the south (right) wall was cemented over at some point. Interestingly, all of the doubled locks on the Girard Canal, except the Girard Outlet, were built side by side. Now, the lock and canal are mere ghosts of what they once were. Even the lock tender's house no longer stands. However, not everything from that time is gone; the small water company that owns the land on which lock 57 sits is still in operation as part of a much bigger operation.

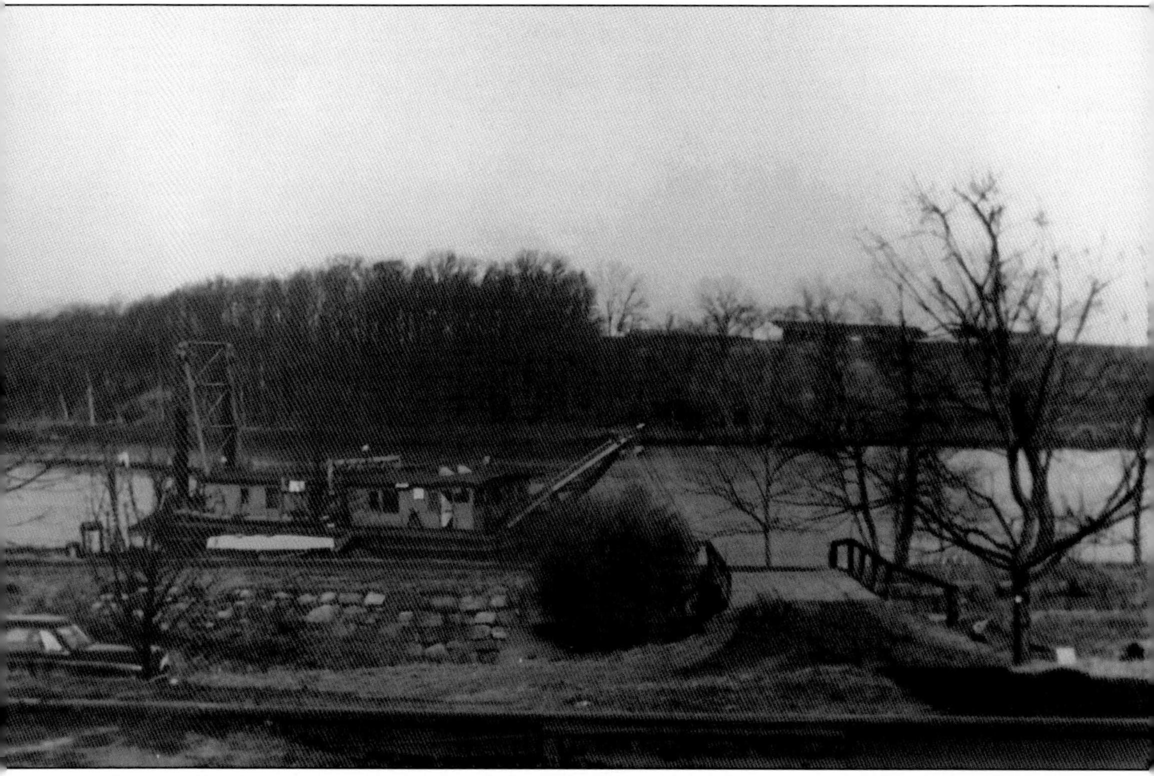

Eventually, the transportation of coal along the Schuylkill Navigation System took its toll, when silt and sediment produced from the washing of coal built up to such an extent that it affected the river's main channel and even filled in canals. Property in or along the Schuylkill River that was owned by the Schuylkill Navigation Company was taken over by the Commonwealth of Pennsylvania in 1945, at which time engineers began the $25 million Schuylkill River Desilting Project. As part of the project, three desilting basins, seven dams, and twenty-six impounding basins were built for the disposal of the dredged materials. In this photograph, taken in February 1950, the dredging operation is under way in the river at the Girard Outlet. Lock 57 was to the right of the small bridge in the foreground. Today, only 28 miles of the original 108-mile navigation system remain.

About the Schuylkill Canal Association

From humble beginnings as a township advisory committee, the Schuylkill Canal Association (SCA) was formed by a group of residents and incorporated in 1985 as a 501(c)(3) nonprofit to protect and preserve the Oakes Reach canal, lock 60, and the lock tender's house. At the time, the canal's banks were eroded, the berm on the riverside had leaks, spillways were broken, and the controls and sluice gates were rusted and inoperable. Wishing to create and maintain a safe and attractive recreation area for the public, the SCA provided routine maintenance to the towpath, trails, and grounds; built canoe launches; created picnic groves; and restored what had previously fallen into a state of disrepair. By 1988, the SCA succeeded in having the area listed in the National Register of Historic Places.

Today, in partnership with Montgomery County, the SCA's members and volunteers uphold the organization's mission to preserve, maintain, and appropriately restore the Schuylkill Canal and its surrounding lands and man-made structures; encourage wide public use of the area and an appreciation of its natural environment; seek ways to further general education in the area's history through programming and interpretation; provide facilities and enhanced settings for various forms of passive recreation; seek the support of individuals and private organizations, and of local, regional, state, and federal governments to achieve these goals; and solicit, receive, and expend funds for such purposes. The efforts of these individuals continues to pay off, as an estimated 25,000 people visit what is known locally as the Schuylkill Canal Park to fish, canoe, bike, hike, picnic, run, and more.

The SCA is run solely by volunteers and with the generous help of new and old corporate sponsors, as well as some 300 dues-paying members.

Consistent with our mission to preserve history on a local level, this book was printed in South Carolina on American-made paper and manufactured entirely in the United States. Products carrying the accredited Forest Stewardship Council (FSC) label are printed on 100 percent FSC-certified paper.